COUNTERPOINT

W. W. NORTON & COMPANY

Independent Publishers Since 1923

COUNTERPOINT:

*A Memoir of Bach
and Mourning*

PHILIP KENNICOTT

For information about permission to reproduce selections from this book,
write to Permissions, W. W. Norton & Company, Inc., 500 Fifth Avenue, New
York, NY 10110

Excerpt from *Selected Poetry of Rainer Maria Rilke* by Rainer Maria Rilke,
edited and translated by Stephen Mitchell, translation copyright © 1980, 1981,
1982 by Stephen Mitchell. Used by permission of Random House, an imprint
of Penguin Random House LLC. All rights reserved.

Excerpts of contemporaneous Bach sources from *The New Bach Reader: A
Life of Johann Sebastian Bach in Letters and Documents* by Hans T. David and
Arthur Mendel, editors, revised by Christoph Wolff. Copyright © 1998 by
Christoph Wolff. Copyright © 1966, 1945 by W. W. Norton & Company, Inc.
Copyright © 1972 by Mrs. Hans T. David and Arthur Mendel. Used by permis-
sion of W. W. Norton & Company, Inc.

For information about special discounts for bulk purchases, please contact
W. W. Norton Special Sales at specialsales@wwnorton.com or 800-233-4830

Manufacturing by Sheridan
Book design by Abbate Design
Production manager: Anna Oler

Library of Congress Cataloging-in-Publication Data

Names: Kennicott, Philip, author.
Title: Counterpoint : a memoir of Bach and mourning / Philip Kennicott.
Description: First edition. | New York : W. W. Norton & Company, 2020. |
    Includes bibliographical references.
Identifiers: LCCN 2019027075 | ISBN 9780393635362 (hardcover) | ISBN
    9780393635379 (epub)
Subjects: LCSH: Bach, Johann Sebastian, 1685–1750—Appreciation. | Bach,
    Johann Sebastian, 1685–1750. Goldberg-Variationen. | Kennicott, Philip.
Classification: LCC ML410.B1 K3 2020 | DDC 786.2092 [B]—dc23
LC record available at https://lccn.loc.gov/2019027075

W. W. Norton & Company, Inc., 500 Fifth Avenue, New York, N.Y. 10110
www.wwnorton.com

W. W. Norton & Company Ltd., 15 Carlisle Street, London W1D 3BS

1 2 3 4 5 6 7 8 9 0

For Marius

For beauty is nothing
but the beginning of terror, which we still are just able to endure,
and we are so awed because it serenely disdains
to annihilate us.

RAINER MARIA RILKE,
"The First Duino Elegy,"
translated by Stephen Mitchell

COUNTERPOINT

ONE

IN THE SUMMER it became clear that chemotherapy would kill my mother before the cancer did. She was making frequent trips to the emergency room, her body was weak, and still she had months to go before concluding the drug trial that was her last, best hope against the disease. She was angry and exhausted, and near despair, and finally she agreed with her doctor and her family that it was time to quit the drugs and reckon with death. But first she was allowed to live again: Within a few weeks, the chemicals cleared out of her body and she came back to life. After many bedridden months, she began using her walker and then felt well enough to send away the hospice nurses. She would rise in the mornings and take a seat by the large windows looking onto the hills outside her home, and wait for birds to come to the several feeders she tended there. By early autumn, she and my father left for one last trip to Arizona, where they had spent their winters, among friends, in the sun, enjoying retirement.

The call came a week before Thanksgiving. The cancer had regrouped, and now it was time for her to return home and finish the dying. My mother begged me to stay away and not waste vacation days on a trip home for a last visit. "I don't want you to see me like this." She had a dutiful sense of self-denial, but the request was more theatrical than sincere, and I brushed it off, just as I had all the others since she became ill three years earlier. I found a ticket on the internet and paid extra for the option to change my return date. Scrolling on the sides of the online travel sites were advertisements for Caribbean vacations and cruise packages, images of turquoise water and beautiful, carefree people in swimsuits.

I realized, as I was packing, that when I put these shirts back into the closet, my mother would be dead, and with that strange realization, almost every trivial thing I did took on a sense of tragic finality. Should I pack this sweater, which she once said she liked? It would be the last time she'd see it. I didn't know how long it would be, days or maybe weeks, but when I returned home a new, unchangeable fact would have been established in my life, a connection that had existed for as long as I had would be sundered. I didn't think much about the clothes I was folding, but I knew I had to bring two essential things: a pair of hiking boots, and some music to keep me company, and sane, in the large, empty house where she was dying.

Without much conscious thought, I threw a recording of Bach's Sonatas and Partitas for Solo Violin into my traveling bag. I had no particular reason to pick this music, though I was mildly interested in the young violinist who was brave enough to record these demanding, dense, and complicated works so young in his career. Perhaps I was drawn to the cover of the recording, a black-and-white image of a soulful man with his hands seemingly clasped in prayer above the familiar, feminine curves of his violin. It had also been a long time since I had listened to these works closely and I was probably happy to bring music that I remembered fondly, but vaguely, great works that remained still somewhat unfamiliar. Music that you have lived with for a long time becomes cluttered with memory and association. For this particular journey, I wanted to pack light.

Pound for pound, Bach is also good traveling music. One or two CDs contain more to occupy the mind than hours of lesser stuff, and it is more emotionally efficient than any other music, with no filler or extraneous matter. For some reason I can't explain, Bach is suited to all my moods, no matter where I am, no matter what mode of life I find myself in, work or play, thriving, surviving, or wallowing in lassitude. His music delights me on the beach as much as it sustains me in a gray desert landscape at the end of November. I could think of a hundred reasons why, while I was there, I wouldn't want to play Beethoven, Brahms, or Wagner; but I couldn't imagine a single reason why I would resist Bach.

When I arrived, my parents' house was quiet, and everyone walked on tiptoes and spoke in whispers. The only noise came from the television in my mother's room, always on, the flickering light clearly a consolation through the night as she passed in and out of consciousness. When she was awake I would sit with her; but much of the time she was lost to the morphine. I never listened to music while I was with her, afraid that I might miss some marker of pain, or signpost of her progress toward death. I tried to tune out the television, droning in the background, and listen to her breathing—"stertorous," said one of the hospice nurses brightly, as if pointing out a rare flower on a walk through the forest. Reflected on the wall above my mother's head, the inanity of the nightly news, the animated weatherman, the frantic banter of the pretty anchorwomen parsing murder, traffic, and parades, was distilled to a dance of blue forms and abstractions. When I looked directly into the wide, flat screen only a few feet away, into this portal to a world that seemed infinitely remote and meaningless, I began to feel untethered from reality.

During the final days, as my mother slid from terrified lucidity into confusion and finally silence, Bach was the only music I could listen to, the only music that didn't seem trivial, insipid, or irrelevant to life. It did a strange, spatial sort of work, defining an interior world apart from the world of chatter and noise, creating a space in which I could separate myself from intense feelings about my mother and watch the unfolding of her death without the distraction of what we oddly call the "real" world. It kept banal things at bay, while bringing profound things close enough to be felt without being engulfed by their dread darkness.

When I wasn't with my mother, or helping out around the house, I listened to the Partita in D minor. The last movement of this five-part work, the great Chaconne, lasts as long as the other four combined, and it became a maze in which I lost myself completely during its quarter-hour span. I returned to it again and again, obsessed with it, sometimes simply hitting the repeat button until after four or five hearings I had to force myself to quit. I listened to it on headphones while walking in the mountains near my parents' house, and in bed while trying to fall asleep. It came with me as I drove to town to pick up some new prescription or more cans of soda, which we would pour into a bowl and stir with a whisk until it was flat, and easier for my mother to drink. Hearing the Chaconne in the car somehow made the polyphony more intelligible. The eyes, focused on the road, kept other parts of the brain busy, freeing up consciousness to listen more deeply, to sort out individual lines from the thickness of the general texture. And the music became a filter for the physical world, almost as if someone had Photoshopped out the gas stations, burrito joints, and gift shops, leaving only the passing landscape, dun-colored and dry, with leafless cottonwood trees spectral against the slate-gray skies of November.

Once, while I was driving on the highway into Albuquerque, the traffic snarled and I was jolted out of the solipsism of music. I slammed on the brakes and stabbed at the buttons of the car's sound system, trying to turn off Bach, but instead I turned on a station playing mariachi music. When the adrenaline subsided, I laughed. Albuquerque was founded in 1706, little more than a decade before Bach likely wrote the Partita in D minor. There is a distant connection between these two things. The Chaconne was based on an early dance form, the *chacona*, likely from Latin America, where some speculate that it was named for the castanets that accompanied it or perhaps the place where it was first discovered. Like the tango some three centuries later, the *chacona* was associated with the lower classes, with vulgarity and licentiousness and untrammeled physicality.

By the time Bach wrote his Chaconne, the dance form was fully domesticated, and the name implied a musical form as well as a rhythmic pattern or dance style. A chaconne, in Bach's day, implied a repeated bass line over which the composer spun out variations, a fusion of an often ponderous idée fixe in the lower register with virtuosic elaboration above. But even in Bach's enormous, complex, and abstract Chaconne, there is still perhaps an echo of the old *chacona*—a rhythmic pattern in three beats, with a distinctive snap of long and short notes—heard in the opening bars. He doesn't sustain it explicitly throughout the piece, but he states it clearly and unequivocally at the same time that he announces the bass line pattern on which the entire edifice will be built. Not every violinist stresses this vestigial, dance-like character of the music, especially the violinists from the early to mid–twentieth century who played it with operatic pomposity. But the best performances, even the most epic, are animated by a memory of the dance rhythms, ingrained, even unconscious, but palpable like a heartbeat.

It's easy to read too much, and too little, into Bach. We always seem to get our measure wrong, anachronistically fetishizing things that would have been of little interest to his eighteenth century listeners, while slighting what Bach would have considered essential. I have been trained, like most critics, to be intellectually skeptical about the connections between art and the artist's emotional life, especially composers such as Bach, who wrote music of endless emotional variety, every day, every week of his extraordinarily productive life, without regard to his own joy or suffering, and in service of an ideal of religious duty that allowed little room for what we now call self-expression. And yet as Bach's Chaconne took over my emotional life, it gathered irresistible metaphorical force.

The music suggested two aspects of life, something essential, immutable, and ever repeated, and something above that grounded truth, a need for variety, elaboration, fleeting connections, and change. It seemed to be music about life, but grounded on the fundamental fact of death, and it felt to me suddenly very profound, far beyond the details of Bach's notes on paper, or the violinist's performance somewhere in a studio, months or years before I came upon his recording. It carried with it centuries, at least, of commonly felt experience, enacting simultaneously the fundamental duality of our emotions, despair and joy, sinking down and clambering up, confronting death and looking back into life, for pleasure, diversion, and purpose.

WHEN I WAS young, and first discovering music, I was enamored of the myths and fairy tales that were often told about the great composers: that Mozart composed the Requiem to encode for the world the anguish of his own demise; that Rossini was so lazy and so prodigiously talented that he preferred to write a new overture than roll over in bed and pick up one that had fallen on the floor; that Haydn wrote the great crashing fortissimos in his "Surprise" symphony to wake up the dreary, sleeping philistines in his audience. They made the music seem more dramatic, and connected my experience of it to a larger sense of history. When I learned to play the piano as a boy, these stories compensated for the tedium of practice. As a teenager, in retreat from the rages of my mother, who was deeply unhappy for reasons I then found incomprehensible, these fables made music seem even more profound. I would pass them on to my friends in vain, breathless attempts to share my enthusiasm for sounds they found old-fashioned and boring. But as an adult, I became allergic to them, not just because many of them were wholly fabricated, but because even those that were true didn't offer any greater access to the music, and only underscored the emotions I already felt. They felt like tautologies: the music is sad because Bach was sad.

And yet it is almost impossible to maintain a cautious, intellectually scrupulous relation to the music we love, especially when we are emotionally vulnerable to it. We want it to tell stories, to speak to life beyond its purely aural realm. Music that merely pleases us may be examined with detachment, but when music possesses us in some deep, overbearing way, it is difficult to submit to scholarly scruple. It must have cosmic importance, and transcend the hermetic and abstract codes of sound. For me, on those drives through New Mexico, Bach's music was absolutely about a dialogue between death and life, an intertwining of the two basic impulses that govern our lives from beginning to end. Even if Bach never conceived of his Chaconne in those terms, he was working within a tradition that delivers to us the possibility of that interpretation. And I chose to hear it that way, and succumbed to the music absolutely, in a way that I hadn't since adolescence. At a time when I desperately needed articles of faith, the Chaconne helped articulate them.

Much of what I was thinking at the time seems banal now. I remember taking some solace from this thought: that the price of admission to life is the acceptance of death. No one lives without dying, and there are no Faustian codicils to this contract. The ticket admits one, it is nontransferable, and there are no refunds or exchanges. For a moment, standing on a rock overlooking the wide, arid plains of New Mexico, I tried to think what it would mean not to have that ticket, not to have been born, not to exist. It was unthinkable. Not only is the ticket premised on death at the end, we also have no choice but to accept it, use it, submit to its limitations.

This was consoling, for a while. It suggested the commonality of our experience of death, as if the meaning of life is to realize that we belong to a fraternity united by one thing only, the fact of our death, and this should make us kinder to one another. Certainly in the months prior I had noticed in myself a new sense of empathy and curiosity about other people who were experiencing death, especially the death of a parent. At parties, in casual conversation, thrown next to a stranger on an airplane, if someone mentioned the death of a parent, I was deeply interested. I asked questions and found myself having genuinely meaningful conversations even with acquaintances whom I didn't like very much. The shared experience of losing our parents casts all of us back into the unresolved residue of childhood, making us children again in some fundamental way. At a time in life when you think you have experienced everything, suddenly there is this one enormous, unsettling thing that is astonishingly new. It is no surprise that almost everyone who has experienced it wants to talk about it, and that the fundamental theme of these conversations about grief is, "I had no idea."

About halfway through the Chaconne, Bach shifts from the minor to the major key, and echoes in a softer way the opening of the movement. The listener is immensely grateful for the simplicity of the first eight bars of this major-key episode, an episode of calm after a long period of virtuoso display, rapid figuration, and widely spaced chords that encompass the violin's tonal range, from growling bottom to the piercing top. But no sooner has the composer allowed us to pause, to consider ideas of tenderness and simplicity, than the animated discourse of musical variations begins again. Mercifully, Bach starts slowly, with stepwise motion, deliberate at first and at a walking pace, moving up then down, almost as if the line is taking stock of itself, checking to be sure that all the essentials are in place. It reminds me of people who feel a powerful sense of duty, who are checking on something they know well, the safety of a home or the care of a family, making sure that everything is in order, everything safe. The simplicity of the line is a reassurance to the listener, a reiteration of the musical essentials, before it again gains speed and complexity and moves on to greater degrees of complexity and elaboration.

If you can believe, as I did at the time, that this passage is essentially maternal, imbued with kindness and care, then what comes next is heartbreaking. In the following variations, Bach begins repeating two notes, A and D, the lower and upper bookends of the first chord of the Chaconne and the essential notes of the key in which it is written. At first these repetitions seem almost accidental, as if they are merely filling in holes in one of Bach's musical patterns. But their reiteration, their gathering force, and finally their emphatic power dispel any sense of accident. Throughout the completion of the basic arch-like form of Bach's Chaconne—in which the music moves from the minor key to the major and back to the minor again—the note A is known as the dominant, the harmonic area of greatest tension, always leading back to D, where the piece begins and ends. The reiteration of A builds tension, insistence, energy, making the ear crave the resolution of D. It feels a bit like thirst, an ever-accumulating craving for the resolution of the tonic key.

Throughout this passage, Bach is shifting the harmonic drama, which for most of the piece is contained in the recurring pattern of the bass line, into the upper reaches of the violin's range. If the music gives us the illusion of multiple voices, it is now the top voices, the ones primarily charged with variation, diversity, and melodic elaboration, that emphatically insist on the fundamental harmonic facts. The distinction—admittedly a very subjective one on my part—between a grounding of the music in the insistence on mortality, and an elaboration of life above, breaks down. And it breaks down in the major key, in the section that at first seemed so maternal and consoling.

I was tempted to think that Bach was complicating the usual maternal attributes of care and kindness. The mother's voice was now speaking about death, echoing the music's fundamental insistence—delivered through the bass line—on a relentless march of life to its terminus. The feminine voice had grabbed hold of the fact of death, held it up in new light, stripped away some of the accumulated anxiety that gathered around it during its ceaseless repetitions in the bass line. The voice that had seemed to chatter so brilliantly before was now grounded, now speaking with a deeper, discomfiting wisdom. For children, the discovery of death is shocking, perhaps in the form of a schoolmate's accident, or a grandparent's failure to appear at some appointed holiday. But with our parents' deaths we rediscover it as unavoidable and universal. Ideally, they help us learn to die, sometimes explicitly, giving us insight, consoling *us* for *their* death, so that ours will be easier when it comes.

But that wasn't my mother. Death brought her no wisdom, life brought her little joy, and when she died it was in anguish, without resolution or any sense of peace. Hers should have been what was once called a "good death," after a long life, filled with children and grandchildren, and surrounded by family. My mother had the best treatment that medicine could provide, and when it could provide no more, she had the kindest and most professional care from nurses who knew how to relieve pain and tend to a failing body. My mother died at home, with all her children fully launched in life, secure and perhaps successful. Not one of her children or grandchildren preceded her in death; not one of them deviated from the usual trajectory of middle-class life. There were no broken homes or abandoned children, no chronic gamblers or heroin addicts. We were by no means a perfect family, but if any ordinary person had come in to assess the fullness of my mother's life, he would have found the balance sheet laden with things that ordinarily make people happy, and mostly devoid of the usual causes of sadness.

But she was unhappy and died that way, unfulfilled and angry about what she sensed was a wasted life. She had wanted to be a violinist, and when I was young she used to play along with my piano; but over time, she gave up on the instrument, just one of many things she abandoned, until late in life even the mention of the instrument would make her grimace with disgust. She also dreamed of being a dancer, but she said it wasn't the decent thing for a girl to show her legs in the 1940s, so nothing came of that. Later she hoped to be a doctor, but her father refused her bus fare to the West Coast, where, she said, she had a scholarship to a good college. A few years after my mother died, when my once-reticent father was surprising all his children by speaking easily and candidly about a past we had assumed was closed for discussion, I asked him about the scholarship story, which I had always doubted. He said yes, it was true, and that my grandfather had indeed crushed his daughter's dream, and though I never met my maternal grandfather and he was, for me, mainly a figure of myth constructed by my mother, I felt a flash of hatred for him, as if he had entered the room uninvited. After that, my mother's life was given over to marriage, raising a family, and being a woman in the 1950s and 1960s didn't help. By the time she was in her forties and had the freedom to do exactly as she pleased, she was embittered, and spent much of her time resentfully cleaning a house that was never dirty. She loved her children, but fretfully and it seemed without pleasure. She was seventy-four when she died, still waiting for the world to sort itself out, to remove its impediments to her happiness.

In the last few days before her death, the futility of this wait struck her with its full, terrifying force. She had always been an atheist, and sometimes stridently so. Now, when we were alone, she asked if I believed in God, if I thought there was anything that came after death. I was horrified by these questions, in part because they struck at my most unresolved thoughts, and also because I didn't know whether to lie and say the consoling thing, or speak a truth that is unnerving even to a healthy person with no intimation of death on the horizon. So I said I didn't know, that nobody knows, nobody has ever known, despite all the certainty of religion, and atheism. I said that the only thing in which I had confidence was that death brings an end to suffering, and a cessation of all things, including regret, worry, and fear. My mother died the day after that conversation.

≡

I BRISTLE AT THE idea that music is consoling or has healing power. It is a cliché of lazy music talk, the sort of thing said by people who give money to the symphony and have their names chiseled on the wall of the opera house. It is the drivel of disembodied voices narrating bad documentaries about Beethoven and Mozart. I don't find music consoling. I'm not sure I even love music. Sometimes I wonder if in fact I hate it, the way one hates a drug, or resents a weakness. It unsettles more than it satisfies, and increases the very appetites it is supposed to sate. At best, it is a distraction from things that are more painful in life. If we confuse its power with consolation, it is through sloppy thinking. Consolation requires a reassuring statement about the world, or life, the kind of philosophical statement that music can't make in any definitive way. Consolation helps us order our thoughts so that life is less painful. Very often these are clichés like the ones I repeated to myself while my mother was dying; for some people they are bromides found on calendars and inspirational posters; for many others, they are the wishful thinking that grounds religion. We think of music as consoling perhaps because it is so often the handmaiden to religion, amplifying our emotional response to religious ideas. But by itself music, if anything, makes us raw, more susceptible to pain, nostalgia, and memory.

Once, many years ago, I used to visit an elderly friend who was dying of cancer, and one evening he asked me to put some music on the stereo, anything I liked. His record collection was vast, and there were dozens of recordings—obscure Baroque operas, rare recitals by singers known only to fanatical lovers of the human voice—that I would have gladly chosen. But I worried that his mood was fragile and his mind cloudy, so I sought out something simple, sentimental, and easy to follow. Bach wouldn't do, Wagner was too heavy, Beethoven too dramatic, so I chose the "Liebesleid," a salon trifle by the great violinist Fritz Kreisler. It is musical kitsch, an Austrian *ländler*, which flows like a waltz, with a melodic line jumping up in hope and expectation, then falling downward by steps, a generic melodic pattern but one that seems to trace the desire and disappointment implied in the title: "Love's Sorrow." It is the sort of music my mother loved, and I thought it innocuous enough to "console," for a moment, a professor of great brilliance, worldliness, and trenchant wit who was struggling with his own mortal fears and regrets. I put the LP on the turntable and carefully dropped the arm on the right track. When I came back into the dining room, where he sat in a wheelchair in front of a cold, picked-over supper, he was in tears. Not the delicate, glycerin tears of Hollywood, but a red-faced mask of quivering lips, swollen eyes, and snot. "Leave it on," he said in a choked voice, and I did. But the evening was over.

Bach doesn't aim at any consolation in the Chaconne. The arch-like form must be completed, the music moves back to D minor, the harmonies become more clotted and the textures more complicated. There is no retreat, only greater intensification of the musical purpose. It ends with a single D, with no harmonic elaboration. None is needed: the many lines of the music, implied or explicit, have given way to a unity, a finality, a single note, vibrating on thirteen inches of sheep gut or metal wire stretched over wood.

We were relieved when it was over, when my mother's breathing grew quiet, undetectable, and finally stopped. Earlier that day, a nurse had told my father that my mother might live for a few hours or a few days, and I could see a sense of alarm and exhaustion flash across his face at the latter possibility. He had tended to her faithfully, with kindness and the precision of a scientist, which he was. Now that it was over, he retired to another room, sat down with his back to the front door, and engaged me in small talk about roads and cars and computers while we waited for men from the city to come take her body away. He grew more animated after the doorbell rang, and as they wheeled her body, encased in black plastic, out of the sickroom and then out of the house, he asked, "How is the old Honda holding up?" The next morning the hospice removed the hospital bed and we carried cases of unused diapers to the garage, along with boxes of unopened soda cans and nutritional supplements. We raised the blinds, aired out the room, and one of the nurses, in a last act of kindness, vacuumed the rug. We decided to forgo a memorial service for a few months, because no one could conceive how that would go, what could be said; no one was ready to speak the platitudes of mourning. For a while, I felt superstitious about the room in which she died, but that faded, too.

On the morning after she died, I took a walk in the hills above Albuquerque, and stood for a while in a grove of aspen trees, their branches animated by a sharp, early winter wind. A poem I had learned many years earlier, and now considered something of a chestnut, kept running through my mind: "Margaret, are you grieving / Over Goldengrove unleaving?" The English poet Gerard Manley Hopkins wrote those words in an 1880 poem called "Spring and Fall," addressing them "to a young child":

Margaret, are you grieving
Over Goldengrove unleaving?
Leaves, like the things of man, you
With your fresh thoughts care for, can you?
Ah! as the heart grows older
It will come to such sights colder
By and by, nor spare a sigh
Though worlds of wanwood leafmeal lie;
And yet you will weep and know why.
Now no matter, child, the name:
Sorrow's springs are the same.

Nor mouth had, no nor mind, expressed
What heart heard of, ghost guessed:
It is the blight man was born for,
It is Margaret you mourn for.

Throughout the fall, as the trees were unleaving, my mother had been unleaving the last of her life. But what haunted me about the poem was its insistence on the deep, self-regarding sense of fear that loss, including the deaths of other people, inspires in us: "It is the blight man was born for, / It is Margaret you mourn for."

Margaret, it is *Margaret* you mourn for.

My mother's death left me terrified about my own mortality, first in small ways, wondering how I will die, whether it will be alone, or in the company of loved ones, in poverty, or surrounded by comfort, in despair, or rich in memories and meaning. But it also aggravated a larger sense of dread, the ever-present but often mute fear we carry with us that our lives have been wasted, that life will simply run out and in the last hours or minutes or moments of awareness we will perhaps feel cheated, or horrified, to have moved so relentlessly and blindly toward nothingness. It was a feeling of panic, followed by a resolution to *do* something, accomplish something, at the very least to understand something like Bach's Chaconne at a level that had until then eluded me.

WHAT, IN FACT, does it mean to *know* a piece of music? When we hear a new work for the first time, we barely scratch the surface of its content. A few more times through and we have a basic road map, a set of expectations and desires, a craving to hear certain particularly affecting passages, a sense of satisfaction to be enveloped for a few measures here and there in increasingly familiar melodies

or harmonic progressions. Multiple hearings may exhaust our pleasure, and some pieces are more easily exhausted than others. Popular music is designed to be spent, arriving everywhere at once with a
built-in obsolescence, and often disappearing as quickly as it came.
Deeper music may exhaust *us* for a time, but remains itself inexhaust-
ible. We may not wish to hear Bach's Chaconne every day for the rest
of our lives, but when we return to it, after years or decades, its power
is undiminished. This basic question, what does it mean to *know* a
piece of music, seems to me very close to all of the questions that really
matter in life. Attempting to answer it—if it is, in fact, *answerable*—
draws one down avenues of thought parallel, or perhaps identical, to
the most fundamental question of all: What does it mean to be alive?

Simply being a bystander, a passive listener to music, isn't an
entirely satisfying form of understanding. For years, I had felt this
way about the great piano works that were beyond my abilities,
among them Bach's *Goldberg Variations*. Like the Bach solo violin sonatas and partitas, and the suites for solo cello, the *Goldberg Variations* encompass everything that Bach has to say within
the parameters of a single instrument. They are comprehensive,
demanding, and infinitely rewarding, and yet I had never quite had
the courage to approach them. Like the Chaconne for solo violin, they are a set of variations, but unlike the Chaconne, they are
mainly in a major key and animated by a wider spectrum of the
happier emotions. Like the Chaconne, they are based on a dance
form in triple meter, a sarabande of haunting beauty, but unlike
the Chaconne, the relation to dance is direct rather than remote,
unabashed rather than vestigial.

People who don't make music, who don't play an instrument or
sing, often sense the presence of a deeper understanding that eludes
them, as if the ability to perform a piece of music might unlock the
real substance of the composer's thought. But the sad truth is that
even the ability to play through a Mozart sonata or sing a Schubert

song leaves one with the same elusive sense of a yet deeper understanding lurking beneath the notes on the page. The musician asks
himself: Have I understood it when I can play it? Or when I can play
it flawlessly? Or when I have memorized it? Or when I can analyze
its structure? At every level of yet deeper engagement, the thing-in-
itself, the musical unknown, remains, taunting us with a sense of
unachieved enlightenment. There is always a nagging feeling that
the reach exceeds the grasp. I had felt this way about the *Goldberg
Variations* for a long time, in love with them from the recordings of
other pianists, yet in love with a definite sense that something was
unrequited. At a moment when it seemed imperative to understand
the world and life more deeply, I wondered if the *Goldberg Variations* might test the possibility of achieving true knowledge of music.
I wondered if perhaps I should learn how to play them.

Certain pieces are performed by great musicians not just because
the music is incomparably rich, but as a kind of badge, or proof of
musical prowess, and this makes those works tremendously intimidating even to competent amateurs. Beethoven's "Hammerklavier"
sonata and Ravel's piano suite *Gaspard de la Nuit* are dazzling music,
but also monuments to the professional daring and accomplishment
of any player who attempts them. The *Goldbergs* have been recorded
dozens if not hundreds of times by pianists and harpsichordists,
and in transcription on every instrument capable of fleet passagework and multiple voices—and on a few instruments that aren't. If
you have any doubts about your own playing, it is foolhardy to try to
learn them. And I had plenty of doubt.

Since I was a boy, I have played the piano. It was a lucky accident
that I was started on the piano, not the violin. My mother hounded
her daughters as they scraped away miserably at their quarter- and
half-sized violins until, one by one, each of them braved her wrath
and put it away, never to be played again. The piano was never her
instrument, so I had some breathing room to learn to love it. By

my teenage years, I was a better pianist than she was a violinist, and music came to occupy far more of my life than it had hers. She encouraged me, though I always felt sad that after a certain point she stopped playing along with me. Eventually, she, too, put away the violin. When I asked her to play, she would look at her left hand with quiet fury, as if the hand itself had willed some mysterious affliction that estranged her from making music.

I've never been able to live without the piano, though at the time of my mother's death I was practicing infrequently. For years, I would decline to play for anyone except close friends and family, mainly because my fingers were barely capable of finding their way through a stable of half-learned or mostly forgotten favorites of Schubert, Chopin, and Liszt. I also made my living, for much of my adult life, writing about music, sometimes as a music critic reviewing the performance of others. It can be an ugly profession if you're not careful, making one hypercritical, turning on music an excoriating scrutiny, leaching it of pleasure. I certainly turned that focus on my own dismal playing, and it only made me play less.

Even as the Chaconne was haunting me, I knew I would never be able to play it, that the best I might hope for was to play a piano transcription of it (Brahms wrote one for left hand), or study its musical form. The Chaconne had served an invaluable purpose during the weeks of my mother's death, but it would always be alien to me as a musician. It was not a piece through which I could pursue this almost manic need to tunnel into the mysteries of music. Yet with my mother's death came a powerful sense that it was time, finally, to really learn a piece of music, to pursue its understanding as far as my limited musical skills would allow.

After returning from New Mexico, I put away my things, the hiking boots into the closet, the shirts into the laundry, and the recording of the Chaconne deep at the back of a remote bookcase, easy to find if I ever needed it again, but not something I ever wanted to stumble over accidentally. I would hate for some well-meaning but oblivious friend to surprise me with it, to take me unawares by dropping it casually into the disc player. But the house was oppressively silent and I needed to listen to something. So I put on Glenn Gould playing the *Goldberg Variations* in 1955, one of the most admired and thorny recordings ever made. With its patina of thin, pre-digital sound, it captures a pianist doing the miraculous, clarifying as with colored light the intertwining lines of Bach's thirty variations on a recurring bass pattern. Even critics who find it sometimes dry, or even tendentious in its almost aggressive flaying of the music's sinews, still stand in awe of it. If it were made today with all the tools available for tweaking and distorting sound, one would suspect the pianist, and his engineers, of studio fraud. As I listened to Gould play, I sensed in the *Goldberg Variations* the same inexhaustibility of emotion and meaning that I had felt in the Chaconne during the days of my mother's death. And the perfection of Gould's playing, his mental tenacity, made me shudder.

Clarity, accuracy, subtlety, these were my failings. The problem is that without them there is no approach to Bach, no way to make his music bring pleasure to other people. Every well-tutored student of the piano learns Bach early, and Bach's music is fundamental to all that comes after it. Through no fault of my teachers, I had managed to make it through this chapter of basic training without ever truly *mastering* anything by Bach, graduating prematurely to later repertoire, fully aware that were I to return to Bach, it would only make the elemental deficiencies of my musical training glaringly transparent. So I avoided Bach almost entirely, but with an increasing sense of shame and sadness. There is, in this music, a universe of beauty to which I felt an outsider.

Bach had always presented challenges that were particularly vexing to me, striking directly at the Achilles' heel of my talent. As a young man, I played big music, nineteenth century music, loud and fast and with lots of drama: music by Beethoven, Schumann, and Brahms, and composers such as Liszt who extended keyboard technique to Olympian heights, music that presented athletic challenges and dazzled listeners who were likely unaware that often what sounds hard isn't all that difficult, and what sounds easy only sounds that way in the hands of a master. It was easy to fake this music, to project the basic, full-throated rhetoric and drama of its romantic appeal, while dropping notes here and there, and smudging or eliding what the fingers couldn't absolutely conquer. But Bach's music doesn't tolerate any kind of bluster, and ruthlessly exposes inadequacy. To study Bach in middle age was to confront a lifetime of bad habits. If I tried to learn this music, I would inevitably be forced to confront an ugly fact: my rusty skills rested on even weaker foundations.

We live in a society that talks a lot of rot about dreams and ambition, awash in the rhetoric of self-realization. There, on television, is a ninety-one-year-old weight lifter bench-pressing almost twice his weight, a blind mountain climber summiting on Everest, a wounded veteran finishing the Boston Marathon. These are no doubt worthy and inspiring ventures, but if we are reasonable and mature about growing old, we learn to shed dreams. By the time I was thirty, I knew with certainty that I would never be a great ballet dancer, in part because I had never bothered to take a single dance lesson, but more ineluctably because my body was past the point of doing the things that ballet dancers must do. By the time I was forty, I felt reasonably certain that I would never be a great classicist spending my evenings reading ancient Greek by the fireside, largely because I had never bothered to learn ancient Greek, but also, because as I looked forward and calculated what I might reasonably accomplish in life, it was clear that there would never be enough hours in the day to master a complicated dead language. I know now with relative certainty that I will never win an Academy

Award, bring home an Olympic gold medal, or drive a team of huskies to the end of the Iditarod.

Each dream we shed stabs us with another small intimation of mortality, but to retain them is to live enfeebled by disappointment and unnecessary self-recrimination. The silly ethos of dreaming the impossible dream is a good way to live in perpetual regret, unable even to muster the energy and will to take on the manageable challenges of a reasonable dream.

Learning the *Goldberg Variations*, however, seemed an eminently *reasonable* thing to do, not a dream, but a project. I had no illusions that I would ever master them well enough to be satisfied by my performance. This wasn't about resurrecting the long-discarded fantasy of being a great pianist. Rather, it seemed a way to test life again, to press upon it and see what was still vital. I wanted to discover if something dormant inside of me could be reassembled, old habits of mind reconstructed after long disuse, if I could concentrate long enough to learn the notes and memorize the lines. I wanted to understand Bach better, and to see if my mind was sufficiently plastic to hear his music not as a wall of sound, but as a network of interrelated voices. In middle age, the question "Can I still do this?" becomes as powerful to our sense of self as the conviction, when we are young, that all things are possible. We must figure out how we will relate to this question, if we will withdraw from the things that once gave us pleasure, or meaning, out of fear that we have grown weak in their execution, as my mother so often did. Or if we must fight to keep learning, keep struggling after fundamental questions like: What does it mean to truly *know* a piece of music?

In our losing battle with death, we must learn to retreat with grace. But music, no matter what our age, is only learned through ridiculous persistence, and persistence in life is key, too. My mother had very little of that, and it worried me that I had inherited the deficiency. Grief unsettled me for a while, but when it began to fade into a low-grade noise in the background of life, I felt competent to search out in the *Goldberg Variations* the mechanical operation of what had seemed to me so mysterious and magisterial in the Bach Chaconne. I would learn the levers and gears of the music and see where that led me, very likely to a more painful awareness of my limitations, but with the hope that there might be other lessons along the way.

TWO

I RETURNED HOME TO my workaday life excited to get back to the piano, but quickly found myself in debt to the world. A month away had left duties neglected, professional promises unfulfilled, and growing deficits to friends and colleagues. A ritual ensued: The ordinary world inscribed me back into my usual place by making a hundred reasonable demands, and I fulfilled them because it seemed the act of measuring up to these expectations might hasten the process of mourning. The grieving was internalized, with no outward markers. Instead, I took up life with the usual, quintessentially American determination to present an image of myself happy and thriving, in hope that the image would become real and supplant embarrassing feelings of sadness. I rejoined the world not because I was done with grief, but because I figured the world, with its fraternity of busy people, would do the work for me.

The holidays came and went, and with them yet more distractions. In the spring, I realized it was time to euthanize my dog, and I marveled at how much better we serve our pets than people when it comes to extending life. He grew increasingly frail over several months, and I told my veterinarian that I would have him put down the moment he began to feel more than passing pain. One day I sensed that moment had arrived and later that afternoon the doctor said it was indeed upon us, and the next day she came to my home and it was done. Love and science tended to the matter, and one small creature passed out of the world without fear, indecision, or regret. At one point, in her last days, my mother begged me to do the same for her, but I wasn't sure if the request was serious. Even in her last days, she was given to histrionic declaration. "Just kill me," she said, so after thinking about it for a few hours I left a bottle of her sleeping pills on the nightstand and said, "You know, these will put you to sleep." But in those few hours she had lost the thread of her own thoughts, and the request to help her slip out of life was already forgotten.

A half year after my mother died, there was a memorial service, so once again I returned to my parents' house. As I got off the airplane, I remembered how before her death I would contemplate what life would be like after she was gone, and how one of the things I imagined I would miss most was no longer seeing her at the airport when I returned home for visits. The first hours of our occasional reunions, when she would pepper me with questions about my life, were always the happiest, even to the point that I would say to myself, *This is what it feels like to have a mother.* And I thought of a future when she wasn't around and no one would greet me outside the security checkpoint. But it had been years since I expected anyone to meet me at the airport, and it suddenly struck me as perverse that I would have decided long before it happened that it was this particular ritual I would miss after my mother died. Perhaps Proust would agree: when we anticipate a coming trauma, we like to think we can outwit our surprise and pain by imagining it in all its details; but when it comes, it never arrives as we have foreseen.

The remains of our extended family gathered at the memorial service, and the pleasure of seeing aunts, uncles, and cousins for the first time in decades, made the event seem more festive than somber. My father, never given to speechmaking, narrated a slideshow of my mother's life, and I was surprised by how many of the pictures were unknown to me, and how little I knew of the basic arc of their lives together. That afternoon, he seemed younger than he had been for years and I was happy to be free of a worry my sisters and I had felt since my mother became ill: that our father, who lived quietly in the shadow of my mother, and who had for decades supplied all the conditions of a happy house but was powerless to make it happy, would downsize his place on earth and die soon after his wife. But here he was, narrating our past in a way that was often new to us, speaking in his own voice, not merely echoing hers. He chose images of my mother when she was happy, or trying to look happy, and this seemed to set the seal on our collective memory of her: a pretty young woman with red hair who married her first love, a young naval officer from Idaho, with whom she had four children and shared a life of freedom and prosperity. No one spoke of the rest of her life, of the sadness and anger and unaccountable rages, of the fights and arguments that, if one were to read back over the transcripts we never kept, always began with her peevishness or fatigue or irritation, and that was fine. Death had severed our connection to her, and with it any hope of understanding her anger; and if we were never to understand that, then we would surely never understand all the rest of her life, and so why not substitute a happier, more comprehensible memory for one that must remain forever perplexing?

So I came back from Albuquerque a second time since my mother's death, this time with a touch of futility mixed in with grief. Not only was she gone, but I had lost energy for the project of understanding her. I was abandoning my mother to a category of things we must inevitably accept in our life, among them emotions we will never feel, objects we will never possess, places where we will never live. Again, I moved on to other things, the dry stuff of life. My intention to learn the *Goldberg Variations* began to join the chorus of life's larger to-do list, murmuring alongside things like "fix the roof" and "lose ten pounds," sinking into the background and growing more remote every day. And then, almost a year later, and quite by accident, I reencountered the intensity of that relationship to music I had felt during the days of my mother's death. I was in Chicago to give a talk, and found myself with a few free hours on a weekend morning. I wandered the city window-shopping and people-watching and was struck in passing that this was the sort of thing that used to make me happy. But I couldn't form a desire, neither for things nor for people. Nothing for sale had even the slightest attraction. Human bodies, even attractive ones, seemed alien. Desire for things, and often for people, operates as a chain of substitutions, leading us to want a new tie or pair of shoes because these objects stand in for deeper, more fundamental desires about connection and power and even immortality. But this chain was broken, and now I wondered what it was that propelled me through the streets at all, what, in fact, had been animating this strange husk that was standing on a corner along Michigan Avenue unable to think of a single thing it wanted in the world.

And then I chanced upon one of the few remaining bookstores that still specialize in classical music, and I remembered how much I used to enjoy browsing through dusty bins of old scores. The shop was full of young people, many of them carrying instrument cases. All around me, people were searching for things, violin concertos by Mozart, string quartets by Boccherini, arias by old Italians long forgotten but for a few lovely trifles that survive in popular anthologies. Each of these searches was evidence that what was dormant in me was thriving in others, and I felt ashamed to be so distant from the impulse to grow, learn, and live. When I walked into the shop I was at first bewildered, as if I had found the right office but forgotten the reason for the appointment, or arrived at the grocery store without my shopping list. I felt a bit of an imposter at first, to be there among so many real and aspiring musicians. But then I stopped and thought that there was in fact something I needed from this store, and as I stood on the threshold of the large, bright space that was humming with activity, I started to search my mind methodically, almost saying aloud what I was thinking: *What are you looking for?* And the repetition of this question, insistently and stupidly, seemed to heat my mind sufficiently to melt the old resistance and apathy, and I remembered a line about an old man's shriveled heart from a favorite poem, George Herbert's 1633 "The Flower." Worn with grief and age, his heart, he writes, "was gone / Quite underground; as flowers depart / To see their mother-root, when they have blown."

In the year since my mother died, I had all but given up on making music. I listened to it, went to concerts, and kept up with new recordings; but I hadn't played the piano in months. It wasn't just a matter of being busy. I couldn't, in fact, blame it "on life," as if life is alien and hostile to us, some mechanical thing over which we have no more power than the pinball does the bumpers. I needed the piano more than I ever had, but as with so many resolutions, the fear of failure had gathered around it quickly, containing and immobilizing it. It seemed ridiculous to buy more music, which would just add to the dust and chaos of the house and remind me how easily life can be held in abeyance. For as long as I stayed away from the piano, my desire to learn the *Goldberg Variations* remained an active if delayed resolution; once I began to play again, however, it would become an active ambition, a real project, and I feared it would join other futile projects, from the half-painted front porch to the unread books stacked on the desk.

The resistance was like what one might feel when calling an old friend after a long absence. A phone call or letter is a simple thing. You know reconnection would be a pleasure. But even between friends who have never quarreled, who could easily take up the thread of dialogue exactly where it left off years ago, silence takes on a life of its own. It grows into something almost palpable, a shared reticence between people too polite or superstitious to disturb the equilibrium. I could have sat down at the piano any hour of the day for the previous year. I passed by the instrument, cold and coffinlike, hundreds of times. I dusted it off and even had it tuned, and tended to the temperature and humidity in the room—to which pianos are as sensitive as plants are to water—more assiduously than the care of my own wardrobe. But to sit down and touch the keyboard would be to start a conversation that I felt would absorb too much of me. The piano and I had achieved a self-sustaining state of mutual wariness.

This wasn't ordinary procrastination, in the sense that we often resist doing something we must do, until the pressure is insurmountable and crisis looms. This was a more fundamental species of resistance, which has been with us as long as mankind has enjoyed the leisure of choosing to do one thing over another. Every day, I chose not to do what I wanted to do, what I knew I must do. To linger in a state of planning and intention may seem like a canny way to outwit the passage of time, always projecting oneself into the future; but it depletes us in the moment. "Remember how long thou hast been putting off these things, and how often thou hast received an opportunity from the gods, and yet dost not use it," wrote Marcus Aurelius, an old Roman soldier near death, trying to talk his way from merely knowing to actually living the truths he had gathered of a lifetime.

The music I knew I finally needed to buy that morning in Chicago was the piece that had haunted me for the past year, a work published with the rather daunting title page: "Keyboard Practice consisting of an Aria with thirty variations for the harpsichord with 2 Manuals prepared for the Enjoyment of Music-Lovers by Johann Sebastian Bach."

The store had a copy of the classic Schirmer edition, with the same dull, old-fashioned yellow cover design the company has been using since before I was born. Even now, so many years after I took my first piano lessons at the age of four from a kindly Welsh lady, the dowdy look of the Schirmer imprints inspired a sense of expectation and excitement. Back in an age when middle-class kids who lived in the suburbs were obliged to learn some kind of musical instrument, students started out with brightly colored musical primers, full of simple songs with titles such as "Indian Dance" and "Irish Gigue," interspersed with pictures and diagrams showing you where to place your fingers. But if you persevered with your studies, you would leave these picture books behind and graduate to "serious" music, by composers such as Clementi, Kuhlau, or Mozart, who wrote little sonatas or sonatinas for young players, accessible music that was, nonetheless, substantial and engaging, music published in old-fashioned books by companies like Schirmer. It was a relief to find the *Goldberg Variations* looking as sober and serious as any of the volumes I had learned from when I was a boy.

Bach never called them "*The Goldberg Variations*," so on the cover the name "Goldberg" is in quotes, an acknowledgment of the biographical mystery and confusion that has grown like a barnacle on this great piece. Johann Gottlieb Goldberg was a student of Bach, but hardly his most renowned or influential acolyte. His name became attached to the piece because of an anecdote in the first Bach biography, published more than a half century after the composer's death. The author, Johann Nikolaus Forkel, tells the following story:

> For this [work] ... we have to thank the instigation of the former Russian ambassador to the electoral court of Saxony, Count Kaiserling, who often stopped in Leipzig and brought there with him the afore-mentioned Goldberg, in order to have him given musical instruction by Bach. The Count was often ill and had sleepless nights. At such times, Goldberg, who lived in his house, had to spend the night in an antechamber, so as to play for him during his insomnia. Once the Count mentioned in Bach's presence that he would like to have some clavier pieces for Goldberg, which should be of such a smooth and somewhat lively character that he might be a little cheered up by them in his sleepless nights. Bach thought himself best able to fulfill this wish by means of Variations, the writing of which he had until then considered an ungrateful task on account of the repeatedly similar harmonic foundation. But since at this time all his works were already models of art, such

also these variations became under his hand. Yet he produced only a single work of this kind. Thereafter the Count always called them *his* variations. He never tired of them, and for a long time sleepless nights meant: "Dear Goldberg, do play me one of my variations."

For this, Bach was supposedly rewarded with a "golden goblet filled with 100 louis-d'or," an implausibly large sum at the time, and about ten times what he was paid for a cantata written for a royal audience. This is one of the many orphaned legends that litter music history, largely disowned by scholars for its many inconsistencies. Bach published his variations in 1741, as part of a magisterial and multivolume series of keyboard works known as the *Clavier-Übung*—an exhaustive encyclopedia of keyboard possibilities and practice. The *Clavier-Übung* was one of several Herculean efforts in the mid–eighteenth century to compile and codify human knowledge, including Denis Diderot's 1751 *Encyclopédie* and Samuel Johnson's 1755 *A Dictionary of the English Language*. Bach took great pains over it, and in a publication of this significance, one would ordinarily expect an elaborate and sycophantic dedication to the man who commissioned it. But there is no mention of Count Keyserlingk, or any other hint of the Keyserlingk-Goldberg story in the *Clavier-Übung* volume devoted to the variations.

Other details seem odd, too. Are these variations really suitable as a sleep aid? While many of them can be played smoothly, others are so "lively" it is difficult to imagine they would soothe an insomniac's restlessness. Nor do the darker variations, where Bach not only casts his material in a minor key, but pitches them well past mere melancholy or sadness, seem suited to somnolence. There are only three minor key variations—the fifteenth, twenty-first, and twenty-fifth—but they have outsized influence on the larger drama, living in a realm of anguish and despair closely connected to the passionate intensity of Bach's most powerful religious music. One doesn't sleep through a crucifixion.

Nor do the variations seem a likely response to a patron who simply wanted some soporific music to flow from the antechamber to his bedroom. In many ways, this is radical music, extending the variation form further than it had been pushed before, exploring new extremes of variety and structural drama. If Bach was indeed fulfilling what was, frankly, a rather patronizing commission—write music that will put an aristocrat to sleep—then the *Goldberg Variations* look like a sophisticated joke. Forkel's colorful anecdote, which still vexes Bach scholars, was published in 1802, after most of Bach's children and all of his sons who had distinguished themselves in the family business of music were dead. Yet scholars still turn to it for evidence, in part because Forkel had direct contact and correspondence with the Bach family, including Carl Philipp Emanuel Bach and Wilhelm Friedemann Bach, whose reputations had surpassed that of their father by the early nineteenth century.

Studying Bach is a bit like studying Shakespeare: There is an enormous imbalance between the depth and breadth of the artistic legacy on the one hand, and the paucity of reliable biographical evidence on the other. Rather like the curious detail in Shakespeare's will, that he bequeathed to his wife his "second-best bed," specific details of Bach's life have been pored over and analyzed for centuries. Our understanding of his life and personality is based on a small, well-abused repertoire of stories, many of them of doubtful authenticity, which recur again and again in the biographical literature. He was once angry enough to berate and throw his wig at another organist; he stole music from his older brother, with whom he lived after he was orphaned; he found money hidden in some discarded fish heads, which staved off hunger and gave him the freedom to travel; he so terrified a French organist whom he had challenged to a musical duel that the hapless player fled town rather than be humiliated by Bach's superior skills.

But if the details of Shakespeare's life are also scant, the plays at least animate hundreds of imaginary souls, each one built up from believable details, each one potentially containing some part of the Shakespeare whom we seek. If nothing else, we feel that we can see the world as Shakespeare saw it, with only Shakespeare missing from the picture. In the case of Bach, the music confirms what little we know of his personality—that he was pious, hardworking, meticulous, and talented beyond any musician of his age or any other. But it is difficult to get the measure of the rest of Bach, his healthy self-regard, his occasional prickliness, his temper, his earthy humor, his love of family and home. The data is there, but not enough to be conclusive, or flesh out a satisfying portrait. And if you were to heap all of it on the table and sort through it dispassionately, you would almost certainly conclude that given a choice between having dinner with Shakespeare and having dinner with Bach, the former would win hands down.

Like so many Bach sources, Forkel's slim biography is a basketful of crumbs, each one of them precious but many of them potentially suspect at the same time. Forkel wasn't just a historian or biographer, he was also an evangelist for a man who, by 1802, was generally regarded as a dry, stuffy, overly intellectual, and aesthetically fussy composer. Even though Forkel knew Bach's children, what he gathered from them isn't necessarily any more reliable than the testimony of disinterested friends or colleagues. Powerful parents shape and even warp their children's memories, and there is evidence from Bach's letters that at least one of his sons felt so stifled by expectations or pressure that he ran away altogether. Duty and filial respect, admiration and resentment, love and grief, are volatile perturbations in the transmission of fact across even a single generation: certainly, I am not to be entirely trusted as a witness to my mother's life, or even my own.

But Forkel's anecdote is surprisingly elaborate, specific, and appealing. Some scholars suggest that the author simply got a few

names and details wrong, that perhaps Bach encountered Keyserlingk shortly after the variations were published, and simply gave
his eminent patron a signed copy. Perhaps Keyserlingk was flattered
by the gesture and began to think of the music as "my variations."
But what does one make of the strangely precise domestic details:
that the young Goldberg served in the house of Keyserlingk, that
his master was sickly and had insomnia, that the teenage musician
played on a harpsichord placed in the antechamber to the count's
bedroom? The anecdote may get all of these details wrong, may in
fact simply invent things that never happened, but it raises fascinating questions about how music was performed in the middle of the
eighteenth century. Were the variations played from beginning to
end, as a single arching narrative, as is almost universally the case
today? Or were they rendered à la carte, a pick-and-choose approach
at the discretion of the performer or the whim of the listener? Keyserlingk doesn't tell his musician to play *the* variations, but rather,
"one of my variations." Even the notion of what kind of music is
likely to help us sleep may have changed in the past several centuries. It's entirely possible that what we might consider musically
laborious—closely following a complex contrapuntal score—was not
felt as work in the eighteenth century.

Then there is the problem of Goldberg himself. He was born in
what is now Gdansk, to a father who was a prominent instrument
maker, and he grew up in a rich musical environment in a culturally
diverse city. The young musician was something of a prodigy and had
come to Keyserlingk's attention by the time he was just ten years old.
Under the Russian count's patronage, the young Goldberg studied
with Wilhelm Friedemann, the oldest of Bach's sons, a brilliant keyboard player and likely the musician for whom the *Goldberg Variations* were written, and with Bach himself. The boy had a reputation
as a virtuoso, an expert sight reader, and a skillful technician, and he
went on to become a composer as well, before he died of tuberculosis

at the age of twenty-nine. And yet, despite evidence of his musical prowess, scholars who are skeptical of the Forkel anecdote cite Goldberg's tender years as still more evidence that the story can't be true. Christoph Wolff, one of the world's preeminent Bach scholars, writes: "The age of the doubtlessly gifted Johann Gottlieb Goldberg (1727–1756), who was brought to Bach in Leipzig by Keyserlingk in 1737 for instruction and was subsequently engaged as the latter's house harpsichordist, would seem to make it highly improbable that Bach had him, barely thirteen years old, in mind when he planned the work." This is curious, given the rich history of child prodigies over the centuries. Of all the arguments against Forkel's accuracy, this is the weakest, but one of the most revealing: it is better, apparently, that the origins of one of Bach's greatest works remain obscure than to believe that he might have composed them for someone so insignificant, so young, so forgotten as poor Johann Gottlieb Goldberg.

Forkel makes it sound as if Bach were grumbling his way through the commission because he disliked the variation form for its repetitiousness ("an ungrateful task" because "of the constant sameness of the fundamental harmony"). And he adds, confusingly, that Bach wrote only one "model" of this kind of work. This last mistake is easy to make. Indeed, Bach had only written one previous work bearing the word "variations" in the title that has come down to us. These were a small set of variations "in the Italian style" on a rather simple-minded tune, and they are rarely performed today. But this was far from Bach's only previous effort at variation form.

Variations were fundamental to a significant amount of Bach's output. The great violin Chaconne and the Passacaglia in C minor for Organ are not only monumental exercises in variation form, but they are grounded on a "repeatedly similar harmonic foundation." The multi-voiced fugues of which he was an unsurpassable master are also exercises in highly structured motivic variation, with individual voices altering the original line as needed for harmonic or dramatic effect, compressing or extending the rhythms, breaking apart and reassembling fragments of the core idea. Many of the instrumental suites follow generally repetitive harmonic schemes, such that each movement, like each variation in the *Goldberg* cycle, is effectively a variation on an existing framework. Given how essential the techniques deployed in the *Goldbergs* are to Bach's larger artistry, how could Forkel suggest the composer found the task "ungrateful"?

What matters, of course, is what gets varied, and how. Unlike later composers, such as Mozart and Beethoven, who tended to write variations based on a melodic line—sometimes a popular song or fashionable aria, including in Mozart's case the tune we know today as "Twinkle, Twinkle, Little Star"—the composers of Bach's day often built their variations around the bass line, sometimes as the "subject" for elaboration and sometimes as an anchor to variations above. The difference between the *Goldberg Variations* and a work such as the violin Chaconne—both of which are built over a recurring bass line—is the length and form of the material that Bach takes as his starting point.

The bass line in the Chaconne is only four measures long, and is repeated again and again, as a harmonic ground, while Bach writes a seamlessly integrated flow of new ideas above it. The psychological effect of the short, repeated cell of the Chaconne is markedly different from that of the variation form Bach was using in the *Goldberg* set. The Chaconne often feels condensed, obsessive, and insistent. The *Goldberg* bass line, by contrast, sprawls over thirty-two bars, twice as long as many of Bach's hymn settings, and like his hymns, this extended line comes to several resting places before moving to its conclusion.

It begins with a descending line that would have been familiar, even to the point of being clichéd, to contemporary listeners—rather like the three-chord pop song is today—but then the music moves on, becoming more elaborate, discursive, and unpredictable. While the aria opens with a dignified, stately walking rhythm, it later becomes liquid, with shorter notes flowing freely, dissolving the song's initial austerity. The music is gently and quietly unmoored, in a way that seems strikingly at odds with what we might think of as "Baroque" music, with its formality, regularity, and even predictability. This moment, when the formal becomes fluent, has historical resonance, hinting at an enormous change in musical style that was well under way when Bach composed his variation, the emergence of a new *galant* aesthetic that was deemed simpler, more accessible, more melodic, and more gracious than the music for which Bach was famous. For many listeners, it is also one of the most moving passages in the entire cycle, especially so when the aria is repeated at the end, and the fluidity of this line becomes an aural symbol for the passage of time itself.

For me, as I was watching my mother die over the course of several days, the short, reiterative repetitions of the Chaconne had mimicked grief, a sense of being in the grips of something primal, commanding, and persistent. Now the *Goldberg Variations* adumbrated something that comes later in bereavement, the elastic sense of confusion that comes from knowing where you are while being lost at the same time. After death delivers its initial shock, one wanders the world exploring loss, how it operates, how it reveals things that were concealed, how loss completes our often limited sense of the person who died and begins the process of fixing that person in our memory. When grief loosens its hold, you return to the world you once knew, only to find it transformed by the thing that is missing; when, at the end of the *Goldberg Variations*, Bach repeats the aria with which it began, it is utterly transfigured. It is like the river in which one can never step foot twice, and Bach seems to say: "You've never heard this thing you think you know so well."

I had no need to purchase a new copy of the variations that morning in Chicago. Almost every note of music Bach wrote is available, for free, on the internet, and I could have simply printed out an old edition of the piece. Bach would be staggered by this development, not just to learn how well he was treated by posterity, but because most of the music he composed never circulated, and wasn't intended for an audience beyond the church, the patron's drawing room, or a small circle of students and colleagues. Bach's music was known only by a handful of published volumes (which included the *Goldberg Variations*), and when he died, he could have had little certainty that his name would outlast the lifetime of his sons or grandchildren. Indeed, almost a century after Bach died, his legacy was so neglected that Felix Mendelssohn gathered funds to erect a monument to his memory in Leipzig. At the dedication ceremony, Bach's last remaining grandson appeared, in his eighties; it was a surprise to everyone that he even existed.

For some reason, that morning in Chicago, I thought it worth paying money for a new copy of the *Goldberg Variations*, and somehow the act of buying it helped dislodge my resistance to making music again. It was a concrete thing, a small, physical stirring after a long period of inertia. During the short flight home from Chicago, I pulled it out and opened to the first page of the aria. There is a kind of superstition that comes with turning the first pages of a new book: that the unknown, contained therein, will change you. It is a fantasy that fades over time, as we grow older, as our identity becomes more fixed, and we emerge more skeptical of novelty. But, opening to the title page of Bach's greatest keyboard work, I remembered the sweet old promise fleetingly, and felt the familiar hope that one might slip into this mystery and slide out the other side newly tempered, cleansed, or shriven.

Over the sound of the engines, I heard the music in my ear, half remembered, half sung silently to myself, a tender line rising three notes before falling down six, a breath of air followed by an extended sigh. It seemed simpler than I recalled, pure and childlike. When I practiced the instrument as a boy, on the small upright piano in the family room, I was keenly aware that my mother was listening. When she was in a foul mood, she listened for mistakes, gathering evidence that I was sloppy or ignoring what my teachers had told me. If she was inclined to rage, then she would descend on me and the piano, furious at my willfulness. I would try to placate her, or make excuses, unless I, too, was angry, in which case we fought. The outcome of these brawls depended on her, and they always went one of two ways: she would thrash me over the neck and arms, pull me by the hair, and then send me to my room; or she would begin crying, angry that I was wasting the hard-earned money she spent on my lessons and in despair at my ingratitude. Once, she pulled my hair so violently that I fell off the piano bench backward and lay on the floor, looking up at her face, contorted by fury. She fled to her bedroom, and I abandoned the piano for the silence of a book.

But the memory of her listening has lasted longer, and mattered more, than the anger, and it remains with me even today when I sit alone at the piano and make music in an empty house. She is my other ear, allergic to music that is fast, complicated, or dissonant, always listening for something simple and sweet, and even now when I play I am aware of her eavesdropping over my shoulder. She chides me and encourages me, and even though it has been decades since I played for her regularly, I still measure my performance by whether she nods off or smiles from the other room. She loves her Chopin and the slow movements by Mozart, is happy to hear a familiar Christmas carol or "We Gather Together" on Thanksgiving morning, and though these things are hidden deep in a box in the attic, I know she would be delighted to hear some of the songs I made up and wrote down as a boy, happy little ditties I composed in imitation of things I heard on the radio, repetitive and cheerful.

As I grew more accomplished at the piano, the music I played appealed to her less and less. She never enjoyed Liszt or Rachmaninoff beyond a few of the preludes or more lyrical character pieces.

Brahms would make her say, "Oooof, too heavy." In college I was in love with the music of the mercurial Russian romantic and mystic Alexander Scriabin, and later the Polish composer Karol Szymanowski, but the sounds they made only vexed her. Opera, which I came to love more than any other music, held no interest for her beyond a few arias made popular by Pavarotti. If I played Verdi on the stereo, she would call down from the upstairs: "What is that awful caterwauling?" And I would turn it off, wondering, where did that word come from?

Over the years, her susceptibility to music was reduced to the most basic things, the familiar classics and simple pieces full of charm and tenderness. My efforts to master technically difficult passages, or muscle my way through bravura display, left her agitated. But when things grew lyrical, when the storminess of a Beethoven sonata subsided to a pastoral episode, or Mozart's quicksilver figuration gave way to a longer, more ardent line, then I knew she might catch the thread and be pleased with my efforts. On occasion, when I was a boy, she would call me by my nickname from another room, saying, "That's nice, Flip." And although I can no longer quite remember the tone of her voice, my mind is as well trained as a faithful dog, so that when the music is beautiful in the way I know she particularly craved, I play it all the more tenderly and still expect to be given my reward: "That's nice, Flip."

By the end of her life, I can think of only one piece that she genuinely enjoyed, Ralph Vaughan Williams's violin fantasy "The Lark Ascending." Music, which had been a large part of her life as a girl and a young woman, was eventually thinned out to a single piece, a musical representation of a bird rising into the air, leaving earth and earthbound things behind, before it "to silence nearer soars"—the words of George Meredith, whose poem inspired the English composer. And though there is a universe of difference between the two pieces, the simple violin fantasy full of melodic afflatus and the *Gold-*

berg Variations with their contrapuntal complexity, I cannot hear
the final repeat of the aria at the end of Bach's masterpiece without
thinking that something in it "to silence nearer soars."

Between childhood and that moment when I sat with the *Goldberg Variations* on my lap, squeezed into the middle seat on an airplane from Chicago, I had created a world of music entirely my own,
learned pieces I never played for her, loved music that would remain
to her absolutely alien and inscrutable: It took me by surprise, therefore, that as I listened in my head to the haunting *Goldberg* aria, I was
overwhelmed by the realization that I would never play *this* music
for her. I might have said the same thing of any number of works I
had learned over the previous decades. But there had always been the
possibility that I *might* play them for her, that she might call from
the other room, "That's nice, Flip." Until now, that voice had always
had some thin but plausible connection to another living being. Now
it lived only in my memory. It was a talisman of adult solitude, sus-
tained by me alone, a thing no one would ever name or notice, or
help me remember, and when I ceased to tend it the erasure would be
utterly insignificant but absolutely final. And the saddest thing was
that this aria was exactly the sort of music she would have adored.

———

I WISH THAT FORKEL'S story about Bach and the young Goldberg
were true, that Bach wrote this music for a young harpsichordist
to play for a sleepless count, ensorcelling him to dreams from a
darkened chamber beyond his bedroom. It is an appealing anecdote
that knits together the composer, the performer, and the listener
in a perfect circle, joining the brilliance of the seasoned artist to
the vitality of the young musician, and the refinement of the ideal
listener. Composers crave performers, performers crave listeners,
and listeners want to believe that the music is made just for them. I

love the unlikely excess of payment, the one hundred louis d'or the count is said to have paid for the music, a blue-blooded tribute to red-blooded genius, a sign that both the patron and the artist knew the worth of what was being exchanged. I'd like to think that Keyserlingk's generosity explains the absence of anything mentioning him on the title page, that somewhere there is a letter from Bach proposing a fawning tribute to the count, and the count's response: "No, the music is enough."

And I'd like to think that young Goldberg saw all of this and was rather in awe of it, that he knew he was the mediator and communicant between these substantial men who were greatly his elders, and felt a terrible responsibility when he sat down to play. Perhaps during the day he wondered about his place in the world, as he stood in the shadow of the count's business and affairs, his work as a diplomat and his stature as an aristocrat. But when it was dark and they had retired from the world, something even greater took place. Then the young Goldberg would sit at the keyboard and, with his mind divided between the music on the page and the fitful man in the other room, he would play as gently and as carefully as he could. Terrified of making a mistake, which might wake his patron, but captivated by the music, which was unlike anything he had ever played before, Goldberg would intone the aria slowly, simply and with the most gracious line his fingers could muster. Perhaps that would be enough to put the count to sleep, but if not, the young man would play on, perhaps skipping the boisterous polonaise of the first variation in favor of the next one, which strolls amiably through a quieter place in the woods. And when he heard snoring from the bedroom, steady proof that the count was finally away, he would be torn: Dare he indulge his own pleasure and continue playing, and risk the chance that some new twist in the music would undo his efforts, some lively variation full of drama and incident would disturb the peace and wake his employer in the adjoining room? Or should he deny himself the pleasure and break off in the middle of things, dutifully sundering the stream of music in favor of silence? But he must stop, and gather the pages of Bach's score, snuff the candles, and leave the room, to sleep no doubt somewhere far less grand and warm than the chamber in which the harpsichord now sat silent.

THREE

MYFANWY LIVED ONLY a few doors away from the house where I spent my first six years, in a suburb of Schenectady, New York. Doubtless her house had been built when all the other split-level houses in the suburban subdivision were built, and its rooms were laid out almost exactly as they were in ours, but it was a very different sort of home. Inside, it was quiet, there were thick curtains on the windows, and the light passing through the sheers was gentle and tinged with color. Her house was full of things, Old World things, ceramic figurines on the shelves, dried flowers in cutglass vases, and on the walls, reproductions of Old Master paintings, which she borrowed from the local library. She was a Welshwoman, in her seventies at least, and a beloved local figure who taught piano to children in the neighborhood.

Down the street, our house was bedlam. When the windows were open in the warm months, you could hear my sisters practicing their violins, scraping out perfunctory scales haltingly on their cheaply made student instruments, with my mother sometimes offering a descant of Vivaldi from some other room in the house. But there was also yelling and fights and doors slamming, and though one might not hear it from the street, there was sometimes crying from my parents' room, which was in a partially converted attic above the main floor. It was a small house, full of wayward people, run by a strong but capricious woman who often said she didn't want to be a mother at all. I was too young at the time to know what the problem was, that a girl of nineteen who had dreamed of a big life had ended up with one of ordinary dimensions, but I sensed something amiss every time I made the short walk home from my piano teacher's house.

I studied with Myfanwy for three years, playing little pieces from colored lesson books on her ornately carved upright piano while she sang along in her lilting Welsh burr. She was plump, kind, and laughed easily. She loved children without ever making them feel like children. When I came into her house she would ask me questions about the little things a boy of four or five might care about. Then she would send me to the bathroom to wash my hands before she picked me off the floor with an exaggerated groan and a low, rolling laugh, like she was lifting a sack of flour, and set me on the round top of her piano stool. Unlike our piano, a Japanese-made box of polished wood with plastic keys and a bright metallic twang, hers had ivory keys and made a dark, mellow sound. It towered over both of us, me with my legs not able to reach the pedals, and Myfanwy in her plush armchair beside me, expanding in every direction but up.

I know I was four or five years old because I could play music on the piano before I could read. Music came into my life like language, unconsciously and painlessly. My sisters must have taught me a few things at home, but I learned the fundamentals from Myfanwy. And yet I don't remember having learned or having been taught anything, only that I would go to Myfanwy's house once a week and we would spend a delightful half an hour singing and pecking at the keys and laughing. I learned to read a few years later, a laborious process that was fraught with anxiety, and I can still recall the moment when my teacher pronounced to the class that "Philip is reading" as I struggled to sound out the syllables of my first-grade primer. But I can't remember a similar moment at the piano when my fingers suddenly did as they were told and someone said, "Philip is playing the piano."

During those years of early childhood, my mother fulfilled all the obligations of motherhood as she understood them, and that included teaching her children music. Her eldest daughters were given violins and she taught them herself, which was a mistake. She would play along with them, growing frustrated and angry, berating them for inattention and sloppiness. After my mother died, I asked my aunt whether she had been a diligent student of the violin. "Oh yes, she was the best of all of us," she said of the three sisters who grew up together during the 1940s. Despite my grandfather's struggling candy store business, he managed to buy his daughters instruments, including a decent used quarter-sized violin from a neighbor. The good violin went to my mother. "I was always getting cast-offs," said my aunt. My mother and my aunt would put on Gypsy dresses and play duets together for parties, not for money, but as a service or offering to friends and family. My mother never told me anything about this, but my aunt remembers it as serious business, with some bitterness: "We got a call once to play a gig and I said we couldn't make it," she says. But my grandmother snatched the phone from her and snarled into the receiver, "They'll be there."

Perhaps my mother imagined fashioning her eldest daughters into something like the duo she had with her sister. Perhaps she felt her daughters didn't properly appreciate their good fortune, to each play their own little violin, newly bought, not purchased second-hand from a more prosperous neighbor. Perhaps she simply had no patience, and with four children in the house, her nerves were frayed, and making music with her daughters reminded her that music had never been her avenue to independence and freedom. In any case, my older sisters struggled with the violin, and came into violent conflict with my mother, who would threaten and belittle and rage at them, until the whole house was shaken by slamming doors and everyone had fled as far as they could from the wrath and tears of the others. For some reason, she didn't inflict the same torture on me or my next-eldest sister. We were allowed to take piano lessons, from a kindly woman for whom music was a form of conviviality and pleasure, and a discipline disguised as play.

Myfanwy was the first of three teachers I had as a child, and I parted from all three unhappily. Shortly after I entered kindergarten, my family left our first home and bought a larger and newly built one a few miles away with modern conveniences like an electric garage door opener and an intercom system for communicating between the rooms, which we never used because we didn't particularly want to communicate with each other, and when it was absolutely necessary it was easier just to yell. It sat in a barren expanse of newly planted grass, with no trees or bushes or flowers of any sort. But it seemed gigantic to me, with a bedroom for each of the four children, and finally a proper bedroom for my parents, who were tired of sleeping in the attic. My mother was enormously pleased with the new house and took to the making of curtains, cutting and sewing, and crafting matching pillows and covers for everything, including the piano, which was draped in a geometric black-and-white diamond pattern that seemed very modern to us at the time. But the new house came with a cost: the younger children, including me, were uprooted from our schools, and we were no longer within walking distance of Myfanwy's house.

So my sister Lisa and I needed to find a new teacher, and because Lisa was older and I was making progress on the instrument, we looked for a teacher who was more than a musical babysitter, someone who taught professionally and would help us advance to the next level. Charlotte was a German woman who lived in one of the better suburbs and ran a bustling piano studio in a room off her kitchen. Unlike Myfanwy, who would appear for lessons as if she had just finished kneading a loaf of bread or stirring a pot of soup, Charlotte ran her studio with brisk efficiency. We would wait at the kitchen table nervously as the sound of the piano filtered through the door, with Charlotte's voice above, counting, counting, counting. Then the door would open and Charlotte would execute a seamless motion with a broad smile, sliding one child out with the right hand and beckoning the next one in with the left, as if reloading some time-saving domestic appliance. After our first lesson, Charlotte sent us home with a mail-order catalog from a music publishing company, with at least two dozen volumes checked off as immediate necessities for our further education. "Jesus Christ," said my mother, when she added up the cost of it all.

Among our new acquisitions was the *Notebook for Anna Magdalena Bach*, a compendium of music compiled by the Bach family in the 1720s. Anna Magdalena was Bach's second wife, and she had been a competent professional singer before they were married. The notebook that bears her name is a potpourri of music including various suites of dances that are among Bach's most accessible works for keyboard, and short pieces by other composers. In an age before the easy availability of printed music, notebooks like this one became rather like family scrapbooks or recipe albums, a motley collection of music made for a variety of different purposes. There was music that might be used to teach dance in the home, arias that were favorites at family gatherings, chorales that served to teach children the basics of harmony, and even works composed by the children themselves, their first essays (along with their father's corrections) saved and cherished like a lock of baby hair or old Polaroids.

The aria that became the basis for the *Goldberg Variations* first appears in the 1725 *Notebook for Anna Magdalena* (though it was likely entered later), along with two minuets that were popular instructional pieces when I was learning the instrument. Charlotte used to say, "Give us, O Lord, our daily Bach," and she intended these minuets as my introduction to Bach. They are simple, gracious, tuneful works, in two parts, but it doesn't take a sophisticated ear to determine that they don't sound much like Bach. In fact, in the 1970s it was determined that they were written by Christian Petzold, a composer and organist who, unlike Bach, traveled throughout Europe. The Bach family notebook gives us an intriguing but uncertain window into the domestic life of his family—some sense, perhaps, of their taste and curiosity. Petzold's minuets occur along with a sophisticated little rondeau by François Couperin, the greatest of the French harpsichord masters, and a composer whom Bach admired, and a minuet ambiguously attributed to "Mons. Böhm," perhaps the famous organist Georg Böhm, with whom Bach may have studied when he was an adolescent. From these and other works, among them arias from various sources, including opera (a musical form Bach never pursued), one gets the sense of a pragmatic, unpretentious household, curious about the larger world, and not embarrassed to cherish music that was easy on the ears and rather trifling when compared to that composed by the patriarch in his professional capacity.

As for the *Goldberg* aria, some scholars have doubted whether it, too, was written by Bach. Curiously, the piece appears in the notebook on two pages that divide another aria in half. It was, apparently, inserted after the copyist of a song called "Bist du bei mir," originally from Gottfried Heinrich Stölzel's opera *Diomedes*, accidently left two pages in the middle blank. Perhaps they stuck together and whoever penned in the *Goldberg* aria didn't want to waste blank paper. But the sentiments of "Bist du bei mir" are curiously evocative of the ingratiating melodic appeal of the *Goldberg* aria, as if the *Goldberg* tune were a sweet filling piped into the aria's darker core:

Abide by me, and I will go with joy
to my death and to my rest.
Ah, how pleasing would be my death,
if your beloved hands
pressed close my faithful eyes.

Philipp Spitta, who wrote what is often considered the first, serious, and comprehensive biography of Bach (and who remains one of the most engaging writers on the subject), went so far as to imply that the *Goldberg* aria was written as a love song. "It must certainly have been originally written for Anna Magdalena," he says, and in using it as the inspiration for his variations, Bach "was probably influenced by special motives of a personal kind." But a robust debate about its authorship broke out in the 1980s, just in time for Bach's tercentennial, with one scholar claiming that the piece "is quite certainly not by Bach but by a so far unknown Frenchman." Others rigorously challenged this, but there is now a slightly unsettled consensus that the aria, though not always typical of Bach and inflected with *galant* delicacies, is indeed by Bach.

I passed by the *Goldberg* aria and "Bist du bei mir" a hundred times as a child, in search of others that were more accessible to me, the simpler dances, including Petzold's minuets. No matter who wrote them, they are lovely trifles, and I learned them under Charlotte's tutelage sufficiently well to proceed on to Bach's easier preludes, and then over the course of the next several years to the first of the preludes and fugues from his grand compendium *The Well-Tempered Clavier*. Charlotte had firm and decided ideas on piano technique, and insisted on a precise hand position, the wrists and palms flat, the fingers rounded, with each digit raising and striking the key with the slight percussive snap of an old typewriter. "Do you know how much weight it takes to press a piano key?" she once asked me, when I played too loudly. I confessed I didn't know. "Two Hershey Bars." Which is to say about three ounces. Once, when I was lucky enough to have two candy bars at my disposal, I tried placing them on a key to see if it would sink down and quietly intone the string, but I couldn't quite manage to balance them properly. I've never figured out if Charlotte was right, but I can still hear her voice in my ear admonishing, "Two Hershey bars," when I played more assertively than was wanted.

Myfanwy had said I had talent, and Charlotte doted on me. It was not the same for my sister Lisa, who had talent but who was treated by Charlotte as the stepchild. Although Lisa had at first enjoyed her lessons with Charlotte, she soon came to dread them, and there were conferences with my mother behind closed doors and conversations in low voices. One January, the tension became critical. My sister remembers it this way: Shortly before Christmas, she told her teacher that she wanted to learn a complicated Beethoven sonata; Charlotte said it was too hard for her. Lisa persisted and learned the first movement over the holiday break, but when she played it at her first lesson after the new year, Charlotte said only, "You played it in the wrong key."

It's hard to know what to make of this. I heard the story secondhand and wasn't party to the confrontation on the other side of the kitchen door. It seems implausible that a child could learn a Beethoven sonata in "the wrong key," which would be even more difficult than learning it in the right key. But perhaps she played it in the wrong tempo, or simply forgot a few sharps or flats here and there. Maybe she misheard or misunderstood Charlotte, or maybe Charlotte was simply being cruel. But whatever happened, my mother and my teacher quarreled and all three of us parted ways with her.

I was bereft, and Lisa was so scarred by the episode that she gave up piano altogether. If Myfanwy had made music fun, Charlotte made it seem important, and she introduced me to serious music, pieces that had weighty labels like "sonatina" and "invention" and "minuet." She made me feel part of a grown-up tradition, something venerable and sacred, and it was while studying with her that, for the first time, I was able to enjoy the music as music, not as a trick a child performs for adults or a chore to be mastered. Success was intrinsic and it meant something more than a star pasted in the page of my musical primer, which was Myfanwy's reward for work well done. It was with Charlotte that I was first able to step outside myself and hear the music independently from my struggle to play the piano, that I was first able to say to myself, *Philip is playing the piano.* Though

Charlotte may have been mean to my sister, that mattered little to me then. She had been kind to me.

———

PIANO LESSONS AS a cultural phenomenon flourished in the United States well into the 1980s. In the first decade of the twentieth century, American manufacturers produced an estimated 370,000 pianos, a number that fell during the Great Depression and Second World War, but rose again to nearly a quarter-million instruments by 1980. By the time I was growing up, in a suburban enclave of tract homes, it was rare to encounter a house without a piano. But the strange ritual of taking lessons, full of social aspiration and the middle-class obsession with self-improvement, has origins that predate the preeminence of the piano as the dominant instrument in bourgeois households. Before the piano came the harpsichord, which was both a workhorse instrument supporting professional opera singers and chamber ensembles and orchestras, as well as a solo instrument. In France of the ancien régime, there was a small industry of teaching the instrument, mainly to the blue-blooded, especially women of the upper classes. The most famous of the harpsichord teachers was also one of the great geniuses of keyboard music, François Couperin, who wrote volumes of short pieces with enigmatic titles that were by turns wry and wistful, scintillating and sardonic, each one a brief sketch of something—a mood, a person, an idea—captured with delicacy, refinement, and poise. Bach, whose musical style and instincts were antipodal to those of Couperin, was an admirer, and though nothing he wrote would ever be confused with the music of Couperin, there are plenty of moments in his keyboard works when alert listeners will feel certain they hear an echo or homage to the French master.

In 1716, Couperin's fame as a teacher was such that he published his own lesson book for young players, *L'art de toucher le clavecin*,

The Art of Playing the Harpsichord. He offered it to the world a bit like sharing family recipes or vital trade secrets: "Perhaps a few people will say that I work against my own best interests in these disclosures," he wrote in his preface. But when he said (in a later edition) that his music had been received favorably by "Paris, the Provinces and foreigners," it was a telling indication of the power of his reputation. At the time, Couperin was as famous outside of Paris as Bach was obscure beyond the reaches of Thuringia, and his little book remains a vital key to much of what we know about harpsichord technique. It details how to hold the body, the hands, the wrists, and the arms, how to ornament, finger, and phrase his music, and it gave useful advice on how to appear graceful at the instrument: "With regard to making facial grimaces, it is possible to correct oneself by placing a mirror on the music rack of the spinet or harpsichord." Music making wasn't just about getting the right fingers on the right notes, but a matter of disciplining the whole body, a physical display of ease and grace from the face to the feet to the fingertips. Music was becoming an integral part of an emerging sense of self-consciousness.

He also gave this piece of advice in his 1717 preface:

It is better, during the first lessons given to children, not to recommend practice in the absence of the person who teaches them. Little people are too inattentive to subject themselves to holding their hands in the position which is stipulated for them. For myself, in the beginning of lessons for children, as a precaution I carry the key to the instrument on which I teach them, so that in my absence they cannot undo in an instant that which I taught them so carefully in three quarters of an hour.

Students of Couperin must have received an exceptional amount of personal attention, at least when compared with the industry that piano lessons would become in the nineteenth century. By the middle of the nineteenth century, pianos were being mass-produced, by rival companies around Europe and in the United States, and they were affordable enough that it wasn't just the young ladies in Jane Austen novels of an earlier generation who learned how to play them. A proliferating and technically challenging solo repertoire was developed, and young people in middle-class families took up the instrument as well. The piano began to extend its discipline more deeply into the people who studied it, even into the home itself, where it became not just a locus of music, but an extension of the Enlightenment's rationalization of the world.

As more people acquired the leisure to learn instruments such as the piano, the cult of intensive practice would take over, and students spent long, solitary hours at the instrument, building on and solidifying what they had learned in their lessons. One of the most famous masters of this early age of popular keyboard pedagogy was Carl Czerny, a student of Beethoven's. Czerny would go on to be the teacher of the greatest virtuoso of the nineteenth century, Franz Liszt, who in turn taught subsequent generations of musicians. Czerny helped standardize a particularly mechanical view of what students needed to master, and the imagery he uses in his book of practical keyboard advice is almost brutal: "For the fingers are little disobedient creatures, if they are not kept well-reined in; and they are apt to run off like an unbroken colt as soon as they have gained some degree of fluency."

Couperin might lock the harpsichord keyboard to prevent pupils from straying from his method, but by the middle of the nineteenth century, piano students were expected to toil alone at the instrument. And they were required to enforce on themselves a scrupulous discipline of surveillance and self-denial. The emotional and existential change this was bringing into the home can be seen in a 1916 painting by Matisse. In *The Piano Lesson* the artist's son Pierre sits at the keyboard of a Pleyel piano with a large metronome prominently positioned between him and the viewer. Pierre stares with only one eye, while the other eye is obscured by a curious triangular gash of flesh-colored paint that mimics in size and shape the pyramidal form of the metronome. Although in a later and related painting, *The Music Lesson*, Matisse would depict a boy sitting at the piano with his teacher, in this image Pierre is entirely alone, except for the painted image of a woman in the background. In his solitude, he is haunted and fractured by the ceaseless mechanical tick-tock of the metronome, which has left its imprint directly on his head. It is the right side of his brain, the part that is predominant in the processing of music, that is obscured by this metronome-like erasure of his identity.

Pedagogues such as Czerny were simply echoing broader nineteenth century arguments about education. Is it through strict focus and discipline that we advance to knowledge and mastery? Or is there a need for emotional engagement and a free-floating curiosity? Advocates of strict discipline weren't necessarily advocating a mechanistic view of education, but their anxiety about freedom and license is palpable, and that anxiety is a consistent thread running through the history of music since the Enlightenment. It can even be heard in figures such as Robert Schumann, who argued for a more holistic view of education based on a healthy regard for discipline and freedom alike. In his "Rules and Maxims for Young Musicians," he encouraged a broad curiosity and engagement with music, not just the keyboard. He advocated a wide diet of listening, including opera and religious music, a thorough knowledge of harmony and musical fundamentals, and the regular performance of chamber music. But he also saw a role for pleasure, indulgence, and occasional improvisation:

> If heaven has gifted you with lively imagination, you will often, in lonely hours, sit as though spellbound, at the pianoforte, seeking to express the harmony that dwells within your mind;

and the more unclear the domain of harmony is yet to you, the more mysteriously you will feel yourself attracted, as if into a magic circle. These are the happiest hours of youth. But beware of giving yourself up, too often, to a talent that will lead you to waste strength and time on shadow pictures.

Schumann was writing during the emerging age of the conservatory, so even his qualified endorsement of the "lively imagination" and the "magic circle" is counter to the prevailing trends at the time. Conservatories began to spring up around Europe in the first decades of the nineteenth century, producing cadres of piano virtuosos, which helped spread a passion for the instrument among amateurs, which in turn led to more people, especially young women, heading off to conservatories. But the conservatory system could be a factory, and soul-crushing. Edvard Grieg, enrolled in the Leipzig Conservatory as a teenager, balked at the conservatism of his teachers and hated the experience, claiming to have learned nothing during his years there. Different schools tended to promote set systems for learning the instrument, and these methods didn't always keep up with the rapidly evolving demands of contemporary keyboard technique. In Stuttgart, students were instructed to hold their arms and wrists absolutely still and raise the fingers like pistons, and then strike the keys forcefully, a method that apparently did untold damage to many of them. The famed pedagogue Theodor Kullak, trained by Czerny, taught a method of keyboard execution that was so taxing that students were told to shake out their arms after practice to release the tension. Amy Fay, an American who studied in Germany in the late 1860s and 1870s, wrote a letter home saying that she was required to play the finger-numbing exercises of Johann Baptist Cramer as fast, as loudly, and as often as she could. Her teacher, whom she admired, was also terrifying: "My hand gets so tired that it is ready to break, and then I say that I cannot go on. 'But you *must* go on,' he will say."

In the United States, teaching piano centered around private lessons. Entrepreneurial teachers ran their own studios, gave instruction sometimes individually and sometimes in groups. Rivalries developed, and teachers often presided over a tribe of passionately loyal followers. By the twentieth century, this system had spread widely, engaging women like Myfanwy, who may have taught to earn a little extra money, or as an outlet for creative energies that would have otherwise languished, given how few opportunities women had for professional accomplishment outside the home. A burgeoning supply of teachers met a burgeoning supply of students, helping to develop a broadly literate musical culture, manifested in local piano competitions, Sunday afternoon musical clubs, and mass-circulation magazines that distributed sheet music. Although by the middle of the twentieth century the emergence of mass media and the spread of recorded music was changing the social dynamics of how people listened to and understood music, these changes hadn't yet displaced the piano as an essential tool for musical appreciation in the home. Within this thriving musical world, now mostly gone, the subculture of piano teachers was a curious and endearing microcosm of the rest of American society, full of idealism and more than a little humbug. Competition could be fierce, branding was essential, rituals proliferated, strange and esoteric systems developed cult-like followings, loyalties were forged and frayed, and somehow out of this there emerged a large, musically curious population, and enough sane, healthy, musically competent people to create a professional class of symphony orchestra and opera performers.

Unlike in the public school system, in which students moved in lockstep with a cohort of same-age children through a standard series of courses and grade levels, guided by teachers who (for the most part) kept a professional distance from their charges, studying music involved a far more personal and psychologically intense relationship with the teacher. Music was art, mysterious and often arcane, and it wasn't uncommon to learn from a new teacher that the old one had taught you everything wrong, from the position of your hands to the method of your practice regimen. Changing teachers often felt a bit like changing religious affiliations: the Sabbath, which had always been on Sunday, was now on Saturday, and whereas hellfire was assured if you didn't stand during Communion, now it was imperative to sit. Sometimes the bewilderment produced by these superficial changes to ritual and practice actually yielded astonishing results in the first few weeks or months of a new relationship. Radical change to any ingrained habit can shake the mind and body out of their ruts. But over time, the proliferation of systems and dogmas came to seem arbitrary, and the best you could say of them is that they gave you a range of options from which to form your own sense of the faith.

My third teacher presided over an ascetic cult that almost killed my interest in music entirely. While Charlotte had been affectionate and encouraging, I was not so fortunate with Joyce. Her assessment of my skills was accurate—I was undisciplined, willful, and too ambitious in my choice of new pieces, which I wasn't able to master sufficiently. But her methods were tedious and diabolically calculated to destroy any joy I took in the instrument. Joyce determined that the only way to rein me in was to feed me music in small, digestible snippets, no more than eight bars at a time. She did this by photocopying each new piece, then cutting it into ribbons and giving me a single new line to learn each week. If I returned with those eight bars sufficiently mastered, she would reward me by pasting them onto a piece of card stock, and slowly, week by week, the full piece would be reassembled. But if I failed to master the previous week's snippet, I would be sent home from the lesson empty-handed, solemnly instructed to return next week with the last week's music fully digested. It was all too much like the nightly ritual at our dinner table, when my mother insisted we finish everything on our plates. When the food was inedible, as it sometimes was, a standoff would ensue for hours until bedtime arrived and the meal would be covered in cellophane, placed in the refrigerator, and returned to us the next evening.

After my first lesson with my new teacher, I took my precious eight measures home and placed the curling strip of paper on the music stand and stared at it dejectedly. I was quite good at sight reading, meaning I could fumble my way through a piece, getting the basics of it mostly by sight the first or second time. I read my way through this first excerpt of a piece by Robert Schumann, dropping notes and approximating the rhythm and missing all the details, and suddenly I came to the end and it felt a bit like watching a film break in mid-reel, or lifting the needle off a record player. The idea was left hanging in the air, a rupture in the melody, a silence, which aggravated my curiosity to an unbearable degree. I wanted to be carried along by the music through to the end, to hear how it came out, and to imagine myself playing it for a delighted audience. I felt like Couperin's young students must have felt, staring at the locked harpsichord, wishing they could hear more of what it had to say.

Instead, I was being forced to set aside the pleasure of making music for the drudgery of learning it. Joyce was right about my musical weaknesses, but she had devised a method to make me loath every minute I sat at the keyboard. The eight-measure fragments of every piece came together only over months, and by the time a piece was finished, I hated every note of it. I would spend my practice time at the piano indulging in the dangerous, onanistic freedom that Schumann had described in his "Rules and Maxims," playing chords to see where they would go, dreaming in the magic circle of shadow pictures, making little progress toward understanding music, but free at least from the drudgery of poring over its lifeless corpse.

My mother grew frustrated with the bad reports Joyce issued on my progress. There were lectures in the car on the way home, and

threats to curtail privileges if I didn't do better. I avoided the piano
when I could, and when compelled to practice would play through
my scales mechanically, until my mother was distracted and I could
lapse into making up my own tunes. Along with the distorted image
of a haunted boy in Matisse's *The Piano Lesson*, there's a patch of
green paint that dominates the canvas, a cut-off triangle that echoes
the shape of the metronome and the strange, effacing gash across
poor Pierre's face. The lower edge of this green region begins where
the piano ends, and it clearly represents the green of the world
beyond the domestic space, a world I craved more and more as the
piano brought me less pleasure. I would delay coming home to avoid
the instrument, and flee outside whenever relieved of my obligation
to practice.

One day, I had an inspiration. Joyce had sent me home with eight
bars of something by Mendelssohn. In those days, a family trip to the
library was, for many of us, a weekly ritual. Why hadn't I thought of it
before? Our library included musical scores, and on our next outing I
found several volumes by Mendelssohn. I leafed through them, page
by page, and it wasn't long until I found the beginning of my piece,
one of the easier of Mendelssohn's *Lieder ohne Worte*, or *Songs Without Words*, written in imitation of the popular vocal songs of his day.
I brought it home with me and set to work on learning everything *but*
the eight bars Joyce had given me.

I anticipated it would be more fun than it actually was to traduce
my teacher. After clumsily pecking my way through the music I had
been allowed, I would barrel on with confidence into the forbidden
territory, smile at her triumphantly, and reclaim my freedom. I would
show her that her method had failed, that the only way I would con-
descend to learn music was on my own terms. No one would lock
away the harpsichord from my unruly fingers. Perhaps I expected
to overwhelm her, that she would draw back, realize her error, and
declare me a little genius. Or perhaps I expected that she would

explode in fury, like the witch I had made her into over months of unhappy lessons. But in the end, it wasn't fun at all. She stopped me as I played on and said gently, "I see you found the music. Let's try something else." So she pulled another page of photocopied music out of her file, took out her scissors, and gave me an amputated piece of it. We spent the rest of the lesson working through it. If I had been less angry, and less ashamed, I might have noticed that she was trying to teach me how to practice.

When the lesson was over, Joyce said she needed to speak to my mother, and I was sent to sit in the car. It was winter, cold, already dark by five o'clock, and it was raining. I was on the cusp of adolescence, I wanted to make music that would shake the heavens, and instead it felt like I was being taught to do needlepoint. Joyce pronounced our lessons a failure, and suggested that I see another teacher. She recommended I find someone who might take a firmer hand, perhaps a male teacher, and she provided a couple of names.

I realize now that my mother didn't much like Joyce, either, perhaps because Joyce spoke to her in a singsong voice with the same infantilizing condescension that doctors often use with patients. Mothers were always sent home with a shorthand reminder of their duties, an encapsulation of the lesson, or homework to oversee. "Pencils and erasers," Joyce would sing out, if I was to spend the week working on fingering, or "Scales and arpeggios," if I needed to brush up on the fundamentals. When my mother arrived at the car after the conference, she tried to be stern.

"Well, you really screwed that up," she said. Apparently Joyce hadn't revealed my deception, because my mother asked, "What the hell did you do this time?" I told her, and I could see her smile, just barely, to herself. I think she giggled slightly when she said, "You little brat." The result, however, was that I was now free of my old teacher, we would find a new one, and I would never have to go back to lessons with Joyce again. For a few minutes, I felt something like joy.

O F BACH'S EARLY musical education, we know very little. He was born into a legendary family of musicians who were so highly regarded throughout Thuringia, and so successful at the internecine game of musical politics, that they were sometimes resented for having a near-monopoly on the many musical posts that were essential to religious life in the early eighteenth century. Bach spent his first years in Eisenach, where he studied in the same school that Martin Luther had attended some two centuries earlier. Luther gave music profound importance, not just to the rituals of religious life, but to the formation of a Christian community, united by a common canon of hymns, many of them almost expressionistic in the intensity of their religious expression. Music was an essential part of daily life, and fundamental to education. School began by chanting the basic catechism, daily lessons included group singing and the fundamentals of how to read and make music, and music played an essential role as a mnemonic aid when learning other subjects.

Bach, an orphan at the age of ten, was taken in by his older brother, the organist Johann Christoph Bach, who held a post in a nearby town. We don't know the impact his parents' death had on him, other than what we can assume any child would have felt. Bach's emotional life remains mostly a matter of conjecture, with the music he wrote providing powerful but ambiguous evidence. His works often have a searing emotional intensity, full of grief and anguish, but it is difficult to disentangle Bach's personal feelings from the heightened emotionalism that was a standard part of the religious culture he served. By the time he was studying with his older brother, we have the sense that Bach was becoming intensely focused, and ambitious. A famous anecdote—taken from Forkel's biography—suggests a boy for whom music had become a kind of hunger or obsession. In an age before the internet or wide-scale publishing, Bach depended on his brother for his musical diet, and according to this account young Bach soon exhausted the music he was given to study and sought more challenging works by the great composers of his day:

> He had observed that his brother had a book in which there were several pieces of the above-mentioned authors, and earnestly begged him to give it to him. But it was constantly denied him. His desire to possess the book was increased by the refusal, so that he at length sought for means to get possession of it secretly. As it was kept in a cupboard which had only a lattice-door and his hands were still small enough to pass through so that he could roll up the book, which was merely stitched in paper, he did not long hesitate to make use of these favorable circumstances. But, for want of a candle, he could only copy it in moonlight nights; and it took six whole months before he could finish his laborious task. At length, when he thought himself safely possessed of the treasure and intended to make good use of it in secret, his brother found it out and took from him, without pity, the copy which had cost him so much pains; and he did not recover it till his brother's death, which took place soon after.

Like the famous account of the creation of the *Goldberg Variations*, this anecdote has a surprising amount of detail—the lattice door, the small hands, the moonlit nights—and some curious mistakes and inconsistencies. Bach's elder brother didn't die "soon after," but lived on more than twenty years, until 1721, when the younger Bach was in his middle thirties. And how did Bach manage to conceal his nightly copying for a full half year?

While the particulars raise doubts, the story isn't wholly unreliable. Almost certainly Bach would have been eager to learn new music; his talent may have so far outstripped that of his brother that there was resentment between them. By the time of this story, Bach would have engaged with composition at least as deeply as he was studying the keyboard, learning primarily through the copying and study of music; musical scores were highly prized and sometimes jealously guarded by working musicians. The fact of impoverishment is touching, of course; Bach had lost his parents, and now lived in a house where no one could spare him a candle. One senses his frailty, his small hands, and his commitment to improving his craft. At the end of the *Goldberg Variations*, Bach included a quodlibet, a musical form that repurposed and wove together popular songs of the day. The extended Bach clan would sing quodlibets together when they gathered for family occasions, likely with the beer or wine flowing freely, and often with ribald or scatological humor mixed in. The quodlibet of the thirtieth variation is a bumptious piece, and more engagingly tuneful than many of the pages that precede it. One of the melodies referenced in the work was a popular drinking song: "If my mother cooked some meat, I'd stay here without question." So the variations, one of the most monumental pieces in Bach's oeuvre, builds to its conclusion with a comic reference to family and a playful allusion to hunger.

In 1700, when Bach was just fifteen years old, he left his brother's house and moved some two hundred miles north to become a choral scholar in Lüneburg, a city near the bustling metropolis of Hamburg. There is a curious anecdote about his time at Lüneburg, where he was required to sing soprano in the school's choir. He had very little money and on one occasion used what little resources he had to travel to Hamburg to hear the great organist Johann Adam Reincken:

> Since he made several trips to hear this master, it happened one day, since he stayed longer in Hamburg than the state of his purse permitted, that on his way home to Lüneburg he

had only a couple of schillings in his pocket. He had not got halfway home yet when he developed a keen appetite, and accordingly went into an inn, where the savory odors from the kitchen only made the state in which he found himself ten times more painful. In the midst of his sad meditations on this subject, he heard the grinding noise of a window opening and saw a pair of herring heads thrown out onto the rubbish pile. Since he was a true Thuringian, the sight of these heads made his mouth begin to water, and he lost not a second in taking possession of them. And lo and behold! he had hardly started to tear them apart when he found a Danish ducat hidden in each head.

Bach's voice broke shortly after he went to Lüneburg, and he was thrown back on his other musical skills, his proficiency at the keyboard and his ability to copy and perhaps compose. He was effectively launched upon the world as a professional musician. If his brother had kept from him the music he surreptitiously copied, if he was unhappy in his brother's house, if the rudiments of the story are true, then one can easily imagine that those moonlit nights he spent stealing music from the locked cabinet brought him deep into a solitude that was foundational to his character. In every picture we have of Bach, he is a portly man; in most accounts we have of his home and family, it was a hive of activity, music, conversation, conviviality. But we know from two anecdotes of his youth that he was at least sometimes hungry and desperate for music, and perhaps these two things were in some ways joined in his mind. When he found the hidden coins in the cast-off herrings, he treated himself to a decent meal, and used the remainder to travel back to Hamburg to hear Reincken perform once again.

FOUR

THE FIRST TIME you attempt a new piece of music, especially music that you have heard but never played before, there is a feeling akin to the flush of romantic love. You may only gather up enough of the essential notes to rough in the melody and bass line, but the sound is enchanting. The conjuring of these voices with your own hands gives them a surfeit of charm, rather like meeting someone in the flesh after having seen only a photograph. Even if the music is entirely new to you, and even if you are playing it poorly, the immediacy of your relationship to this new thing, unfolding in time, is like the rush of discovery and uncritical pleasure we take in conversation with an appealing stranger. The music flows without any foretaste of the complexities and pain that lie ahead.

On the music stand of the grand piano is the aria of the *Goldberg Variations*. Bach doesn't label this gentle dance a "sarabande," as he does similar movements from his keyboard suites, and he gives no indication of its tempo or expressive character. All of this would have been obvious to musicians in the eighteenth century simply by looking at the contours of the melody and the rhythmic profile. Today, pianists take full advantage of Bach's reticence, shaping the aria by whim or instinct, extending it into an agonizingly solipsistic meditation, or playing it with pompous solemnity. But in that they are simply furthering the historic evolution of the piece from its origins. Like the chaconne, the sarabande supposedly came from the New World, and it also had a reputation in the sixteenth century for being louche and lascivious. If it did originate in the New World, it was quickly put through the cultural machine of France and Versailles and tempered in the larger spirit of political absolutism that was sweeping Europe; it was pressed and refined into something perfect and fragile, suitable music for an elite society that was as insecure as it was insistent about its own claims to being civilized. So early descriptions of the dance—full of wild movements and overt passion—bear almost no resemblance to the form that was finally domesticated in France. By the late seventeenth century, the stately, slow-moving sarabande was a standard part of the Baroque suite and had taken on the character of a melancholy lament. Contemporary choreographers attempting to resurrect a historical sense of how it was danced create a tension between static elegance in the upright body and isolated motion in the hands, arms, and lower legs, as if the torso is suspended like a puppet on invisible strings, with the extremities free to move seemingly without weight or encumbrance. The only vestige, if any, of the old wild form of the dance is in the tendency of the music to topple, gently, from the third beat back to the first, in a mildly syncopated pattern, and perhaps in the thick ornamentation, which metaphorically substitutes the ballistic precision of the fingers for the wild movement of arms and legs.

By the time Bach wrote his sarabandes, including movements in his French and English suites, the melodic contours of the dance were fairly standardized, often a simple, plaintive line with a slight stress on the second beat and a tendency to resolve in a cozy way into the basic chordal pattern underneath. This austere framework was then developed, and in the case of the *Goldberg* aria, embellished to a high degree. Ornamentation in music of this period involved discretion, taste, and improvisation, but it wasn't optional or extraneous in the way we often think of it in architecture, mere filigree tacked on to prettify something ordinary or undistinguished. Ornament was part of the language of the music, and Bach's sarabande without its ornaments loses much of its plasticity and tenderness.

Debate about whether Bach wrote the aria misses an essential point: whether he wrote it or not, he at least *chose* it as the starting point for this work, and that choice is in itself fascinating. The aria seems to point both to the past and the future, playing curious temporal games. Its elaborate embellishment suggests that there may be an earlier, simpler iteration of the piece, as if the aria is itself the first variation on an unheard, imaginary precursor. The Bach scholar Peter Williams drafted a compelling version of that prototype, an appealing but rather generic sarabande that might have been composed by any number of Bach's contemporaries. At least one pianist, Wilhelm Kempff, who released a recording of the work in 1970, seems to hint at that precursor by stripping away much of the ornamentation and placing the simplified melodic contours in high relief. It was an interesting experiment, making explicit what is implicit, but it sounds odd and awkward, like seeing a once-elaborately-coiffed show dog shorn for the summer. If the aria intimates an earlier version of itself, it also seems to evolve even as it unfolds. The clear sarabande rhythm and profuse ornamentation of the opening give way in the second half to the more fluent melodic contours of the *galant* style, echoing perhaps Bach's own sense of larger musical changes in the world around him. Bach may have earned a reputation as a conservative musician, but he was aware of and often deeply interested in new musical currents. The *Goldberg* aria, whether written by him or not, could be part of a personal investigation of new ideas.

It was also a daring choice to use such an extended piece of music as the ground for variations that would encompass so many different stylistic gestures and ideas. The first eight bars make use of a bass figure that was standard material for composers of Bach's day, including Handel, who composed a keyboard chaconne on the same descending line. But this eight-measure trope is greatly expanded, to thirty-two bars. Those thirty-two bars are then divided by twos to create a series of periods, or episodes. The aria is divided into two halves, each lasting sixteen bars. Each of those is divided into two eight-bar periods that come to a rhetorical resting point at their conclusion. Those eight-bar sections are also divided into four-bar phrases that each reach a satisfying if not entirely stable conclusion. And those four-bar phrases are divided into subunits of two bars each. This deliberate structure is a bit like the organization of a formal poem, dividing the music into neat stanzas, couplets, and regular metrical feet. But it also sets enormous challenges for the composer, who must fit into this framework not just character pieces and dances, but canons and a fugue (as well as an overture that includes a second fugue passage), which have their own way of unfolding and an innate dynamism that resists arbitrary architectural restraint. A poet who sets out to write an epic, which must include explication, character development, philosophical rumination, interventions by long-winded divinities, and perhaps love interludes and battle scenes, might wisely choose a flexible, short-scale poetic form, like couplets. Bach, from the outset, commits himself to a musical structure at least as constraining as a sonnet.

I missed those niceties the first time I played it, and even after months of practice it took formidable concentration for me to squeeze in all the ornamental figures without the music sounding plodding and pedantic. But in the first few weeks I spent with the variations I didn't bother much with details. I happily devoured a new movement every few days, skipping over the canons that require careful plotting and precise fingering to render the voices distinct, and bypassing the more virtuosic variations, especially those that Bach wrote for the harpsichord with two keyboards. When played on the piano, these "arabesque" variations require crossing the arms, interlacing the digits of both hands, and frequent reconfiguration of the voices to avoid entangling the fingers. But the first, second, fourth, and seventh variations came relatively easily, at least in the sense that I could play them well enough to recognize what the music was about.

There was no polish or finish to them. I was merely paraphrasing them, and as I turned yet more pages of the book I felt a nagging and familiar sense of guilt. The hard work of getting beyond the basic lines of the music was left undone, and this kind of laziness can be debilitating. The first approach to a piece of music will be necessarily superficial, but to continue in a superficial relationship is to ingrain the music into the mind in a crude, unfinished form. When competent musicians sit down to practice, they have in their head a to-do list: the rough spots, the complicated passages, the transitional places that need special attention. But I was playing merely to indulge myself.

Almost every sin that you can commit against another person, especially one to whom you are particularly close, you can also commit against a piece of music. Among these is the sin of not listening, or hearing only what you want to hear. There is a kind of narcissism we indulge when we first approach a piece of music as strikingly beautiful as the *Goldberg Variations*. The mess you are making, the actual notes that you are sounding on the keyboard, is lost in the rapture of hearing yourself produce an approximation of the real thing. For a while, so long as the music beguiles your ear with novelty, you remain self-mesmerized, listening to yourself, perhaps admiring yourself, thrilled to be a conduit for what Bach wrote centuries earlier.

This trance disappears instantly upon trying to play the piece for someone else. As soon as there is need to take full control of the music and present it with clarity and confidence, as soon as there is an audience to keep you honest, all of that initial joy disappears. A few months after I began making my first attempts to play the piece, I had neighbors over for supper. There was wine, and later digestifs, and we all slumped onto the sofas in the living room. I volunteered to play, which was foolish. My head wasn't clear and any basic knowledge of the piece that might have seeped in through simple repetition dissolved entirely, my fingers were sluggish and thick on the keys, and what emerged was a parody of the variations. My guests recognized the music, seemed indifferent to the flaws of my performance, and they clapped. But I felt like a fraud.

It was a familiar feeling. Until I was an adolescent, I could play in front of people without nerves of any kind. Music came easily, almost unconsciously, and so long as I was under the spell of enthusiasm and reflexive self-confidence, the music flowed freely, as if from an automaton. Hormones and self-consciousness undid all of that. I can't remember exactly when I first felt fear at the keyboard, but I can remember one of the first times I understood the full power of fear to undo anything in the music that wasn't fully learned and under complete mental control.

One summer, when I was about eleven or twelve, my family traveled west to visit the many relatives whom my parents had left behind when my father, a scientist, took a corporate research job in an industrial town in upstate New York. Among them was my great-aunt Clara, an artist and eccentric who rode herd over a shy, dignified husband who had made a small fortune as a lawyer in San Francisco. Clara lived in a house as artistic and eccentric as she was, and the house had a grand piano. She had studied the piano seriously as a young woman, which I learned later when I inherited many of her music books. She had essayed Bach and Beethoven, and Chopin and Debussy, and her scores were filled with the notes of someone who was knowledgeable and attentive to the details, including tempo indications she had culled from recordings by Walter Gieseking and Rudolf Serkin, both of them not just keyboard titans, but musicians deeply revered for their subtlety and integrity. Clara had been a young woman of considerable accomplishment and beauty, with a striking degree of independence and willfulness. She spoke in a glittering patter, a singsong of irony and wit, much of which was lost on us, though I remember thinking: *When I grow up I want to talk like that.*

My mother had a fraught relationship with her aunt, whom she adored and distrusted. Clara, who lived in the hills north of San Francisco, brought glamour to the lives of her adoring nieces as they were growing up in Salt Lake City. Her visits to Utah, where my mother's family struggled to make ends meet during the Depression and the war years, unfolded like cinematic spectacles. She came with luggage and hatboxes, descending from the train with imperious confidence and cosmopolitan hauteur. My mother and her sisters awaited her arrival with feverish anticipation, but her visits often seemed to end in tears or bitterness. I was told one story I find hard to believe, though it makes sense when I try to fathom the depths of hurt and resentment that coursed through the maternal side of my family. Clara, my mother said, had gathered her nieces and enjoined them to pack for a long trip, and to pack very carefully, sparing nothing they might need for long days of walking in the city, meals at restaurants, overnight trains, and a sea voyage. They were going to Europe. The girls were thrown into a frenzy of excitement. They were quite poor at the time and there was no money to fit them out properly for a trip to the Continent. But they did their best, sewing and mending and borrowing this and that from friends and neighbors. When the day of departure came, they stood with their luggage on the sidewalk awaiting Clara's arrival, but she never arrived. They waited for her for hours, and wondered if they had the day wrong. But Clara had left town, and the girls went back to their humdrum lives. Like many of the stories my mother used to tell me, this one sounds too perfect in its cruelty and distillation of character. Whether or not it is true, it probably stands in for something that was true, in some way. Exaggeration and fabrication were how my mother struggled to convey a pain that was deeper than she could express with mere truth.

Perhaps that explains why she was so eager that I play the piano for Clara. She wanted to prove herself to her aunt, to show that she was doing well in life. There was some effort at vindication involved, and perhaps she hoped that Clara, who had never had children, might envy her just a little bit. My mother may not have been a musician, or an artist, or wealthy, but she had a large family, a comfortable house, and her children were learning the refinements of life. Shortly after we arrived, as we were sitting in Clara's large and sunny living room, I was encouraged to sit down at the keyboard. I thought nothing of it, and went to the instrument, which was a far better one than any I had played on before. I assumed that I would place my fingers on the keys, the music would flow, and my aunt would beam at me radiantly. Earlier that year, I had studied one of Beethoven's two easy sonatas from opus 49, pieces that students often use as an introduction to the longer, harder Beethoven works, the larger and especially the late sonatas, and the concerti. But for some reason, when I got to the piano, the trance didn't come, the music didn't flow, and I had to skip things and make up passages to connect the few tattered bits of the sonata I could remember. I sensed my aunt watching me, and I knew that she knew that I was making mistakes, and it seemed I couldn't make anything but mistakes. I butchered the exposition of the first movement. Rather than politely letting me finish, Clara got up and said, "Enough of that." My mother was mortified. I flushed red with shame and couldn't take any pleasure in the rest of the visit, which included a fine meal and a tour of the studio where my aunt painted and carved, with passion and facility. As we were leaving in the late afternoon, Clara submitted to having her photograph taken with my sister and me, and she hugged us close to her, joking that she wouldn't look so fat if we hid her bulk from the camera. She was airy and ironic again, but I felt only my own failure, and it lasted for days. In the car, my mother spoke sharply to me. "What the hell got into you?" she asked.

This was a persistent fear we keenly felt, those of us who belonged to the legions of children shipped off for piano or violin lessons during those decades of suburban aspiration and pretension that defined postwar America. The fear of total breakdown. I had seen it several times. A young pianist would sit at the keyboard and launch confidently into music that would for a few minutes dazzle us with its complexity. Then, if you were alert to the performance, you'd notice that somehow something got stuck. A modulation that led from one section to another kept leading back to the same place, twice, three times, maybe four, until the player stopped and started over from the beginning. And again, the music found itself looping around, twisting helplessly, as if caught in an eddy forever cut off from the main current. Eventually he or she would look up frantically, and everyone in the room would be gripped with fear and fascination and sometimes cruel pleasure. Perhaps the teacher or a bustling parent would bring up the music and place it on the piano, and the hapless musician would start in just where the problem had derailed him or her earlier. With the music as a crutch, the pianist would start over, eager to get through the wreckage and escape the shame of failure, playing with a frantic determination, and sometimes rage, that annihilated any beauty or pleasure. More than a few times, that was the last time you ever saw them at the piano. The humiliation was complete, and they were done with music, or at least done with trying to make it themselves.

Music, in these moments, was occult in its power, neither pleasure nor pastime, but a demonic game of chance into which we were thrown. In the face of this unknowable, mercurial thing that tormented us, practice functioned more like prayer than medicine. You practiced for the same reason that people once wore amulets or repeated superstitious incantations, you did it to appease the furies who would punish you at your next lesson or recital, you practiced just like our ancestors once performed certain rituals to be sure the sun would arise in the morning, and that the seasons would follow one another in their ordinary succession. But the power of prayer is fickle, and so we went out to the piano, and bowed to our teacher and submitted to the malicious surveillance of our fellow students, and placed our fingers on the sacred geometry of ebony and ivory and hoped that we would not, in that moment, become the obligatory sacrifice.

———

I DIDN'T LEARN HOW to practice properly until I was in college. My teachers had done their best to teach me the complex and mentally exhausting skill, but something never clicked in my head. I was more than willing to sit for long hours at the keyboard, and to perform the drills they gave me. I played endless exercises, scales, arpeggios, and the dreaded *Virtuoso Pianist* by Charles-Louis Hanon, a French pianist and pedagogue who promised miracles: "This entire volume can be played through in an hour; and if, after it has been thoroughly mastered, it be repeated daily for a time, difficulties will disappear as if by enchantment, and that beautiful, clear, clean, pearling execution will have been acquired which is the secret of distinguished artists." Hanon was the bane of piano students at the time, who balked at its relentless streams of meaningless notes, without melody or harmony or any musical charm. I didn't find it nearly as torturous as the others did. The exercises were mindless and formulaic, endless streams of rapid figuration played at first by both hands in parallel motion and later in contrary motion and with the hands separated in different ways, but it seemed to me the promise of enchantment and the clear, clean, pearling execution of a distinguished artist far outweighed the drudgery of repeating these musically vacuous drills.

But they didn't work, even after mastering all of them, and then playing them in all twelve major keys. Nor did any of the other mechanical things I tried, the dutiful repetition of troublesome passages, or recasting them into different keys or with rhythmic variations, or with exaggerated articulations like the sharp pecking sound of staccato fingers. Teachers who assigned these exercises never suggested that they were a substitute for mental effort.

Only by stopping, focusing, and diagnosing problems would I make progress. If I forged ahead without fixing what came before, the unsolved problems would merely accumulate, and with them the threat of disaster during performance.

Still, as I grew more serious about the instrument, I would devote hours to these exercises, falling back on them when I was too tired or unfocused to work on more complicated, challenging things. In the hours before school, when the house was still quiet, I would sit at the piano in a state of semi-wakefulness and play through yet more Hanon, waiting for the miracle of virtuosity to descend. All the while, the pieces I needed to learn for upcoming recitals were neglected as I pursued the vain hope that finger calisthenics would somehow make the delayed work of musical learning easier and more efficient. I even felt virtuous in the process, subjecting myself to a rigorous athletic discipline. But this, too, was a sin against the music not unlike sins we often commit against those we love: we pretend that the sacrifices we are easily able to make are somehow an adequate substitute for the sacrifices that are actually needed. There was also the sin of false hope, that things would improve of their own accord, or that by faithfully showing up to the piano bench I would be granted some kind of epiphany as a reward for good attendance. Many a relationship has ended that way, too, after years of dutiful attention but emotional neglect.

Unfortunately, hours of finger work were not only inefficient or useless, they left me defenseless when it came to actually performing music before an audience. Sometimes, as the date of a recital or piano competition grew closer, I would test myself to assess my actual progress. I would stop and say: *Play it now as if you were before an audience, and see how it goes.* And then the results were almost always dismal. The fear of the looming recital would gradually eat away at things I had thought were already mastered. Everything would be a shambles, and I would go to my lessons and put my hands out as if they were some kind of mechanical device that needed oiling or repair, and beg for help.

Years later, in college, I made friends with a violinist and would accompany her in her lessons. She was far more accomplished than I was, and she studied with a famous teacher who had enjoyed a substantial career, making several recordings still admired by connoisseurs. Somehow, playing the subordinate role of accompanist lessened my nervousness, and I was able to bash my way through the orchestra reductions of violin concertos by Vieuxtemps and Wieniawski. But when I confessed to her my enormous fear of performing, and the endless hours of work that yielded such minimal gains, she asked incredulously: Do you know how to practice? She told me to take my hands off the keyboard and see a difficult passage in my mind. Imagine my right hand playing the notes. Imagine every muscle, how it feels to stretch the fingers from one key to the next. Do it so slowly that every note is disconnected from the previous one and only a fully conscious memory of the music will allow you to move forward. Hear in your head the note that comes next before you mentally play it. This was to be done silently, with the hands folded in the lap. And this was all for mastering one hand playing part of one passage. Later, I would have to imagine the left hand, in the same painstaking internal way, and then, while playing the music of the right hand, imagine the left hand silently accompanying the right, and then reverse the two hands and repeat the process.

For some reason, I took her advice, perhaps because nothing else was working. I had been playing the piano for more than fifteen years when, for the first time, I sat down in an underground practice room, at a battered old Steinway, and started working on a complicated étude that required both hands to leap around the keyboard in opposite motion. Someone listening at the door would have heard very little noise coming from the room, and almost nothing that sounded like music. The notes were disconnected and the lines spare. For much of the time I sat making no sounds at all, with my hands folded in my lap. And then, when I did begin to play, I saw in a flash what my teachers had tried to tell me for years: the power of a visual and auditory image of the hands in motion.

While playing one hand very slowly, I sensed that I was in command of things. Not total command, but I knew the steps, what came next. It seemed that I might play this short passage with the same confidence with which I went through the ritual of making a cup of coffee in the morning. I kept at this for about twenty minutes, certainly no more. By then the world around me began to crowd in once again. Despite the thick walls of the practice room, I could sense the presence of people outside, and a painful self-consciousness flooded over me. In a quarter of an hour, perhaps, I had managed to learn one half of one line of music. The piece wasn't long, only a few pages, but even so, the small accomplishment of the morning seemed negligible compared with what was left to master. And then, like an addict, I put both hands to keyboard and launched into the piece to see whether what I had learned would still be secure when played at full speed. Alas, it wasn't, and not only was the rest of the piece still insecure, but when I tried once again the passage on which I had worked so diligently a few minutes before, it, too, was weaker and more flimsy. I left the piano, shaken by the enormity of what was left to be done, and exhausted by my first real effort at serious musical work.

Still, I celebrated with my violinist friend, as if she had baptized me anew as a musician, and in the thirty years since that breakthrough, I have struggled to replicate that kind of work. It remains for me a touchstone of what I could do if everything in my life were placed in order, the messiness of my mind most of all. The drama of those few minutes three decades ago—a sudden intuition, a sense of growth and understanding, followed by a reckless frittering away of most of the small victory—seems now the shape of my life, the trope of my existence. I have spent decades returning to the piano, struggling to find the concentration and peace of mind necessary to move a piece forward, and never, in all those many attempts, scattered through every chapter of my life, have I managed to find more than a few quarters of an hour when I was actually in control of the music.

Music is now something at which I am always starting over, always beginning again. After a long absence, there is no telling in what state I will find my mercurial relationship with the instrument, and so every return is fraught with anxiety. Sometimes, as we find our bodies refractory when we return to exercise after months of idleness, everything is flaccid and weak. But that isn't always the case with the piano. Strangely, there are times when things seem improved, as if the work interrupted months ago has set and hardened and is now a foundation on which new things can be built. Knots will have loosened, and passages that always flummoxed you, that had worked their way into your habits so firmly that there was simply no playing them correctly, will feel loose and pliant, and if you are attentive to them, it will be possible to disentangle them and put them in order.

But more often, there is simply a daunting sense that you must start over again and work twice as hard to get to the place where you left off, and hope that by the time you have recovered what was lost, you will still have just a bit more time to push on a little further. Some people have projects that occupy them in this way for life, an antique car forlorn in the backyard, to which they return year after year, to tinker with and patch up and perhaps incrementally improve, but never make roadworthy. Or a house to which they repair once or twice a year, always in want of improvement, always a bit more dilapidated than last time. There is always that disheartening first moment of return, when we pull the cover off the car, or push open the creaking front door, and see the ravages since the last time we encountered these curious pilgrims who accompany us in our scattered lives. Some people manage to cast off these things, if they bring them no pleasure. The car is taken to the junkyard and soon the grass grows over the ruts it left in the backyard, the old cabin is sold off and the nagging thoughts about the leaky roof or the pipes that need draining fade away, and there is a sense of relief.

But music is more tenacious in its claims on us. It is not an object, or a thing, something we possess and can give away. It is a relationship, and to cut it out of our lives is to cut away some piece of ourselves. We return to it because, fundamentally, it is bound up with hope, with the persistence of our forward motion in our lives. The violin, which my mother had played for much of the first part of her life, stayed with her until the end, even though she had long rusticated it to the shelf. It made her feel inadequate and sometimes angry to think of it, but it was a permanent fixture in her world. The piano has been the same with me, and the *Goldberg Variations*, with which I have struggled for years now, have become the locus of that relationship, the place where music and I meet once again, month after month, year after year, and try to rekindle old love.

It is almost a ritual now. Sensing the imminence of one of those moments of rebirth, when life seems to give you the chance to start over again, to buckle down and really focus, I clear off my desk, sort through bills, carry old magazines to recycling, and remove from the piano everything but the now-dog-eared copy of the *Goldbergs*. Perhaps it is a long weekend, or I know the house will be empty for a week; often it is simply an inexplicable, intuitive sense that I am ready to work again. To clear my mind, I set the cell phone alarm for an hour, so that I can focus without distractions, and then I turn off the ringer. By now I know where the weak spots are, and perhaps always will be, and I turn directly to them. There are variations, such as the fifth and the twenty-third, where speed and clarity are the primary challenges, and others, such as the seventh, where the ornamentation is the principal difficulty, and yet others, including the sixth and the ninth, that are slower and yet require strategizing with every finger.

In the fifth variation, a rapid line heard first in the right hand and then in the left, is threaded through a simple but charming dialogue between what sounds like two woodwinds, perhaps a bassoon and a flute clucking and cawing at each other as they pursue the same idea. At one moment, near the end of the first half of the variation, where the left hand rises to a high point in the line, capped by a jaunty little mordent—a quick snap of ornamentation—is a detail I have never managed to get right consistently. I play the passage slowly and realize that if I slow down just slightly and give the troublesome three-note figure just a little bit of extra space, I might be able to fire it off without it seeming too belabored. It's a trick, but I try it, first in my head, then slowly with just one hand. And it works.

And now on to the canons, the heart of the variations but also some of the most difficult pieces to pull off. The first canon appears as the third variation, and it is one of the oddest of canons, with a busy, florid, loquacious bass line supporting the canon figures above. I have spent hours wrestling with its two interlocked voices, which follow one another at the same starting point, identically unspooling a long, plaintive melodic line. They don't so much echo each other as create a curious sense that the music is repeating itself even as it is making its first statement. Psychologically, the ear hears the initial melodic line, and no sooner has it registered its shape and purpose, it hears it again, creating a kind of perceptual delay. Unlike other canons or fugues, in which the voices seem to speak to one another, this one feels more like a single voice caught up in a dreamy feedback loop.

Because the upper two lines are playing exactly the same notes, and it falls to the right hand alone to play almost all of them, they are constantly getting in each other's way, and this seems to be where the problems lie. But often, when we gravitate to what initially seems most difficult, we neglect things that may be easier, things that if left untended become the weak link. The bass line of the first canon is restless and complex, and it needs attention. So this morning I decide to devote myself to the bass line alone, commit it to memory and play it while imagining the other two voices in my head. Without the upper voices it feels barren and dry, which is why I've probably neglected it. But after half an hour I have half of the bass line memorized, and to my delight, when the voices are reunited, there is a new stability in the piece.

For a moment I celebrate, imagining that this fresh start will be the one that lasts, the beginning that leads, finally, to unlocking and mastering the rest of the piece, rather than just another stalemate. But as I turn to memorizing the rest of the canon's bass, my concentration flickers and my mind follows this path: An old friend called last night; I was for many years close to her and her husband, both of whom meant a great deal to me; he died recently and she is moving on, courageously, but I know it can't be easy after decades of marriage; I worry about her because no sooner has she started to put her life back together than she discovers that one of her close friends is also sick and near death. Did my mother suffer dreadfully? What was her fear like? When she woke up in the morning, during those last few months, was there any pleasure to be taken in the world? When she gave up hope, was it all at once, or was the hope persistent, something that needed to be beaten back again and again until it died? My left hand is still playing the canon's bass line, but mechanically, and now death is in the room.

And so I put the music aside once again, and wonder what will remain of this scant hour of progress.

FIVE

HE SNOW BEGAN well before dawn and when the alarm rang at six-thirty there were several inches on the ground. School was canceled and I was euphoric. I stayed in bed, warm and sleepy, and free for once of the fear that filled me each morning before classes began. I was fourteen, in junior high school, and subject to the caprice and cruelty of a gang of bullies. But this day was mine.

My mother kept to her room, which made things even better. In the morning I went downstairs to where she kept her old books from college, and pulled out a copy of Dante that I had never read. I was surprised to find it so accessible and soon I was lost in his *Inferno*, amazed by it, horrified and thrilled to discover the sullen, the wrathful, and the blasphemers, the angels too fickle and frightened to take a side in the divine struggle and who were thus caught forever between heaven and hell. Some of the names I recognized— Dido, Tristan, and Achilles, and others were new to me, Semiramis, Tiresias, and Nimrod. I wanted to know them all, these sad, glamorous figures of myth, history, and legend bound together in suffering. Later, I practiced the piano, playing a Schubert impromptu on the out-of-tune piano, focusing on the softer parts for fear of rousing my mother, even though it was coming on noon. When the lunch hour arrived and passed with no sign of her, I went to her door and knocked lightly and asked permission to make myself a sandwich. I was always hungry.

Our house was full of rules, rules about food, about clothes and laundry, about doors (which must always be left open), about towels, about lights, about the radio, the telephone, the television, and the mail (letters were opened for inspection before being passed to us). Most houses have rules, and we had all the usual ones: no feet on the table, wash your hands before supper, never leave dishes in the sink. But we had dozens of others, rules about reading and sleeping and bathing, rules about money, about play, and about friends. The rules governing food were the most strict, and we were forbidden from eating or drinking anything without explicit permission. When my mother consented to let me make my own sandwich, I was euphoric, because I knew I might break the unspoken but adamantine rule that required our meals to be scant, austere, and unappetizing.

I ate well that afternoon, my hunger subsided, and still the snow was falling. I wanted to be out in it, revel in it, and give thanks to it for one of the best days I could remember, so I decided to surprise my mother and shovel the driveway and walks without being told to do so. The snow was wet and heavy, and well more than a foot of it lay on the ground. It was hard but exhilarating work, and I sang to myself as I shoveled, snatches of Schubert and other things I had learned recently. I imagined my mother's surprise and delight when she discovered that I had voluntarily undertaken and meticulously performed a grueling and unpleasant job. In the gray light of late afternoon, I felt both vigorous and virtuous. When I finished, I took off my boots and left them by the front door and went off to my room to slip beneath the covers of the bed and back into the *Inferno*.

I was lost again in Dante when she called my name. She often grew agitated when I spent time alone reading in my room. She had studied literature, and most of the books I read were her books, full of notes in ballpoint pen in a small, well-practiced, elegant script. But along the way, for reasons I could never understand, she grew suspicious of reading, especially the reading of others. My father, who had an insatiable appetite for popular novels, especially thrillers and spy capers, took to hiding books around the house and reading them surreptitiously. When I was small, and could still fit into the narrow gap between the sofa and the wall, I would hide there and read for hours, or at least until she discovered I was missing and began calling my name. I had come to expect that my reading would always be interrupted, especially if there was no hope of passing it off as homework. I was so used to this that whenever I read, part of my attention was alert to her presence, always anticipating her interruption. If she knew I was reading, she would invent some task that needed doing immediately, make-work jobs that were suddenly urgent, like sweeping the garage or arranging the magazines by size and color so that they looked tidy on the shelf. Occasionally, when she called my name and dispelled the reverie, I would go to her and find that she was at a loss to invent anything that needed doing. So she would shuffle through her mind until it came to something—wipe out the window tracks on the second floor, run a wet paper towel along the grooves of the baseboards in the living room—and I would say, "But I did that yesterday," and she would give up and let me return to my book.

When she called me this time, I anticipated her pleasure and delight and perhaps even a reward. But there was anger in her voice, and when I found her by the front door she was in a fury. Boots, she said, must always be left at the back door. "We're not animals," she said, sobbing. "We don't live in a barn." I didn't know this rule, and perhaps she just made it up that afternoon. I stammered something about having shoveled the snow, but her anger was still mounting. She slapped at me with both hands, striking my chest and my head and driving me down the hallway, boots in hand, toward the back door. She was small, and when she beat us, it rarely hurt, unless there was some object ready to hand, like a broom handle or a hairbrush. It was humiliating to be beaten, but it rarely meant much more than a lot of yelling, flailing of arms, and a few slaps with an open hand.

This time, however, she was angrier than usual, or perhaps she misjudged her own force. When I got to the other side of the house, where a sliding glass door opened onto the patio and backyard, I noticed her boots were neatly placed on the mat, and I leaned down to put mine next to hers. She struck me hard against the back of my neck, and I staggered forward to the floor. I lay there, hiding my face, with my arms clasped tightly against my head. I was crying now, and ashamed to be crying. I tried to shout at her that she had hurt me, but my voice was still changing and the words came out in the squeak of a child.

"Don't be so goddamned dramatic," she said, and stormed off. She was, I think, angry at herself for having exceeded the usual limits of her violence, and I was angry at myself for crying. I summoned what dignity I could, the dignity I always asserted at school when boys tormented and beat me. I stopped crying and forced down the twitching ache in the throat that leads to sobbing. I was exhausted, not just because of the hard work of shoveling snow, but from the ruin of a perfect day. My mother had fled back to her room and once again I had the house to myself. I rolled over on the floor and stared up into the sky, whence the snow continued to fall in thick, heavy flakes.

It seemed to go on forever, filling an infinite sky, emerging from a swirling gray confusion, as if every flake were being born at just the moment I perceived it. I was hypnotized by it and lay there in the last of the afternoon light trying to imagine myself someplace else. I wanted to tell some friend I didn't have about Dante. I wanted to ask someone who knew more about books why Dante's hell was so unforgiving. Why did the unbaptized have to suffer even though they were good and kind and had led exemplary lives? Why did so many of the damned continue to rage and rail, against each other and even against God, once the reality of hell and the force of divine fury had erased all doubt of His existence? Perhaps, I thought, they were angry at Him, angry at His capricious rules, angry at His cruelty. They had their pride and in their hearts clung to one certainty: that they were better than this.

In his *Berlin Chronicle*, Walter Benjamin grapples with the oddities of how we remember places. "Nothing prevents our keeping rooms in which we have spent twenty-four hours more or less clearly in our memory, and forgetting others in which we have passed months. It is not, therefore, due to insufficient exposure time if no image appears on the plate of remembrance." Habit, in fact, can dim impressions, suppress memory, while shock can suddenly illuminate a space so brilliantly that the photographic "plate of remembrance" retains the image. I spent hours of every day in the bedroom of the house where I grew up, but can hardly remember it. But I think only once did I ever lie on the linoleum floor of the kitchen and look up into the sky through the sliding door, yet that is the most powerful memory I have from more than a decade in that home. "It is to this immolation of our deepest self in shock that our memory owes its most indelible images," writes Benjamin.

I date to this moment a monument in my personal mythology. Whether or not it was precisely then, lying on the floor on that particular snowy day, that I decided to withdraw from childhood doesn't matter. That is how I've chosen to remember it, and if it wasn't then, it was about that time in my life, perhaps after some other beating, perhaps after she did it in front of people, which was even more mortifying. In any case, I decided that I was better than this, better than the tawdriness of lying on the floor, crying and angry. Earlier in the day, reading Dante and taking on myself the duty to clear the snow, I had felt independent and grown-up, and then suddenly I was a boy again, under my mother's power. So I decided to cancel the rest of my youth and devote myself only to things that mattered. What those things were, beyond, say, Dante and Schubert, I wasn't sure. But I vaguely sensed that there was a life to be lived in books and music and art that was more substantial than the lesser, messier life that had led me to this particular moment, this particular bathos.

I made my own rules that afternoon. I set myself against my

mother, never to be seduced by her occasional kindness, never to speak with her of anything that mattered, never to trust her. I saw with clarity that she would tear me apart if I didn't root her out of my life. I would be proper, well behaved, and above all dignified. But I knew I must keep my distance. And I knew I had to get out and never come back. These resolutions weren't easy to put into practice. I was bound to my family and my home for years to come, and the best I could do was retreat into a self-imposed exile, into silence and inscrutability. But when it came to devoting myself only to serious, meaningful things, I had the opportunity and the means to do that, and I began to keep that resolution scrupulously.

I was utterly unequipped to know what was great and what was trivial, to make any kind of authentic judgment about music or literature or art, but I could look out into the world and adopt the most catholic taste of others. When I visited my older sisters at college, I studied their bookshelves and came home with copies of what I found there. When I visited other people's houses, I scoured their record albums and books, looking for those things I had vaguely heard of, things that registered on the far horizons of the intellectual world as I knew it. When I heard people whom I considered sophisticated speak, I listened alertly for the exotic names of thinkers and artists, and took dutiful mental note. Mostly, I trusted to a single intuition: that if it was difficult, it must be important.

In retrospect, it all seems rather silly to build one's emotional life on such a flimsy and borrowed foundation. But I had no other, and over the years we may come to own things that first we borrowed, and own them as authentically as anything else in our lives. All taste is adopted, whether we set out into the world looking for the best models or merely absorb what is around us, unconsciously and uncritically. But what was at first a survival skill, an escape into things so esoteric my mother could never follow me there, became a life's habit, inseparable from my genuine sense of self. I don't honestly enjoy bad books, or even merely entertaining ones; nor have I ever developed any taste for popular music beyond that which is indelibly associated with old love affairs. And although I am entirely aware that it is a superstition, at best, I still believe every good book or great piece of music carries with it the possibility of redemption.

＝＝

THE IDEA FEELS old-fashioned now, that there are greater and lesser things in our aesthetic lives, but it was still current and semi-respectable throughout much of the last century. I grew up in the 1970s and 1980s, with the music criticism of Harold Schonberg at the *New York Times*, and with his books *The Lives of the Great Composers*, *The Great Pianists*, and *The Great Conductors*. We had on our shelves several cardboard-boxed sets of *Great Books*, Mortimer Adler's quaint effort to condense the Great Ideas for a mass audience, books that served as Sunday school fodder when we attended the Unitarian church for a few years in the 1970s. The word "great" permeated the art discourse of public radio and television without causing embarrassment well into the 1990s. I remember spending a summer in a small cabin in northern New Mexico when I was in my late twenties, with only one radio station that played classical music available on the dial. Every morning, it would broadcast *Adventures in Good Music*, hosted by the Jewish German émigré to the United States Karl Haas, who spoke with a rich Old World accent about the greatness of Beethoven and the sublimity of Bach and the profundity of Brahms.

But as the audience for classical music began to dwindle and age, as a new generation of musicians and music promoters sensed that with talk of greatness came the odor of snobbery, the word "great" fell into disfavor. When applied to high culture, greatness became increasingly connected to ideas of patriarchy and class, and avoiding the word became part of a necessary atonement for centuries of hierarchy and racist exclusion. And yet, the word simply migrated to popular culture, where there is no shame in magazines like *Rolling Stone* charting the 100 Greatest Artists, and where the old concept of greatness came back in disguised form like "must read" books or "Oprah's favorites." It remains a fundamental category for most people today, and even if there's little or no agreement on what is great, and while standards for greatness change from moment to moment and radically across demographic, cultural, and stylistic lines, it still structures the public conversation about music.

It's hard to live without the idea, not only because it is deeply ingrained in how we think, but because we fall back on it when we make decisions about how we listen and what we listen to. Life is short, and we all want great rather than ordinary things. I can pretend, like many of my colleagues and friends, that I don't think in terms of great music, and acknowledge only that some kinds of music are more or less appealing on a personal basis, or serve a particular function (to entertain, distract, animate, relax, or provoke) more or less well. But when I examine how I actually behave with music, it is clear that greatness is as important to me today as it was when I lay on the floor of my childhood home, hoping to find something sacred in the world that was larger than petty misery. I may enjoy all kinds of music, but when I *need* music, it is always great music that I need.

If Bach's *Goldberg Variations* are not great, then nothing is. Man has a curious habit of not just making music, but talking about music, and for centuries, Western cultures have proposed different theories for analyzing and evaluating music, which has inevitably led to ideas about what makes some kinds of music better than others. Some say it is all about formal perfection, which privileges things like complexity and order and balance; others advocate for emotional impact, which stresses the rhetorical or affective power; and there are other claims about how music reflects sacred or cosmic things, how it may be an analogue or sonic embodiment of the solar system, or reflect ideas about mathematics and geometry, a picture of the mind of God, or a metaphor for the spiritual architecture of the cosmos. The *Goldberg Variations* were written at a key moment in the history of these three fundamental tendencies in musical aesthetics, and Bach's music has inspired interpretations based on all of them. Scholars have looked to treatises on formal rhetoric to explain Bach's musical devices and expressive gestures, to numerology to make sense of everything from the composition of his musical motifs to the tonal structure of the large, multipart works. They have borrowed ideas from the ancient Greeks, the Renaissance, and the Enlightenment to explain his music, looked to his knowledge of Latin and science, even proposed Bach as a kind of Newton or Kepler of the musical sciences. But during much of the twentieth century, Bach criticism has been particularly concerned with the formalistic perfection of his music.

So even if we live in an age that resists any single standard for judging the greatness of music, we might also say: pick any standard you like, and almost certainly Bach's music will still be great by that standard. When I struggle to explain why I think it is great to people who resist the idea, I am more than happy to shift standards to meet the needs of the argument. Is his music charming, engaging, and melodic? Listen to the gigue of the seventh variation, the spinning song of the nineteenth, or the tripping dance of the twenty-fourth for proof of its easy charisma. Is it complex, rigorous, and finely wrought? The evidence is there in every line on every page. Does it have a grand spiritual meaning that transcends other kinds of music? That is a harder question, but I can say this: the *Goldberg Variations* certainly reflect my own personal cosmology.

Let's start with structure. The overarching form of the work is one of the most sophisticated and subtle ever imagined. The thirty variations are flanked by the aria, heard twice, once in the beginning and once at the end. This creates a total of thirty-two sections, which are divided in the middle at the sixteenth variation, forming a hinge that connects two large wings of a musical diptych. Each variation is, in turn, divided into two sections, and each of those sections is repeated. This fractal-like pattern is greatly complicated by the appearance of nine canons, in which two voices are heard playing the same line, one slightly delayed from the other, like the old nursery song "Row, Row, Row Your Boat" sung as a round. Each of these nine canons sets the two interlocking voices a scale degree higher than the last, so that the first begins at the unison, the second is one note higher (or in musical terms, separated by the interval of a second), the third is a third apart, and so on until the last canon, where the voices are separated by a ninth. After the initial three variations, a general pattern holds: each canon is preceded by two other variations, an arabesque that is fast and fleet and challenges the physical skills of the player, and another one, usually a dance of some form, or a reference to other genera of music popular during Bach's lifetime.

The form of the work is thus both symmetrical and open-ended, and divided into multiples of two, and multiples of three. The larger division at the midway point, and the repetition of the opening aria at the end, gives one a powerful sense of balance and closure, but the pattern of two variations followed by a canon could be repeated ad infinitum (if the keyboard was wide enough and the arms long enough to encompass widely spaced voices). So the work's plan has both the static balance of an architectural façade and the dynamic openness of a mathematical pattern, such as 1, 3, 7, 15, 31 . . . Look to almost any formal analysis of the variations, and one finds them arranged like an arch, often with tortured efforts on the author's part to organize them in perfectly symmetrical groupings of two or three variations so that not only is the arch balanced, but even the brickwork matches side to side. But we might also think of the structure as a circle, and anyone who has felt shivers at the return of the aria at the end of the piece may remember these familiar lines, about the conflation of beginnings and endings and the paradoxical nature of our cyclical existence, from the last of T. S. Eliot's *Four Quartets*:

> *We shall not cease from exploration*
> *And the end of all our exploring*
> *Will be to arrive where we started*
> *And know the place for the first time.*

And yet all these formal metaphors for describing its structure—the symmetrical arch, the open-ended mathematical progression, the closed circular loop—are premised on understanding the work as a whole, as a single, intentionally structured piece meant to be comprehended as if from a great distance or height, from beginning to end. It's not clear if Bach intended the piece to be understood that way, as a unified masterpiece, and very likely that isn't how the piece was used by musicians during Bach's time. I know of no record of an actual performance of the *Goldberg Variations* from any time around its creation, or during Bach's lifetime. But to the extent that the *Goldberg Variations* were played at all in the years or decades after they were published in 1741, they were probably played piecemeal, with the musician making a selection of them rather than performing the work in its entirety. The work definitely circulated in printed form during the late eighteenth and early nineteenth centuries, and we assume that Beethoven not only knew it but admired it deeply when he wrote his magisterial *Diabelli Variations* some eighty years later. But it wasn't until the second half of the twentieth century that the variations became a standard concert piece, as we know them today, played from beginning to end as a unified composition.

Even when they are played that way today, the larger, macroscopic structure holding the variations together isn't perceptible unless the listener has already studied it. Casual listeners may notice something significant happening at the midpoint of the work when the sixteenth variation announces the second half of the diptych, if only because this variation, written in imitation of a French overture, is self-consciously grand and even pompous. And most listeners are deeply touched by the closing aria and recognize its importance to the larger structure of symmetry and return, even if they don't articulate it to themselves in those terms. But beyond that, the piece seems more a collection of related episodes, a succession of ideas, rather than an arch or a progressively repeating tripartite pattern of two variations and a canon. It may feel monumental because it is complex and long, but listeners will experience it as a catalog of great ideas rather than a fixed structure.

Bach certainly gives the listener no assistance if the goal is to hear his underlying architecture, especially the open-ended division into units of three. The careful progression of the nine canons is lost on casual listeners not just because the canon is a complicated form, but because Bach often elides the difference between the canons and the other variations, and writes several of the canons in ways that don't sound particularly "canonical." The twenty-fourth variation, the canon at the octave, in which the top voice makes a clear statement of theme before the second voice joins, sounds very much like a canon, with clearly demarcated imitation between the two voices. But in the sixth variation, the canon at the second, the voices are so closely intertwined, and follow each other so intimately, that the effect is more like hearing a single idea slowly turning in space, such that one senses two sides or aspects of the same thought, rather than two discrete voices in dialogue. In the twenty-first variation, the canon at the seventh, the second voice often seems to finish the thought of the first, picking up where it left off, like two people who have been in conversation so long they finish each other's sentences. Yet other canons are subverted by their bass lines, as in the third variation, the canon at the unison, in which the near-constant sixteenth-note motion of the bass figuration creates a delicious murmur or rumbling in the background that confuses apprehension of the interlocked voices above, or the ninth variation, the canon at the third, where the bass line imitates key details of the canon voices, in such a way that the ear wonders if all three parts are involved in some kind of three-voice fugue. In the eighteenth variation, the canon at the sixth, it seems we are getting a lesson in old-fashioned part writing, with Bach refreshing and reinvigorating the kind of music he might have found dull if he had ever been taught formal composition by a pedantic schoolmaster. To further complicate things, Bach also throws in a couple of exercises in counterpart that feel at least as contrapuntal and formally structured as the canons, including a fughetta in the tenth variation, the fugue conclusion to the overture of the sixteenth variation, and the alla breve of the twenty-second variation, which imitates an old-fashioned motet. Someone who is new to the piece and approaches it determined to search out the nine canons might well think these are among them, and he would be wrong.

Why does Bach go to such lengths to subvert our efforts to comprehend the formal structure of the variations? Perhaps because he didn't think that kind of mental effort was essential to the enjoyment of the music. And indeed, the actual experience of music doesn't seem to include the perception of many of the things that have long been said to be determinant of its greatness, including complex architectural forms. We listen to music in the moment, aware of what just happened, and alert to what is about to happen. The range of our musical perception is remarkably focused on the immediate moment. If we are honest about how our mind actually responds to music, we find it is akin to picking our way through a large museum, noticing this and that on the walls as we pass, vaguely remembering the pleasure of the room we just left, perhaps anticipating something we remember from a previous visit that awaits us in the next gallery, but utterly incapable of experiencing the totality of the space and its contents in any meaningful way. We believe, or hope, that the larger patterns Bach has built into the music are available to us in some unconscious way, and we may study them to make them more available as we listen; but the ear tends toward pleasure and surface, while the mind admires from afar.

———
———

IT IS CURIOUS how our metaphors for appreciating art have tended to associate ideas like warmth and cold with mental states and experiences, how much the clear, crystalline idea of ice is associated with intellectual effort, as opposed to the warm fluidity of pleasure, and how much pride and shame is attached to different modes of artistic appreciation. In a 1914 book called *Art*, the Bloomsbury Group critic Clive Bell laid out a hierarchical and moralistic view of art, with pure formal appreciation the highest, and indeed only worthy experience, and all the rest of the pleasures degraded and insignificant. Art was capable of inspiring emotion, but not through its immediate, sensuous content; rather, we are moved by appreciation of its formal complexity. He was primarily interested in visual art, but tried to apply the same sense of intellectual purism to his experience of music. He analyzes his state of mind at a concert when he finds himself "tired or perplexed" and prone to "weaving into the harmonies that I cannot grasp the ideas of life." This is, he believes, a vulgar habit:

> I have tumbled from the superb peaks of aesthetic exaltation to the snug foothills of warm humanity. It is a jolly country. No one need be ashamed of enjoying himself there. Only no one who has ever been on the heights can help feeling a little crestfallen in the cozy valleys. And let no one imagine, because he has made merry in the warm tilth and quaint nooks of

romance, that he can even guess at the austere and thrilling raptures of those who have climbed the cold, white peaks of art.

A century later, this idea still haunts us, even as most descriptions of how people listen to music are firmly rooted in the warm tilth and quaint nooks of immediate experience. As musical analysis has moved to incorporate not just ideas of architecture and structure, but the psychological perception of how we actually listen, scholars now speak of "syntactical" or "quasi-syntactical" understandings of music. Music is apprehended not as a language that can convey specific meaning, but as an aesthetic object that behaves like language, and which we experience not in paragraphs or chapters, but fundamentally at the level of sentences. But since the age of Bach, at least, philosophy has debated whether or not deep structure—the grand arches of Bach or the dialectical forms of Mozart and Beethoven—is perceptible to listeners, if they can somehow detect it on the "surface" of music, which is the only place we actually experience music. One school of musical analysis works assiduously to connect surface to structure, so that if a symphony is at its most fundamental level a progression from A to B and back to A again, we will find that grand drama manifested again and again in larger and smaller ways, with each of its movements, or chapters or paragraphs, also articulating that A-B-A narrative, and each smaller subunit, too, so that every constituent part is somehow an iteration of the same A-B-A pattern that governs the whole.

In a 1985 journal article, researchers described using the *Goldberg Variations* to explore how ordinary listeners perceive key aspects of interpretation and structure. After playing different interpretations of the work, on different instruments, to 112 undergraduates at the University of California, San Diego, they found little difference in the pleasure reported by the test subjects. Even more striking, they also reversed the order of some of the variations, mixing up the three-part units that culminate in a canon, and again found the pleasure substantially the same. They concluded that "modifying the piece had only a minimal effect on subjects' enjoyment of it. It would seem, then, that the pleasure produced by the piece results from something other than what the music authorities suggest."

And yet I don't believe structure is irrelevant and that attempts to explain the structure of music and connect it to listening are wasted or hollow. Despite the icy chill up on the peaks of Clive Bell's Parnassus, there is still something powerful about perceiving the grand structure of a work. It gives us insight into the conscious ways in which Bach brought order to large-scale pieces of music, and it also helps us remember the piece in ways that may be more definite and lasting than the memory of pleasure in its immediate perception. And it is rare that some aspect of the music that you perceive as a lovely surface detail with immediate sensuous appeal isn't also directly connected to the larger formal pattern of the variations.

No single understanding of what makes the *Goldberg Variations* great is necessary, or sufficient, and yet many of them apply in some way, or when the work is understood in some particular context. Even if we set aside the idea of architecture altogether, and think of the variations as a collection of enticing musical vignettes, the work remains great by a host of other standards. Many of the most appealing variations are rather simple dance forms, and among the most simple are some of the most sensuously appealing. The gigue of the seventh variation is a strongly marked dance in a lively triple meter, which exerts a ferocious pull on the body. And yet even in this rather overeager little dance, the harmonic line of the *Goldberg* aria is passed between the two voices with astonishing dexterity, landing at one point in the upper register where it is transfigured into melody. Bach has intentionally caught up his formal material in the ebullience of the dance, so that it makes no sense to think of a ground below and a caper above, but rather of some new, organic thing. For the few minutes that it lasts, a variation that seems at first a mere trifle feels like an incarnation, whole and integral, of everything that matters in the *Goldberg Variations.*

Long after I had been working on the piece, I sat down with the score away from the piano and studied another one of my favorites, the thirteenth variation. While it seems one of the most transparent and even sentimental of the variations, I discovered with delight that it is also one of the variations that most closely tracks the original aria. If you have been struggling to stay attuned to the bass line since first hearing the aria some twenty minutes earlier, here you will find it strangely intact, and at times quite close to its original statement. Even the top line, which begins with a graceful turning figure reminiscent of the little mordents heard in the opening of the aria, seems to track the rising and falling profile of the aria's melody. But for all of its apparent similarity on the page, it is difficult, and perhaps perverse, to play it in a way that underscores its close connection with the original aria. If in many of the variations Bach says, "I have changed everything and still it is the same," in this one he seems to say, "I've changed little, but it is utterly different."

We live in an age that believes art is a communal experience, that the pleasure of music only exists in being shared. But a work like the *Goldberg Variations* also brings with it a deeply private sense of discovery, pleasures that are difficult or impossible to share, that may not be pleasures at all, but simply moments of intuition and awareness that are meaningful to us alone. Part of its purpose may be to throw us back upon our most inward, private, solitary selves, in a way that mimics how death parts us from the world. The feeling we have when we experience beauty that is incommunicable, which we can only perceive in absolute solitude, helps us anticipate that other, absolutely private experience of our life. We experience art in many ways, but one way, and perhaps one of the most profound, is through an intimation of beauty that we can never hand off or pass on to other beings.

I don't love Clive Bell's metaphor for exploring art, of time alone on an isolated, snowy peak, but I understand what he was trying to explain, and I confess I'm sympathetic to the idea that it takes a heroic effort, with feats of self-denial and discipline, to get there. For years it seemed to me that there was nothing more important in life than making my way to that place, wherever it was. While I was still living at home, I read another of my mother's cast-off books, Virginia Woolf's *To the Lighthouse*, and was deeply disturbed by a scene in which the author lays out the perils and costs of a life spent seeking that high ground of perfect understanding. Woolf describes with sharp and austere irony the "splendid mind" of one of her central characters, Mr. Ramsay: "For if thought is like the keyboard of a piano, divided into so many notes, or like the alphabet is ranged in twenty-six letters all in order, then his splendid mind had no sort of difficulty in running over those letters one by one, firmly and accurately, until it had reached, say, the letter Q." But what comes after Q? And what follows R? "How many men in a thousand million, he asked himself, reach Z after all?"

When I lay on the floor, looking up at the snow falling down relentlessly from the gray sky almost forty years ago, I thought survival depended on something like Mr. Ramsay's quest to reach Z. He was standing, at that moment, on the terrace of his house in the Hebrides, looking at his family through a window as he smoked a pipe on a summer evening. He was a philosopher. I was a formless thing, full of shame and fury, and determined to bring order to what little of the world I could command. I didn't yet have the sobering example of Mr. Ramsay's failure to temper my hopes. Woolf, whose sister was married to Clive Bell, describes Mr. Ramsay's failure in terms similar to Bell's description of the great heights of aesthetic experience. Her philosopher undertook his heroic mission to reach Z like the leader of an expedition to some great alpine summit, a doomed venture: "Feelings that would not have disgraced a leader who, now that the snow has begun to fall and the mountain top is covered in mist, knows that he must lay himself down and die before morning comes, stole upon him, paling the color of his eyes, giving him, even in the two minutes of his turn upon the terrace, the bleached look of withered old age. Yet he would not die lying down."

Nor I. When I got up from the kitchen floor, I had a new sense of purpose. I dropped out of school a few years later and went off to college early, to escape the house I hated. My inner life developed independent of my mother's scrutiny, and I never spoke to her of love, or beauty, or what I desired in life. I never shared my intuition that there were great things in the world, nor, when I discovered one of those things, did I bring it to her for her delight or approval. We still made music together, from time to time, but I accompanied her as if she were a stranger, diligent, proper, disengaged. And once I left the house in which I grew up, I returned only a few times. My parents sold that home and bought another one, in New Mexico, and I was glad to find I had no feelings for either one. I was in my forties before I went back to the town where I was born. It was warm, the weather soft and clement, but I thought: *I miss only the snow.*

SIX

WHEN BACH WROTE the *Goldberg Variations*, there were three different kinds of keyboard instruments commonly being used in Germany. The first, and the one on which his formidable reputation was based, was the organ, which uses compressed air to make metal and wooden pipes resonate at specific frequencies. Bach began his career as an organist, and he understood the instrument not just as a vehicle for his compositions and performance, but as a mechanism, and one of the most complex machines in Europe on the eve of the Industrial Revolution. The second, and the one for which he wrote the *Goldberg Variations*, was the harpsichord, which uses wooden jacks and, in Bach's day, little bits of crow quill known as plectra to pluck the strings. Bach also used the clavichord, a smaller, more intimate instrument, which produces tones by striking and holding the strings with metal tangents, rather like the faint sound made by pressing a guitar string sharply against the metal fret. Unlike the organ and harpsichord, the clavichord could render gradations of loud and soft, and could imitate expressive devices like the slight warbling or vibrato of the human voice. But the clavichord's tone was spare and delicate in comparison to the organ and the harpsichord, and thus it was considered a domestic rather than a performance instrument.

There was another keyboard instrument beginning to circulate in Bach's day, as well, the piano, which had emerged in Italy around the beginning of the eighteenth century, and spread into Germany a few decades later. Bach tried a piano made by the eminent craftsman

Gottfried Silbermann, and a written account of that event demonstrates how highly Bach was esteemed in his lifetime:

> He praised, indeed admired, its tone; but he complained that it was too weak in the high register and too hard to play. This was taken greatly amiss by Mr. Silbermann, who could not bear to have any fault found in his handiworks. He was therefore angry at Mr. Bach for a long time. And yet his conscience told him that Mr. Bach was not wrong. He therefore decided— greatly to his credit, be it said—not to deliver any more of these instruments, but instead to think all the harder about how to eliminate the faults Mr. J. S. Bach had observed. He worked for many years on this.

The story of Silbermann and his pianos continues, and it ends happily. The famous instrument maker improved the mechanism, Bach tried the new model, and Silbermann apparently "received, in turn, complete approval from him." But that was late in Bach's life, and as a composer his principal loyalty was always to the organ and harpsichord.

Today, the *Goldberg Variations* are played on both the piano and the harpsichord. There are abundant recordings of the piece on both instruments, and listeners have a choice: Do they want the brighter, more brilliant sound with its prismatic play of overtones produced by the harpsichord, for which the work was written, or the greater range of dynamics and articulation but more blunt and sluggish sound of the modern piano? On the harpsichord, the music seems to pop and sparkle, while on the piano it becomes almost symphonic in its richness but less precise in its details. Until the revival of the harpsichord tradition, which came to fruition in the 1980s, the choice was easy. The resuscitation of the *Goldberg Variations* from obscurity in the twentieth century was due mainly to Glenn Gould's 1955 recording of the work on the piano. This was not the first recording made of the piece—the Polish-French harpsichordist Wanda Landowska had recorded them in 1933, the first time ever on that instrument—but it was Gould's recording that established the *Goldbergs* as a fundamental part of the contemporary piano repertoire.

But the work wasn't written for the piano and playing it on the modern piano presents, at times, daunting challenges. At the head of most of the variations, Bach wrote one of three recommendations: "a 1 Clav.," "a 2 Clav.," or "a 1 ovvero 2 Clav." These refer to the two keyboards that were common on larger harpsichords in Bach's day, with some variations meant to be played on a single keyboard, on both keyboards, or at the performer's discretion on one or both. A two-keyboard (or double-manual) instrument gives the player significant advantages in at least two ways. The two keyboards on a harpsichord have slightly different tone qualities, with the lower one producing a fuller, rounder tone and the top one a slightly brighter and more twangy sound, a bit like an oboe in contrast to the lower manual's clarinet. The difference in tone quality also helps the player distinguish different lines, both in those variations (such as the thirteenth and twenty-fifth) that imitate a solo voice or instrument playing against an accompaniment, and in the fast-moving arabesque variations in which the contrasting tone quality between the keyboards helps clarify the two rapidly moving, frequently intersecting independent lines (as in the eighth, fourteenth, and twentieth variations).

Bach's hand-crossing variations come in two sorts. One uses the left or right hand to grab a note or two from above or below the opposite line, which can be managed easily on one keyboard. These hand crossings have a visual as well as musical purpose, adding to the spectacle of performance such that "the eye shares in the pleasure that the ear receives in it," according to Bach's near-contemporary, the French composer Jean-Philippe Rameau. More troublesome are the variations in which two independent lines frequently run up and down the keyboard, crossing in the center, and sometimes lingering there such that both hands must negotiate the same shared keys, with ten fingers occupying the space usually allotted to five. A second keyboard makes this relatively easy, giving each hand its own traffic lane. But these variations aren't difficult just because the hands collide, they also challenge the brain in a peculiar way: With the arms crossed, the right hand is performing in the left hand's space, and vice versa, and this can create a surprising disconnect between the eyes, the hands, and the mind. At times, it unsettles the usual dominance of one hand over the other, or "handedness," and without practice and particular effort it can make it difficult to coordinate motor control between the two hands. Passages that would be relatively simple if the hands occupied their usual space relative to each other can become maddeningly difficult when they trade places across the vertical line that divides the body in half and gives it laterality.

The difficulty of transcribing the *Goldbergs* from two keyboards to one is invisible to listeners. The danger zones sound no more challenging or virtuosic than any other passage in the music. The hard work of figuring out how to divide up the lines, which fingers will drop which notes, whether one hand will play over or under the other, nearer or farther from the edge of the keys, is inaudible in performance. Early in my efforts to master the *Goldbergs*, I encountered these challenges in the eighth variation, like coming across a roadblock or a washed-out trail while hiking. All forward progress was arrested when I reached the twelfth bar of the variation, where the right hand plays downward in a chain of sixteenth notes that articulate an A-major chord, while the left hand mirrors the same motion and harmony in the opposite direction. These two bars, and a similar passage later in the piece, absorbed every bit of mental energy available and it took weeks to decide on a workable strategy for playing them. These measures, which together pass by in less than ten seconds, left me with a familiar sense of desolation, and even after I had learned them I had a premonition: *This is where I will fail.* No matter how hard I work on them, no matter how well they are mastered in the privacy of my living room, no matter how many hundreds of times I play them without trouble, when I play them for an audience, they will fall apart. Precisely here, every time, without exception.

I T SEEMS PERVERSE and self-defeating to allow part of one's mind to determine failure in advance, but the habit has been deeply ingrained in me since adolescence. This degrading mental routine follows a familiar script: I identify the danger in the music, I see the crash coming at me inevitably, I resist the self-fulfilling prophecy, I fail in my resistance, and I feel a familiar despair. I've done this so many times, in so many pieces, and suffered the same results in almost every attempt I've made to play in public that I've become fatalistic about it. In some perverse way, it's almost a talent, to be able to divine in any new piece, with perfect and instant clarity, the site of my future humiliation. In the fifth variation there is a little right-hand mordent that I know will be the source of misery; in the ninth variation, there is a trill that must be played with two fingers of one hand while other fingers of the same hand execute a smooth line above; in the twenty-sixth variation, there are several places where Bach makes tiny alterations to a regular, running six-note pattern, and I am quite certain that each of these small deviations will cause grief no matter how thoroughly they are practiced. And, of course, in the eighth variation there are the hand crossings that I know I can master technically, but will never manage to play cleanly for an audience.

The longer I live with a piece of music, the more it seems that some part of my consciousness is keeping a criminal file on my fingers, a dossier of treachery that will always show itself in the end. The pleasure one might take in Bach's music is reduced to a grim, diagnostic picture of weakness and future failure. I might master 99 percent of it, but the 1 percent that is self-ordained as a site of catastrophe seems more significant than anything else. I know this is foolish.

I knew it was foolish forty years ago, when I invented this strange behavior. It developed rapidly, when I was about twelve or thirteen years old, and by the time I was in high school I could almost define it and name it as an ineradicable part of my psyche. It was an established bugbear in the months leading up to a recital I was to give at the local public library when I was a freshman or sophomore in high school. I was one of four or five students participating, and my contribution was Beethoven's Sonata No. 8, Opus 13, a stormy work with a thunderous opening and fiery exposition, one of the composer's most glorious slow movements, and a fast, quicksilver finale full of strange twists and surprises. Early in the school year when I was assigned the sonata and first opened its pages, I was ecstatic. Here was music significantly more advanced than anything I had learned before, music that was part of the standard repertoire of serious, professional pianists. But I had spent barely a few hours with the score before I determined the one bar that would always embarrass me. The sonata opens with a slow, grand, impassioned introduction, at first portentous, then lyrical, rising to a high point from which it tumbles precipitously into the main body of the work. That falling motion, a rapid chromatic scale played about as fast as humanly possible, is a flourish, a brief, scintillating sweep through all the keys, black and white, that sets up the principle theme of the first movement. It didn't just look menacing, a dark gash of notes slashing downward across the page, it was the kind of detail I feared most: short, dramatic, exposed, and in some ways not terribly important. It would be over in a blink, a mere moment of musical data, but I knew I had found the perfect spot for conspicuous failure.

I practiced this sonata for months, all through the fall and over the Christmas holidays. My mother was particularly taken by the

beauty of the second movement and sometimes, when I was playing it, I would notice her standing nearby, just inside the kitchen,
where she would pause from her daily ritual of scrubbing and scour-
ing its spotless surfaces, as if on the edge of some kind of obsessive-
compulsive disorder. She was particularly sensitive to music, which
either addled her or assuaged her restlessness. She would lurk within
earshot, and despite the anger between us, I would change my playing
to keep her engaged, leaning into the hymn-like simplicity of Beethoven's ecstatic melody just a bit more, taking things more slowly than
usual so that she might savor the pleasure of its repeated melodic line.
Despite the breach between us, these moments of wordless communion carried on, and perhaps we both sensed in them some relic of
the past. I would make music for an ideal mother who didn't exist,
and she listened to a son who, through music, spoke without irony, or
condescension, or the studied formality of a preternaturally grown-
up adolescent.

I fought the diabolical passage week after week. I tried it slowly,
I played it through in strange groupings of three or four or five
notes, with different configurations of dotted rhythms, hoping
to defamiliarize it enough through distortion that when I tried it
as written it would be somehow stronger and more secure. Early
efforts yielded some success and sometimes, if I played the passage
in isolation, out of its musical context, it was almost easy. But once
I started trying to integrate it into the flow of the music, the results
were much more unpredictable. Perhaps one out of every three
times, it would go as planned, especially if I didn't think about it
too much. But these occasional successes were all the more maddening because they suggested that the ability to play the music
was available to me, that the music was *in there* in some fashion,
that the problem existed between the mind and the fingers, not in
the fingers themselves. When a problem is intractable, it is little
comfort to realize that it is mental rather than physical. If it were

merely a physical failing, we could focus on strengthening whatever is weak, and the problem would disappear; but with a mental failing, one confronts a superior but pernicious strength—the mental block—that must be defeated, and the enemy is not something that can be externalized, but seems to be consciousness itself.

As the concert approached, and I grew more superstitious about it, the passage got worse. In the weeks before the recital, I would occasionally put the music away, stand up, take a few deep breaths, and then sit down to the piano as if I were sitting down to play the recital, imagining an audience, forcing myself to anticipate the nerves I would feel that evening at the library. I would force myself to play without stopping, without going back to pick up dropped notes or take a second pass at something I'd missed. *This is exactly how it will go at the recital,* I told myself, and then I would listen for every flaw and blemish in my performance.

When I had only a few days left to fix things and still the passage was intractable, I became desperate and angry. I was so angry one afternoon that I slammed my fist on the keyboard and shouted some expletive. I wasn't aware that my mother was close by, but suddenly she was in the room, furious with me. The piano wasn't a toy, it was an instrument, it was fragile, and I might break it. "Don't you ever hit the piano!" she screamed at me. I was angry at myself at this moment, but still her fury shocked me, as did her uncanny insight into my dilemma. You're making it worse, you're doing it all wrong, you're fucking it up big-time, and you're going to blow it at the recital if you keep doing this to yourself. She seemed to know exactly what I was going through, the torment I was suffering, as if she had experienced the same thing. "You're doing this to yourself." As I often did when she yelled at me, I went into a trance, listening to her as if she were far away, in another room, behind an arras, or in some deep hole in the ground. She wasn't angry just because I had hit the piano, or frustrated with my self-defeating habits. She was angry at my anger. She knew the toll that rage could take on a person and I suspect she was sorry to think it might be taking root in her son.

The recital was on a Friday night, and I spent the last few days before doomsday in a state of grim stupefaction. The looming failure oppressed me from the moment I woke up in the morning to the final filaments of thought before falling asleep at night. The last days of anticipation grew darker and darker as my frustration mounted, and my fears deepened into a low-grade, ceaseless panic. I ate little, and took no pleasure in anything, and eventually gave up practicing altogether. What was the point, when every minute at the piano seemed to uncover new problems, and no amount of effort had been sufficient to master the passage that beleaguered me? Instead, I bargained with the fates, and put more faith in games, like avoiding red tiles on the hallway floor, or challenging a car to pass my window in the length of time I could hold my breath.

The ride to the library with my parents, the milling about before the event began, the performance of the players who came before me, all passed in a state of sickening nerves. I wiped my wet hands on my pants legs, rubbed my ice-cold fingers, took deep breaths, counted patterns in the ceiling, and struggled not to reveal my dreadful state of mind. My father sat quietly, absorbed in the music, no matter how tentative and flawed the performance, while my mother scowled at my all-too-visible nerves. As the player just before me finished her piece and took her bows, I thought of a tall rock at the lake where we sometimes vacationed, and the erasure of time and existence in the moment one pitched oneself from the terrifying height into the cold water, and how it seemed the only thing that separated the fear aforehand from the triumph after was pure will and resolution. Finally, it was my turn, and I went to the instrument like a zombie, sat down, and promptly forgot my teacher's advice to always take a moment and think through the first few bars of the piece and fix the tempo in my head before putting my hands on the keyboard. The passage I knew would fall to pieces came early in the first movement, and when I got to it everything went as planned. The fingers of my right hand tangled into knots and I did my best to fake it and managed to miss most of the notes between the top and the bottom of the chromatic scale, but still ended on the right note, a bit like a gymnast botching his routine but sticking the landing.

And then, after that calamity, things went fairly well. I was too drained by that early failure to care about anything that followed, and with that came a kind of freedom. I was miserable and angry at myself, but all of that emotion was tied up with one bar of music that was now safely in the rearview mirror. The second movement went off without a hitch, and the third, which is just as challenging as the first, was relatively unscathed by lapses of attention. The sonata ends with a tender, plaintive melodic fragment repeated softly, twice, as if fading into nothingness, followed by a furious C-minor scale and fortissimo final chord. I loved this theatrical ending and played it with fervor, extending the whispered reminiscence of the lyrical line and the long pause before the crushing final statement. Then there was the applause, which shocked me. It was almost as if the audience had forgotten the signal failure of the performance some twenty minutes earlier in the evening.

The enthusiasm seemed genuine, which was disconcerting. So, too, the pleasure of my mother, who hugged me and beamed with pride when I got back to my seat. I was embarrassed by it, took a reluctant and guilty pleasure in it, and then chastised myself for succumbing to it. The audience clearly didn't know Beethoven very well if they could reward me after I made such a hash of the last beat of the tenth bar of the introduction to the first movement. As the next player went to the piano, my mother whispered to me that the second movement was very beautiful. *Of course the second movement was beautiful*, I thought. *It's easy.*

The next pianist was a boy about my age with dark, curly hair and fair skin, who moved like a cat. I had never seen him before and he seemed a bit sad to me. He gave the audience a slight smile and sat down and played a piece from the twentieth century, a jazzy étude with a fast tempo and a catchy recurring melodic line that somehow fit the pianist perfectly, graceful and melancholy. I was captivated by his playing, and his presence, which disturbed me. If he made any mistakes, I didn't hear them. I don't know how long he played, but I was lost in his performance and sorry when it was over. The clapping of the audience brought me back to awareness of the room and myself, and as I watched this young player take his bows with the same half smile, I felt two things: *I wish I was him, and how nice it would be to make him feel less sad.*

After the recital there were refreshments, which my mother had organized. Only when I saw the homemade cookies and punch did I realize the effort this had caused her during the days when I was lost in my anxious solipsism, and it would be decades later when I realized how odious these displays of conventional motherhood were to her. She never relished the role of servant to her children, she hated to bake, and she rankled at being lumped together with other mothers. In the aftermath of every recital, there was a buzzing social scene of women who taught piano, who competed with each other for the best students, and for whom the world of music lessons, recitals, and local competitions was as hierarchical and stratified as Versailles. My old teacher Charlotte was there, and Charlotte had taken a keen dislike to my mother, which, perversely, she demonstrated by doting on me as if I had been tragically orphaned when we moved on to another teacher. She would cluck and fuss and tell me what great potential I had, with the obvious implication that this potential was now being squandered. Another local doyenne of the keyboard had the odd habit of referring to all the mothers not by their names, but simply as "Mother," and I am sure my mother took no pleasure when this eminence surveyed the table with its refreshments and said to her, "Good work, Mother."

During the reception, I scrupulously avoided the boy with the dark hair. People said nice things to me, compliments that I received warily. But one woman, considerably older than all the others, dressed rather like my grandmother, old-fashioned and precise, with thick glasses that made her face deceptively benign, was gently impatient with me when I deflected her praise. No, she said, the second movement *was* very well played and that is not an insignificant accomplishment. Everyone misses notes. Missing notes is not what music is about. Between this curious woman and me, there was a gap of perhaps some fifty years or more, and when she spoke I realized I couldn't place her in any of my usual categories, neither motherly nor grandmotherly, and certainly not just another of the bustling teachers who were working the room. For a moment, I listened, and considered her words.

My mother praised me again on the way home. It was Friday evening, and the weekend lay ahead, a weekend free of the torture I had felt for months. I was exhausted and full of the lazy contentment that floods in when some great anxiety has been removed from one's life. I felt I could luxuriate in the everyday stuff of life again, take pleasure in reading, daydream without guilt, and know that when I woke up on Saturday morning, although my first, reflexive thought would still be one of dread, my next thought would erase it and I would feel only relief. Looking out the window of the car at the lights passing by, and with my parents chatting happily in the front seat, I felt safe.

That night I was tired and restless at the same time, and lay in bed struggling to fall asleep. I was excited to start life again, to take up new projects and even dive into a new piece of music. But I couldn't tame my mind. And so I tried an old exercise that occasionally worked, which was to remember a feeling of great pleasure I took listening to a summer thunderstorm a few years earlier. Something about remembering the distant ferocity of the tempest, safely outside the window, calmed me and made it easier to drift away. I could see the rain beating against the glass and the trees bending in the wind and as my brain began to shut down for the night I could hear muffled rumbles of thunder. My arms and legs began to feel heavy and my body sank into the bed and wakefulness was almost extinguished when, in an imaginary flash of lightning, I opened new eyes to see the boy with the dark hair lying next to me.

WITH ADOLESCENCE, YOUNG players become prey to new fears and anxieties about performing. I've spoken with friends who are professional musicians, and with others who once played an instrument but no longer do, and they report similar stories. Different people articulate it in different ways, as a newly felt need to please, or an emerging sense of the possibilities of success and failure, or simply as a side effect of the self-consciousness that accompanies the dawning of sexual awareness. The memory of having been able to play in public without anxiety before adolescence is common, too. "I could do anything when I was eight," a friend tells me. But by thirteen, that invincibility was shattered. There is more than just anecdotal evidence for this. Some theories of musical creativity suggest that giftedness may be related to prenatal exposure to uncommonly high levels of testosterone, and that rising testosterone levels in boys during adolescence can cause that same creativity to deteriorate.

I may not have been gifted, but whatever talent I had underwent a curious deformation during adolescence. I had long since passed the stage of music making in which the child is capable of nothing more than mechanically marching through the notes like reciting a meaningless poem, and by the age of eleven or twelve I could play with some facility, feeling, and expression. When I would sneak glances at people who were listening to me, family and friends mostly, I began to notice that the old look of studied patience was sometimes replaced by signs of actual engagement and pleasure. I may have disgraced myself in front of my great-aunt on that one afternoon, but on other occasions I think I genuinely touched the emotions of at least some people. But the better I got, and the more I was rewarded for my playing, the more reward I craved. The piano had become a part of my sense of myself, which made me infinitely more alert to the reactions of other people.

With greater skill came greater awareness of the possibilities of music. As I came of age I began to wonder if I might make a career of the piano. When I was fourteen, Hollywood released a dreadful film called *The Competition*, starring Richard Dreyfuss, who was nominated for a Golden Raspberry Award for his performance as a young pianist trying to win a major competition. He gets entangled in a romance with one of his competitors, and there's a tedious back-and-forth of desire and rejection and promise and betrayal, before it ends happily. Like almost every other Hollywood film about classical music, it romanticizes ideas of inspiration and dedication, and minimizes the tedium of work and loneliness that makes music possible. But it offered a vision of the world beyond the insular confines of suburbia, a world full of artists and eccentrics, big dreams and vibrant cities, and it left me wondering if the piano might be an avenue to that world.

But the more one invested in the dream of music as a means to escape, the more ominous were the consequences of failure. What if you lacked talent? Today, there is a tendency to think of talent as innate in everyone, a hidden resource that can lie dormant or be drawn out, depending on whether you believe in yourself, find the right teachers, and have the means and opportunity to develop it. In the 1980s, talent was commonly seen as much more a genetic given, like hair color or height or shoe size: it was distributed capriciously, and absolutely, and you either had it or you didn't. This was the same cultural moment as Peter Shaffer's popular but crudely reductionist 1979 play *Amadeus*, which proposed a rigid caste system of talent that governed the arts and was apparently divinely sanctioned. The reality of talent may lie between these extremes, but when I was growing up the question of one's innate skill felt a bit like that silly game of poker in which each player is dealt one card and then places it unseen on his or her forehead. Everyone but you knows if you're holding an ace or a deuce, and you only learn the value of your card after blindly risking your wager.

The piano recital was the moment when you showed your cards, and learned your fate, so of course playing in public was fraught with anxiety. Today, psychologists who study performance anxiety call my kind of stage fright "catastrophizing," the irrational tendency to fear the absolute worst before a performance. The recommended remedies include confronting the irrationality of the fear and thinking through the actual worst that could happen, which is far less terrifying than your apocalyptic fantasies, or creating a script in your head that focuses on essential aspects of performance that aren't related to the danger zones that inspire panic. But no one used the term "catastrophizing" when I was in the grips of this debility, and no one proposed a remedy for it, either. Fear was something to be mastered, fought back, and beaten down.

There is an enormous literature available to people today who confront their self-limiting anxieties, and a large subset of that is devoted to performance anxiety, which afflicts not just musicians, but actors, dancers, athletes, and people who are obliged to give public speeches. A lot of what is written is based on the idea that we have a pure, uninhibited self, which is corrupted over time by adult self-criticism. The solution is to find one's way back to the child who took pleasure in things, a prelapsarian self with limitless, untapped power. Some authors offer stark, Manichaean schema for the mind, divided between a vessel of pure, innocent potential and a cruel, self-critical overlord. Others suggest ways of outwitting the brain's bad habits, finding zones of freedom and detachment from self-destructive thoughts.

One popular book that touches on many of these themes is *The Inner Game of Music*, which owes its title to an earlier, 1974 book *The Inner Game of Tennis*. The latter has sold millions of copies and is still among the most popular self-help volumes written for athletes. The tennis book, which spawned an empire of related self-help manuals, doesn't delve all that deeply into tennis, but posits a new kind of mental hygiene for players, urging them to exist in the now, to stop overstriving to achieve things that their bodies already know how to do, and to seek out a state of relaxed concentration that allows them to reach their inner potential. *The Inner Game of Music* borrows a succinct formula common to the larger *Inner Game* franchise: $P = p - i$, an equation in which your performance (P) is equal to your potential (p) minus your self-interference (i). "Isn't it reasonable to think that our performance would improve tremendously if we could eliminate that critical voice altogether?" the authors ask. If failure is what you fear, then try to fail, confront the reality, and see how it feels: "You have released yourself from the fear of failure and are now able to focus your attention one hundred percent on making music."

Throughout the book, and others in the self-help genre, there is a curiously American habit of seeing enlightenment through the prism of authority and freedom. Borrowing, perhaps, from Freud's idea of the superego, the author suggests we suffer because we have internalized the barking authority figure who chastised us as children. "As anyone who teaches the Inner Game quickly finds out, it requires effort and attention to teach without prescribing 'shoulds and shouldn'ts.'" The problem, of course, is that without some deference to authority, there really is no hope of learning most complex skills, and classical music, with its focus on a set of written musical texts that must be exactly mastered, is particularly bound up with discipline and the transmission of tradition. The *Inner Game* is never quite clear how far we should pursue the liberation from authority. Is it a matter of tone and temperament—finding teachers who can nurture rather than overawe and terrify—or do *Inner Game* advocates really believe in the possibility of learning without teaching?

Other self-help approaches advocate using fear, rather than fearing it. Fear, properly understood, is your friend, a kind of white-hot energy that one taps into, deliberately and judiciously, to bring the proper edge to your concentration and performance. This, too, seems particularly American, to convert everything into a resource, something to be mined and refined and put to good use. Like the "inner game," tapping into fear as a resource requires dividing the self into pieces, so that one part can exploit the other. Yet other self-help theories suggest giving voice to your fear, letting it speak and be heard, as if fear is a problem child within us, an unruly demon who goads us to self-destruction but who would mend his ways if given the proper acknowledgment and attention.

The Inner Game of Tennis was published in 1974, just as the self-help book genre was beginning to explode. These books brought the blessings of pop psychology off the airwaves and out of the coastal enclaves of self-improvement into neighborhoods like the one where I grew up, treeless tracts of suburban houses advancing relentlessly and amorphously from city's edge into forests, deserts, or farmland across the country. They were read by exactly the sort of people who surrounded us, upwardly mobile new members of the middle class, many of whom came from small towns, farms, ranches, or urban ethnic enclaves, close-knit communities dissolved by the corporate world, with its frequent dislocations, job transfers, new opportunities, and occasional layoffs. When my mother was nineteen she got married and moved with her twenty-one-year-old husband some nineteen hundred miles away to Pensacola, Florida, where my father was in flight training. During the years that she was sick, she began to reminisce about that chapter of her life, acknowledging the fear she felt at moving so far away. In earlier accounts of her marriage, the move was a parable of personal responsibility, and sometimes an intimation of her unhappiness about being thrust into motherhood. "We did it because we had to do it," she explained. But as I sat with her during her final illness, and heard these stories once again, I realized how deeply the scattered nature of modern life—which people of my generation take for granted—had traumatized her.

But not so much that she would ever bother with self-help books, which were not seen in our house. My mother, who suffered from anxiety, depression, and sleeplessness, had internalized not only her father's authoritarian parenting, but her mother's prickly contempt for overt emotion. Psychology, my mother firmly believed, was a racket. There were people in the world who were "sick in the head," a moral category distinct from mental illness, capacious enough to include not just criminals and the criminally insane, but the homeless, hippies, Democrats, the Catholic Church, and most of San Francisco. Self-mastery was essential to growing up, but self-help was hocus-pocus. To a large degree, I have internalized her views, as well. Not her prejudices, her disbelief in mental illness, or her contempt for the mental health profession. But I have little patience with the ideas in any of the self-help books I've read about performance anxiety, especially those that seem to divide the self into simple dichotomies, and come suspiciously close to being fables about our larger cultural ideas of authority and freedom. They graft cheap narratives onto something far more complex than a bifurcated inner life that needs only liberation or kindness to find equanimity.

Of all the changes that come upon us with adolescence, even more than the need to please or the fear of failure, the most profound is the emergence of desire. More than anything else, this seems fundamental to explaining the fear of performance that became crippling for me sometime around the beginning of high school. It explains the self-consciousness, the self-defeating habits, the urgency and panic to achieve self-mastery, the dreadful sense of isolation and failure, and the inexplicable craving for beauty that is thwarted by the body's awkwardness. When children who are immersed in musical performance (and surely other arts, too) come of age, they do so equipped with a language to speak thoughts far bigger, more intangible, and more erotically charged than anything ordinary language can contain. Music equips them for a grandeur and tragedy of feeling that is bewildering and terrifying.

For years, I've been haunted by an image by Titian, which recurs in different forms in several paintings, depicting the goddess Venus reclining with a musician sitting close beside her. In some versions, the musician is a young man on the left side of the canvas playing the organ, and in others he is playing the lute. Venus, nearly or entirely naked, lies recumbent on a luxurious bed to his right. Behind them, variously, are a wild landscape, a mountain scene, or a garden. In all of the paintings, spread among galleries from the Prado in Madrid to the Gemäldegalerie in Berlin and the Metropolitan Museum of Art in New York, there is an overtly sexual engagement between the young man and the voluptuous goddess. He is elegantly dressed and enraptured by her, turning away from his keyboard, or twisting his head in the opposite direction from the neck of his lute, to look directly at her exposed flesh. I've known the version at the Met, in New York, for decades, and I've made pilgrimages to see the ones in Berlin and Madrid. I love the Met's most, because (like the one in Berlin) the young man isn't staring quite so intently at the goddess's genitals, but rather up into her face, with tenderness and perhaps a pang of jealousy as her attention is drawn away by Cupid, who crowns her with a wreath.

Critics often interpret these works as an allegory of the power of sight versus the power of sound, and the superiority of visual to aural beauty. The musician, after all, seems distracted from his playing by the beauty of the woman. But the erotic power of the image is the more fundamental message. The young man craves something, and he expresses that craving through music. And yet, even music isn't sufficient to carry the weight of his want and desire. We see music not just as an attribute and refinement, like his fine clothes and a carefully clipped beard; we see music not just as an effort to embody and convey his desire; we see music as pointing to something beyond music, a beauty beyond art, which is his ultimate aim.

When I first saw this painting as a young man, still in college, still roiled by romantic ideals of love and desire, I thought it captured the entirety of love, jealousy, want, and need. Now, though I still love it, I think, *The poor boy*. He has worked so hard to capture her attention, and still she turns away. He has polished himself, perfected himself, and refined every aspect of his mind and manners to charm a lady. His narcissism enchants me, but I see it for what it is. A few centuries after Titian and his workshop painted these works, Immanuel Kant wrote a book on education, and he put music in what seems a dubious category: "Some accomplishments are essentially good for everybody—reading and writing, for instance; others, merely in the pursuit of certain objects, such as music, which we pursue in order to make ourselves liked." It is a brutal thought, to reduce music to something on the level of perfume and joke-telling, social niceties used to entrap the affection of others.

Venus is all too often with me when I practice. Not the goddess, of course, or even Titian's representation of her as a naked woman. But the thought of something beyond music, the craving for connection, to play for the dark-haired boy, to be made more beautiful through the agency of music, to be younger or in a different place, to feel as intently as I once felt, to recapture things lost or never possessed at all. She is a distraction, an instigator of daydreams, pulling the eyes and the mind away from the keyboard and the music. And she is importunate, for what she asks is horrifying to contemplate: Are you doing this just to be liked, loved, wanted, needed? Is that all this is about?

SEVEN

WHEN THINGS ARE going well, there is extraordinary pleasure in playing Bach. The fingers feel plastic, stretching to
take in notes far from the center of the palm, one hand now borrowing bits of the melodic line from the other, now pivoting silently on
a single key so that the more supple digits can stretch out into new
territory. The pinkie changes place with the thumb, and, with a slight
turn of the hand, the third and fourth fingers produce a smooth crab
walk up and down the keyboard. In his teaching, and in the music
he left to posterity, Bach demanded absolute independence of the fingers, which must nonetheless work in close collaboration. When the
notes are securely learned and memorized, the player sometimes has
the uncanny sense that the two hands have become a single organ-
ism, a ten-legged centipede or an octopus moving smoothly over the
surface of the keyboard, with a mind of its own.

On good days, when the music is both familiar and fresh and
hasn't faded from the memory through neglect, the fast passages will
feel elegant and infallible, the motion of the fingers both automatic
and deliberate, the skips and jumps sure-footed. Patterns over which
you labored for hours as if they were arbitrary facts in some incomprehensible argument now sound logical, obvious, and inevitable.
To snap a little mordent or quick trill at the top of a line while the
other hand executes a flurry of figuration below yields a superfluity
of musical delight.

When things go well, Bach emerges and the self retreats and one
can imagine that the incredibly sweet chains of mild dissonance and

tender resolution he works into the twenty-second variation, sevenths sliding into sixths only to have the bottom slip again into another delicious seventh, gave him exactly the same pleasure they are giving you, and that perhaps he, too, was inclined to linger over them, draw them out, even exaggerate them a tiny bit, so that no one in the room would miss these fleeting moments of tension and release. When, at the end of both halves of the thirteenth variation, he unexpectedly flattens the sixth so that the resolution of the chord becomes inflected with a frisson of darkness far in excess of the merely piquant, brief, but engulfing moments of bleakness that, perhaps, given this is the *thirteenth* variation, have something to do with the numerology of Christianity, one wonders if he felt them in his chest and arms the same way you do as your body tightens under their spell. Even in the solitude of practice and the absence of an audience, the pleasure persists and one has the sense that the perfection and autonomy of the music summons the composer himself: this is between us, whoever I am, so faulty and scattered, and whoever Bach was, so remote and inscrutable.

This feeling—that the rigorous beauty of the music puts us in communion with a higher intellect—is a controversial one. In the history of writing about and interpreting Bach, a history complicated by nineteenth century ruptures and twentieth century revolutions, there is fierce debate about whether there is some higher degree of abstraction or objectivity in Bach's work that compels performers to serve it in a unique way. Must they suppress the ego and disappear into the music that, if played well, somehow allows a transparent window into the mind of the composer himself? Words freighted with religious and spiritual significance come into play: Bach demands that we be humble, pure, and self-sacrificing. But why should Bach's music be different than that of any other composer? Isn't the performer always intervening in the music? Does music even exist without the performer? And if not, why should the interpreter be reduced to a mere acolyte in the instantiation of the composer's ideas? But even musicians who acknowledge the philosophical weight of these arguments may also confess that with Bach, a special, or at least unique form of humility is wanted. And that humility is sometimes rewarded by the illusion that you are the only person in the world at that moment so perfectly aware of the incomparable greatness of some small detail in the music.

Since the nineteenth century, Bach's music has been embroiled in a larger philosophical debate about art, and about whether it reflects objective ideas of order and rationality in the world, or expresses an inner, emotional landscape of subjectivity and feeling. The belief that Bach's music is an exemplar of aesthetic abstraction has sparked fanciful theories, including one that posits the *Goldberg Variations* as a reflection of Ptolemaic cosmology, reflecting the order and character of the moon, sun, and planets. But one needn't go that far to sense that there is something more on the order of facts than feelings in Bach. One doesn't play Bach in order to get closer to Bach the man, whoever he was; nor does his music offer a playground for uninhibited self-expression. The pianist Jeremy Denk, who has made an exemplary recording of the *Goldbergs*, describes Bach's music this way: "All other composers seem to be writing novels, but Bach writes non-fiction."

The objectivity, or facticity, or "non-fiction" quality of Bach's music seems to raise the stakes when it comes to performing and interpreting his works, as if the thousands of small decisions a performer must make have greater moment and consequence than they do with other kinds of music. If Bach's music is nonfiction, then the performer's decisions are bound up with ideas of truth. Instinct and inspiration may be satisfactory guides to the romantic music of the nineteenth century, to music that is written with the narrative sweep, unstable subjectivity, and emotional immediacy of a "novel," but they are insufficient for Bach. And this decision-making process isn't just essential to how one plays the music, it reveals the character of the musician.

Of course, the performance of any complex piece of music requires careful plotting and myriad small choices about execution. You decide which fingers will fall on which notes, the manner of articulation and dynamics, how distinct the lines will sound, how fast the piece must go, where its climax (if any) lies, what texture it will have, how much drama you will coax from it or perhaps force into it, whether it will be Apollonian or Dionysian. Some of these choices are strategic, calculated attempts to finesse the effects you want to achieve. But many of them are ethical choices, decisions that reveal the fundamental moral underpinnings of your relationship to music. Are you faithful to the text? May you elide or even skip that which you cannot manage? If there is an easy way that offers slightly less of what is intended, and a harder way that yields more, which one do you take? Do you learn only those pieces that you know you can play well enough to serve the music, or do you stretch yourself into music that you may never adequately master? Do you steal from other players, mimicking the best of what they do and claiming it for your own? Or should you at least strive to make every choice original to you?

There are no absolutely right answers to any of these questions. There may be no fixed musical text to honor, and the texts that have come down to us often represent an amalgam of what the composer wanted, what the copyist reproduced, and what the engraver fixed on the plate. What the composer desired wasn't stable, either, and a single piece can exist in multiple versions, each presumably as authentic as the next. Great musicians don't always play everything that is on the page, and sometimes play things that aren't on the page at all. Artur Schnabel, a pianist whose interpretations of Beethoven were legendary, missed notes and hit clunkers through sonata after sonata, and yet despite all their infelicities, his recordings are magisterial. An artist out of his or her element may produce a thrilling, seat-of-the-pants performance, while performers who work faithfully in their comfort zone often leave us cold. The old adage (attributed to various artists and poets) that "good artists borrow, great artists steal," applies to musicians as well. Has there ever been an entirely original performance? Even the first performance of a new piece often distorts the novelty of the music with a hodgepodge of ideas borrowed from other works.

But even if there are no right answers to these questions, the pattern of how you answer them defines your ethical makeup as a performer. Some players tend to a messy extroversion, full of drama, sweeping all before them, even the details of the music itself; others are austere and reserved, creating epochal events with the most minimal gestures, though their abnegation exhausts all but the most dedicated listeners. Some players consistently choose to exaggerate the showy effects and skimp on precision and detail, while others play dutifully and accurately, constantly missing the forest for the trees. When I was young, I adored Vladimir Horowitz, who played like a wizard, brilliantly and with terrifying virtuosity, yet he warped the music to his purposes, forcing it to dynamic and expressive extremes, and creating new textural effects with no sanction from the composer. As an adult, I blush at the enthusiasm I once felt for his playing. Horowitz's choices usually ran to the indulgent end of the ethical scale, not absolutely wrong or indefensible, but more demonstrative and megalomaniacal than inward and poetic. Today, I find his playing exhausting, like suffering an extrovert at a party who has an opinion on every subject.

I FIRST DISCOVERED AND fell in love with Horowitz's playing when my parents sent me off to a summer chamber music program in Maine at age fifteen. It required an audition tape to get in, and so for days I recorded and rerecorded the same Brahms rhapsody until finally I produced a version that had both a daring tempo and a reasonable degree of accuracy. This felt a bit like cheating, capturing the best performance without the pressure of an audience, and I wondered what would happen if the selection committee asked to hear me produce the same music live. But I sent off the tape with great anticipation and it was indeed good enough to secure me a place at the camp. I was thrilled, not just to explore a new kind of music, but to escape my home, live on my own, be surrounded by peers, and perhaps have a girlfriend.

The acceptance letter came with news that I must learn a Beethoven piano trio before I arrived in July for the six-week program. The tuition cost over a thousand dollars, which my parents paid without complaint. My mother was diligent in preparations, buying new clothes, packing a trunk with care, explaining to me the logic of her provisions, sunscreen and insect repellent, hats and sweaters, sneakers and boat shoes. When she packed a pair of pajamas, which I never wore at home, I asked her why, and she hesitated before saying, "Wear them every night. I don't want any sickos looking at you." I had never thought of myself as a thing that might be looked at, and the idea intrigued me. As she closed the trunk, I put in a fresh, untouched copy of Tolstoy's *War and Peace*, which I finished during the summer, despite the unusual distraction of having friends, with whom I walked to the town nearby, went sailing on the placid bay, and, one evening late in the summer, played spin-the-bottle.

The campus for the program was a maritime academy, a tidy brick school far larger than the musicians needed, full of empty rooms and dark hallways through which we ran after slipping free from our nightly curfew and the college-aged counselors who enforced it. The grounds were open and grassy, stretching down a hill toward the water, where one could borrow small sailing tubs when not practicing or rehearsing. More than the Beethoven, which I learned competently, or the private lessons I took, or the mornings I spent practicing, or the afternoons I whiled away with Tolstoy,

I remember sitting on the lawn after dinner, talking and listening to students who were greatly more sophisticated than I was. They debated the merits of various artists, and they had strong opinions on whether Horowitz or Rubinstein was the greater pianist, whether Rudolf Serkin or Wilhelm Kempff was the true keeper of tradition, and where in the pantheon one placed sui generis figures such as Glenn Gould. They were New York City kids who spoke of going to the symphony and the opera, who had heard famous singers like Beverly Sills and Joan Sutherland, and waited in lines for Horowitz tickets, and they gossiped about conductors, violinists, and even critics, many of whom they seemed to know intimately and sometimes called by their first names.

I studied them closely because I wanted to belong. Even in their teens, these young musicians were making the choices that would determine whether they would have careers in music, and what those careers would be like. There were some with effortless talent, who seemed never to need practice, who could play flamboyantly anytime, anywhere, but with a recklessness that distressed their teachers. There was a young woman whom I tried to court, who was quiet and introspective and a dazzling violinist, and when she showed no interest in me, her friends offered this consolation: she cares only for music. She went on to be a successful artist. There was a girl who wrinkled her nose at most everything, including the other members of her string quartet, and sometimes at the music itself, which she dispatched with grim efficiency, and perhaps a bit of contempt. Her self-assurance and the sweep of her opinions terrified me. And there was an older boy, rumored to be gay, who played the cello with warmth and generosity, always smiling and embracing everything around him, though we kept our distance because, of course, of the rumors. He never failed in his affection for the world even if the world didn't return it.

At the end of the summer, we were to perform with our assigned ensembles in a public recital, and the whole community was abuzz with anticipation. I worked with my trio frantically in the last two weeks to push through to the end of the Beethoven and bring some polish to it. We were shocked and elated one afternoon to play the whole thing through credibly for the first time, and for once I actually looked forward to a performance. But a few days before the event, my mother called to say that she would arrive early with my sister to fetch me and my trunk, and we would have to leave before the concert. The members of the trio were furious with me. I was spoiling things not just for myself but for them, too, and their parents who would be there as well. I pleaded with them to understand that I was subject to my mother's caprice, and had no say in the matter. I wanted nothing more than to stay to the very end, to enjoy every last minute of this idyll. I tried to explain my mother to them, her odd whims and unaccountable decisions, but I found myself confused in the process, unable to offer any anecdote that defined her strange behavior, or a label that captured her character. Through the summer, other students had spoken of alcoholic parents, absentee fathers, mothers with breast cancer, and bitter divorces, but I was suffering from none of these challenges, and it seemed inadequate to repeat what my mother had always said of her mother, with a touch of admiration and affinity: "She can be mean."

I promised I would beg my mother's indulgence, I would plead with her to let me stay just one more day. I was embarrassed in front of people whom I admired, and desperate that they understood my powerlessness. Curiously, after my mother and sister arrived, it was the latter who insisted that we should leave early. My mother, to my surprise, was sympathetic to my pleas, looked at me affectionately, and relented. By the time the recital was over, it was too late to start the eight-hour drive home. That evening, my mother proposed we have dinner together away from the school. We found a restaurant on the water, but a giant Maine lobster sat on her plate all but untouched through the evening, which unfolded mostly in silence.

The next day, as we drove through the rain, I learned that staying for my recital meant my mother had to postpone an appointment that same morning with an oncologist. It was melanoma, she said, and things didn't look good. She was calm and matter-of-fact about the cancer, her composure was strange and uncharacteristic, and it worried me deeply. Illness sobered her and it brought out the best in her. Caring for sick children quickened her maternal feelings more than anything else, and long after I had insulated myself from any emotional connection to her, she kept up an intimate and touching interest in my health. On this cold summer morning, her fear of cancer seemed to clarify her mind, and made her kind. The anger in her became simply sadness, and the sadness felt like wisdom. As we drove home along the Maine coast, I wondered about my complicity in whatever might happen to her, about my selfishness and the missed doctor's appointment. I checked the skin on my arms and legs for any alien spots or marks, and prodded at a lump in the back of my neck that sometimes I could feel, and sometimes not.

The Beethoven, which had gone well, was a distant memory, as were my friendships, the first alliances I had made with people who seemed to understand me. The evening conversations on the academy's darkening greensward, with dozens of pianos, violins, and cellos murmuring a delicate cacophony in the background, seemed alien and remote, even trivial, given the new fear that had entered my life. Over the coming weeks and months as my mother went from doctor to doctor and finally to Boston for a specialist's care, as we waited for a verdict and I imagined the worst, I listened to a recording of Horowitz playing Liszt, with the same hunger and absorption as I would listen decades later to Bach's Chaconne. And at that age, given those feelings, it was the right music, a stream of pure feeling that captured the only truth I could recognize in the world, which was the truth that existed in that particular house, at that particular moment, a house full of fear and anger, resentment, longing, regret, and guilt.

And somewhere at the bottom of all that mess, a few thwarted feelings of tenderness and love.

———

IN 1964, AT the age of thirty-one, Glenn Gould chose never to perform in public again. Live performance was a strain on his nerves, and he considered it an inadequate and undignified medium for music making. He remained a public figure through his writings and radio appearances, and a pianist of colossal importance through his recordings. He was a cerebral pianist, and perhaps no other artist in the past century has so intimately connected his artistry to a deeper sense of ethical choices about music, about performance, about technology and modern life, and his own way of existing in the world. And no pianist has had a greater impact on public perceptions of the *Goldberg Variations* than Gould. It was the first piece he recorded, in 1955, after signing with Columbia Records, and a work he returned to at the end of his life for a thoroughgoing reappraisal. Those two recordings, bookends to a meteoric and idiosyncratic career, offer an encyclopedia of choices a pianist can make about the music of Bach.

Gould's first recording of the variations is fast, fleet, and spirited, and it came as a tonic to the full-toned and ponderous way that Bach was usually played in the middle of the last century. Gould's manic tempos enlivened the dance rhythms that run throughout the cycle, and his unerring mastery of the virtuoso demands in the faster variations had a brilliance that allowed new generations to discover the work not just as a revered monument to polyphony, but as a scintillating showpiece. But it was Gould's clarifying of the musical lines that made the most lasting impression. Critics and listeners spoke of an X-ray of the music, and though the original recording was released in the two-dimensional monaural sound that was standard before the later 1950s, Gould's playing seemed to give Bach's music a three-dimensional presence. His astonishing independence of fingers and finicky attention to articulation and dynamics rendered the music with a contrapuntal transparency that was new to most listeners, and established its talismanic power as an artistic act fitted to an age of science and reason.

Gould used a light, often staccato touch, and brought out the middle lines of the three- and four-voiced variations, forcing them insistently into the listener's awareness while allowing the more easily discerned upper and lower lines to recede a bit in the texture. His piano sounded dry and even a bit delicate, and though he claimed to be more interested in the logic of the music than in the textures and sonority of the instrument on which he played, his distinctive touch imitated the bright, plucking sound of the harpsichord. Although his career spanned the rise of new scholarly interest in the history of Baroque music, and new generations of musicians adept at performing on historical instruments, Gould stuck to an ideal of music that transcended history. He chose the piano, rather than the harpsichord, because he felt the piano was better suited to bringing out the complexity of Bach's canons and fugues, and he chose to communicate with his audience through recordings because he felt that recording technology was better suited than live performance to convey Bach's complexity and nuance. The microphone, he said, "permits you to cultivate a degree of textural clarity which simply doesn't pay dividends in the concert hall."

Gould connected all of this to a personal ethic of music and life. His distaste for live performance came, in part, from disgust with the way in which music amplified ugly, egotistical aspects of the temperament, the thirst for acclaim and competitiveness. When he spoke of the pianist Rosalyn Tureck, who made definitive recordings of the *Goldberg Variations* but never achieved the fame and renown of Gould, it was in moral terms: "It was playing of such uprightness, to put it into the moral sphere. There was such a sense of repose that had nothing to do with languor, but rather with moral rectitude in the liturgical sense." He abhorred what he called the "adrenal" aspects of life, the biologically and chemically complex stew of emotion that drives men to all manner of barbarism, small and large. In the middle of the Cold War, with the world on the brink of annihilation, he wrote that the age of technological warfare was preferable to the grappling and stabbing of primitive battle: "A war," he said, "engaged in by computer-aimed missiles, is a slightly better, slightly less objectionable war, than one fought by clubs or spears" because the participants would be "less engaged by it" on the hormonal level.

His voluminous interviews and writings are punctuated with this kind of provocative statement. Gould's voice, familiar from interviews and his radio shows, is gentle, articulate, and reassuring; his ideas and opinions are often extreme. But he also strove to live out the rational consequences of his idealistic view of music, committing himself to a repertoire of rigorously intellectual music, with Bach preeminent. But even Bach failed to live up to Gould's standards at times. Gould would emend Bach's works when he felt the master had engaged in distracting asides, or failed to clarify his own contrapuntal structures. He cut fourteen bars from the Toccata in F-Sharp Minor, which he felt were too improvisatory in their repeated sequential figures, and added notes to the toccata from Bach's Partita no. 6 in E Minor to make certain lines more explicit and audible. Gould even found fault with the *Goldbergs*, which he called "a grab-bag of subgrade Bach," according to a journalist who interviewed him in the early 1980s. He acknowledged the work contained "some of the very best moments in Bach, which is saying an awful lot, but I think there are also some of the silliest." Among these were the virtuoso variations at the end of the cycle, which Gould said "are as capricious and silly and dull and as balcony-pleasing as anything he wrote."

I discovered Gould's playing long before I knew anything about his hermetic and puritanical musical life. I was introduced to him by a favorite professor who embodied a studied rationalism, a man for whom the rules of physics, chemistry, and biology were never mere abstractions but the guiding principles of daily life, to the point that he would rather offend the pieties of polite company than lapse into inconsistency, hypocrisy, or cant. The second law of thermodynamics, with its promise of increasing chaos and entropy, ruled over his world, making him as intellectually pessimistic as he was instinctively cheerful. If, at the end of a long and tense conversation about the inevitable decay and corruption of liberal democracy, you tried to effect a graceful transition from political philosophy to small talk with a vague suggestion that perhaps things would turn out for the best, he would observe sadly, and sometimes with irritation, that you had learned nothing about physics or behavioral science or philogeny. Gould's Bach was, for him, the summit of musical art.

Late one evening, over a bottle of brandy, my friend played the 1955 recording of the variations, and I was mesmerized. Unlike Horowitz's piano, which thundered with the force of an orchestra, Gould's instrument sounded remote and slightly metallic. His tempos were breathtaking, as was the dexterity of his fingers, though I didn't realize at the time the collateral damage—to the individual character of different variations, to the larger mood and drama of the whole—that his rapid-fire execution was causing. Rather, the music felt like an analogue for the orderliness of life that I admired in my professor, an enticing world of adulthood that was bright, clean, organized, and stable. I sensed that there was something important not just in the music, but in the playing as well, something that I aspired to achieve in my own life, but lacked the resolve and mental facility to accomplish.

I filed away Gould as I filed away all the possible lives that I might lead, alternatives to my messy existence. If I were better than myself, more disciplined and diligent, more balanced in my emotions, less given to sloth and self-indulgence and periods of scattered lethargy,

I might learn to play to some small degree like Gould played. I might keep a tidy little house and work productively in the mornings and advance through life with the cheerful determination to face reality with poise and levity. The piano might become a kind of stenographer's keyboard on which I registered my understanding of the music's structure, rather than a medium merely for self-expression. I might, in short, be less of what I was, which was my mother's child.

Late in life, Gould made his second studio recording of the *Goldbergs*, in which he extended rational control more thoroughly over all its dimensions. In this autumnal interpretation, he offered his view of a central debate about Bach's variation cycle that still divides musicians, theorists, and listeners. And that is: Are the variations a single, coherent work, consistent and unified in all their parts, or a collection of diverse ideas assembled to show the variegated breadth of musical possibility? Is this a unity with subdivisions, or a suite of diverse pieces with common elements? For a performer, this isn't an abstract debate, but critical to key decisions made about interpretive details, tempo paramount among them. Although Gould would say of the *Goldbergs*, "As a piece, as a concept, I don't really think it quite works," his second recording was his attempt to *make* it work, to unify it and present it not as a string of delightful episodes but as an integrated whole.

In his 1955 recording, Gould moved through the variations as if each one precipitated the next with a breathlessly effusive logic of association. One thought inspired another and another one after that, as if Bach were thinking with an adolescent's pure enthusiasm for seeing connections in the world. In the curious program notes he wrote for his 1955 recording, Gould used an extended metaphor to describe how the generative material of the aria related to the rest of the piece. The aria, he said, was like a genial but self-involved and detached parent. He warned listeners not to "become entangled in the luxuriant vegetation of the aria's family tree" and suggested they be wary of the aria's dominion and influence, and "examine more closely the generative root in order to determine, with all delicacy, of course, its aptitude for parental responsibility." Struggling to find an image for the variations as a whole, he offered up something like a solar system, with the aria at its center—remote, indifferent, even a little stupid in a ditzy way ("totally uninquisitive as to its raison d'être")—from which the variations radiated outward, circling their bad parent with celestial independence. By the time he made his second recording of the variations in 1981, this radial metaphor had become in practice a linear conception, and his view of the piece was more integrated and holistic.

In the original printed score of the *Goldberg Variations* there are curious markings at the end of some variations, but not others. They look like a horseshoe with a dot inside it or a child's rendering of a sunset. These are fermatas, and they may be indications to the performer to pause or linger, rather than plunge directly into the next variation. The fermatas suggest Bach may have wanted some variations to flow into each other, and others not, thus establishing smaller subgroupings of the variations. If that's the case, then it's reasonable to assume that the tempos within these groupings were somehow related, so that a common pulse threads its way through both fast and slow variations alike. In Gould's last recording, he went even further, in an attempt to bring an internal logic of consistent pulse to the entire work, reflected in orderly (though not always simple) tempo ratios. "In the case of the *Goldbergs*," he said in a 1981 interview with the critic Tim Page, a conversation Gould mostly scripted, "there is one pulse that runs all the way throughout."

In some ways, Gould's second recording merely continued what his first recording began, which was both a rejection of the past and an extension of his distaste for the affective and adrenal. If the young Gould reclaimed Bach from a tradition that he felt was too self-indulgent and romantic, the older Gould attempted to distill out of his earlier version many of the same sins. When Page asked Gould about his 1955 performance of the twenty-fifth variation, the most anguished and complex of the three minor-key variations and, for many listeners, the summit of the entire work, Gould dismissed it as sounding "remarkably like a Chopin nocturne." Unlike most young virtuosos, who would announce their arrival with something splashy and romantic or well loved like the music of Chopin, the young Gould chose for what was effectively his debut recording to record Bach, and one of Bach's most complex and least familiar pieces. Now he was finding intimations of Chopin in his own playing, which he was determined to eliminate. "There's a lot of piano playing going on there and I mean that as the most disparaging comment possible," he said of his earlier version.

Gould set standards for himself and by implication for other performers and listeners, too, that can seem inhuman. In the puritan's progress of his career, even "piano playing" becomes something extraneous to pure musical insight. Things like sonority and expression were distractions. When he first sat down to record the aria of the *Goldbergs*, the thirty-two bars of music that many listeners will acknowledge is the guilty pleasure of the piece, so simple, melodic, and graceful, his goal was to "erase all superfluous expression from my reading of it, and there is nothing more difficult to do." His ethos was severe: "The natural instinct of the performer is to add, not to subtract." And he kept subtracting from music throughout his career, until he managed at the end of his life to bring Bach's music in some ways full circle, producing an account of the *Goldbergs* that many find as ponderous as the readings against which he had rebelled almost three decades earlier.

No pianist can play these works without at some point grappling with what seems a rigorous syllogism: Bach is to music as Gould is to Bach. Both are exemplars of perfection, abstraction, and purity. But both sides of that syllogism are distortions of the truth. Bach was not "the supreme arbiter and law giver of music," as a popular biographical dictionary once defined him, any more than Gould's ideal of Bach is the only rational or ethical one. Even so, most pianists crave the level of intellectual control over the music that Gould claimed he possessed, and to a large degree demonstrated in his playing. Even if they don't want to play like Gould, even if they find his interpretations in some ways abhorrent, most pianists would acknowledge admiration, even envy, for his control over the keyboard. As I grew older and tired of my own emotions, and increasingly suspect (though never to the same degree) of what Gould called the "adrenal" aspects of life, I increasingly admired his flinty and austere musicianship.

Learning to admire Gould meant facing up to the consequences of having avoided Bach for so long. When I finally turned to Bach I grasped for the first time the vastness of my musical failings and I understood my neglect of Bach not just as a youthful oversight, but as a willful decision that had cost me years of unnecessary struggle. If as a boy I experienced musical failure rather like the unfortunate protagonists of Homer's *Iliad*, suddenly disarmed in the pitch of battle by the random visitation of some vengeful god or goddess, now I understood it to be of my own making, the result of my choices, my habits, my neglect. So when I started to learn the *Goldbergs*, I set about to change not just my playing, but myself.

Because it may take us years to effect a change in our habits, it is difficult to know when our efforts amount to genuine growth and self-transcendence. It may be that through self-denial or other discipline we have simply done violence to our nature, lopping off or walling in some vital aspect of our character. Gould has been dead for decades now, and the world has changed so fundamentally since he died that parts of his legacy seem deeply problematic. Not the recordings, but the ideas, and the cost of his self-sacrifice. Most musicians today crave direct contact with an audience more than ever, and Gould's idealization of the recording medium seems rather quaint in an age of media saturation and universal access to digitized entertainment. And his asceticism is increasingly difficult to interpret. In a 1993 film called *32 Short Films About Glenn Gould*, director François Girard includes an interview with the great violinist Yehudi Menuhin, who collaborated with Gould on recordings of Bach, Beethoven, and Schoenberg. Menuhin admires Gould, but with a genial, even sad sense of irony. He explained Gould's decision to retire from the stage as essentially a self-indulgent one, which led to him creating an elaborate justification that in some ways took over his life: "I think that like all people who try to rationalize their position, who do what they want at any cost, and then seek some sort of universal justification, he fell into a trap, a trap where he dwelt a little too much on the morality of his decision."

Menuhin gently chides Gould, who had died a decade earlier, for his self-justifying intellectualization of a decision driven by emotional vulnerability rather than rational choice. Perhaps there were other ways to deal with the strain of giving concerts. Perhaps Gould simply needed psychiatric help. But instead he not only gave up performing in public, but created an entire identity and ethos around it. And Menuhin found that rather sad: "I am not of his stature, creatively. I could not create my own life and lead it to the exclusion of the rest of the world."

Not long ago, a cancer scare made the condition of my viscera of intense interest to certain doctors, who recommended various tests, including an MRI, and so one afternoon I was pushed feet-first into a large metal tube with my legs bound together and an intravenous drip in one arm. The attendant asked if I was claustrophobic and I said no because I had never felt that fear before. Inside the machine, I understood in a flash what claustrophobia is, and struggled not to succumb to it. The MRI made fearful clanking noises that continued for five and ten minutes at a time, punctuated by brief respites during which the attendant called through a loudspeaker to ask if I was okay, queries that only added to my nerves. To find some sense of serenity, I tried to listen to the *Goldbergs* in my head, something I do often while walking on the street. As the machine banged on, I struggled to hear its familiar patterns of three, flipping through the variations to find one that would fit whatever arbitrary tempo the machine was inflicting on me.

My mother had been dead six years. Throughout her illness, I admired her fortitude and courage when facing doctors and medical procedures. As I was confined in an MRI, struggling with fear, fighting off a consuming sense of pessimism, struggling for some measure of emotional discipline, it seemed to me that what she had done some thirty-five years earlier, choosing to hear me play the piano rather than keep an important doctor's appointment, was nothing less than heroic. She didn't often find what she needed to rise above her fears, which consumed her slowly and thoroughly throughout her life. She lacked the power, or the will, to reinvent herself as a different person. She only seemed to transcend herself during moments of illness, hers and others'. But she found the power she needed that day in Maine, and often enough to keep fighting during the last years of her life.

I could not make anything of Bach fit the shifting patterns of grinding noise coming at me from all sides. The effort to summon the *Goldberg Variations* only added to my frustration and addled my nerves. So I tried a Chopin mazurka, a simple, forceful piece, dance-like and exuberant. It was one of the last pieces my sister learned before she quit the piano, and she practiced it with determination for weeks, to the point that everyone in the family dreaded to hear its opening dotted rhythms banged forth once again, prelude to a few minutes of music that had become so familiar we came to hate it. And yet, it became a family earworm, something any one of us can begin humming and expect the others to finish. It is a silly piece, a delightful piece, an inconsequential piece, and as I listened to it perhaps a dozen times in my head before the MRI was over, I was thankful that this kind of music exists, a colorful joyous distraction, bearing memory, giving pleasure, and nothing more.

EIGHT

BY THE TIME I was entering high school, and dealing with the emotional and musical changes of adolescence, I had become a problem student. I loved to play the piano, but practiced without efficiency and to little effect. I had outgrown my first teacher, burned bridges with my second one, and exhausted the patience of my third. There were only two options for me: quit the instrument, which I was loath to do; or audition for one of the two men in town who had earned a reputation for being serious pedagogues, preparing students potentially for professional careers. Perhaps there were also women in town who were also serious pedagogues, but if so their reputations never reached us. In any case as a boy, and a problem student, there was general agreement that I needed "to study with a man."

One of these two upper-level teachers taught at the local university, in a bright, modern studio on campus; the other, deemed more eccentric but the better pianist and a composer of distinction, taught out of a basement studio in a musty house that he proudly declared was "on the wrong side of the tracks." And indeed it was, a small house, weathered and overgrown, it sat across the railroad tracks from the larger, better-appointed middle-class homes in our town. I auditioned for both men and was accepted provisionally by the former, to study first with his graduate assistant and then, perhaps later, with him. I was also accepted by the other teacher, who didn't employ assistants, with whom I would work directly, without being palmed off on a young protégé. I chose this latter course, fearful that if I became part of a large factory studio I would sink into the background, eventually lose interest, and quit.

And thus began a lifelong friendship, with an enormous impact on not just my musical abilities, but my larger interest in the world, in books and literature and all the other arts, my sense of humor, my understanding of self, and my musical conscience—that deep sense of right and wrong that governs our relation to music, steering us variously toward perfectionism or license, diligence or indulgence. Joseph Fennimore had studied with Rosina Lhévinne at Juilliard, and Lhévinne had studied with Vasily Safonov, who had studied with Theodor Leschetizky, who had studied with Carl Czerny, who had studied with Beethoven. I didn't know about these connections when I began to study with Joe, but they emerged later, when I was an adult and we spent hours talking late into the evenings. Joe was ironic about his pedigree, and in later years would tell funny and sometimes ribald stories about the eminent figures with whom he had worked, including the formidable Rosina, who numbered Van Cliburn, James Levine of the Metropolitan Opera, and John Williams, composer of the *Star Wars* soundtracks, among her students.

These lineages say more about an emotional connection to tradition than they do about any authentic knowledge or practice that is passed down from generation to generation. I am sure Beethoven would blanch to think that I might claim to be a sixth-generation disciple. But tracing these connections isn't just a parlor game for musicians, and it isn't about invoking some fictive apostolic succession from the great geniuses of the past. Rather, it foregrounds the historical process by which art has been transmitted from generation to generation, how it has survived when the worst forces of man's nature were inimical to it. It encourages students to take the idea of pedagogy seriously because pedagogy, in the arts, is about far more than just passing on a body of facts. Teaching music is not only intimate and psychological, it is bound up with ideas of right and wrong, with character and a sense of purpose, and it requires more of both the teacher and the student than other forms of learning.

Joe was an unmarried man who lived much of the time in New York City, and his dress and manners were exotic by suburban standards. He wore fingerless gloves and scarves in warm weather, and when he spoke he was curiously droll, both self-deprecatory and playfully aggrandizing, such that one suspected he took pleasure in language. His studio terrified me at first. He had wedged two grand pianos into a basement, and used curtains and hanging beads to separate the instruments from a wall of hand tools, garden rakes, hedge trimmers, and other household implements. Only later did I learn that the more officious defenders of good morals in town whispered about his "lifestyle" and had warned my mother about allowing her teenage son to be alone with him. In the beginning, she would stay during the lessons, but if Joe took offense at her monitoring the proceedings, he never showed it. When she came for my first lesson he indicated a sofa opposite the piano and invited her to "bask in my exalted aura," and when she moved to sit at the far end, he added, "Not so far, it won't reach." He suggested she take notes, which she did, faithfully.

She hung on his words, laughed at his jokes, and would repeat through the week the more memorable of his bon mots, many of which went over my head. She could be intensely judgmental, and took a powerful dislike to many people I knew, including close friends and teachers of whom I was fond. She was a homophobe during those years, even more vigorous in her bigotry than the general tone set by the Christian partisans of Ronald Reagan. But she was mesmerized by Joe's playing, and perhaps felt a connection to him as an outsider to the conventionality that she both scrupulously upheld and resented at the same time. Her interest in the lessons led her, for a while, to take a greater interest in my practicing, which annoyed me. She wanted to monitor my scales and arpeggios, and make sure I was practicing my assignments from Clementi's *Gradus ad Parnassum*, a collection of athletic études with substantially more musical interest than the usual books of finger exercises. Joe often broke with the received wisdom from my earlier teachers, who insisted on nothing but the slow, methodical practice of scales. He suggested I endeavor to play them as rapidly as possible, to develop agility and velocity. As he demonstrated what I should practice at home, his hands rushing up the keyboard in parallel motion, he playfully barked at me, "Throw up those scales, throw them up!" For weeks after that, when I played my scales, my mother would call to me from the other room in much the same tone of voice, "Throw up those scales!"

I wasn't pleased with her participation or enthusiasm, which intruded on a part of my life that was becoming increasingly a private realm. I was relieved when she was too busy to drive me to lessons and left that task to my older sister. She would ask me later how they went and if Joe had said anything funny or clever and what I had been assigned to work on, and I would respond in monosyllables. She was eager to be part of the fun, and I would have none of it. When Joe moved to another studio some twenty miles away, she attended lessons less frequently, and I encouraged her absence. When I learned to drive, my mother stopped coming altogether, and I was glad to be free of her. My relationship with my teacher wasn't easy during these years. "You never suffered from an excess of practice," he said later. But it became a refuge from the rest of my life, an adult space where I was fully responsible for my actions.

He could be a demanding teacher. One afternoon, when he was frustrated by my indifference to details, he tried to show me how to practice. We spent almost the entire hour on a single measure, going over it again and again, starting over each time I played a wrong note, or held a tone too long, or neglected the articulation and dynamics. I think he wanted to make clear that there was a world of musical matter even in the tiniest scrap of a piece, and the mind can only assimilate this plenitude of music through strenuous activity. But I was frustrated and my brain went elsewhere and I found the lesson excruciating. It would be at least ten years before I gained an intuitive understanding of what that lesson was supposed to be about.

Another time, while playing something I hadn't sufficiently mastered, I said, "Sorry about that," as I blundered on, missing note after note. He stopped me.

"Apology not accepted," he said. There followed a discursus on intention, actions, and apologies, a summation of his rigorously rational view of human behavior, a view he holds still today, and much of which I now believe, too. Which is: Intentions don't matter, only actions. There are no accidents when it comes to how we comport ourselves in the world. The phrase "I didn't mean to do that" is meaningless. Though we may not have the honesty or clarity of self-perception to acknowledge our true motivations, we always do exactly as we wish. I missed notes because I didn't practice; and I didn't practice because I didn't want to practice. Ergo, I meant to bring him shoddy work, so I mustn't apologize for it. This mechanistic understanding of behavior was maddening to a teenage boy. I felt I had perfectly valid excuses for my lack of progress: there were exams at school, I had a report due, my family was leaving on vacation, I wasn't feeling well. But all of this added up to a pattern as clear to Joe as it was eventually clear to me: I had other priorities.

He made it clear that he didn't like to have his time wasted. Often, I knew before I arrived for my lesson that I hadn't done enough work to merit his attention for an hour. How could I avoid wasting his time? I contrived what I thought was a clever strategy: rather than play through a piece, I would ask specific questions, request help with particular passages, divert his energies to small, localized problems. He saw through this, of course, but he also indulged me, not for my musical talent, but for some other reason. Perhaps he intuited my need for intellectual company or adult conversation. So our lessons proceeded, sometimes focused on the music, often devolving into conversations about life. I made sporadic progress and managed to play a few more complicated pieces in annual recitals, including a Liszt polonaise, preludes and études by Chopin, and one of Mendelssohn's piano concertos. I was motivated by my occasional successes, but unlike with students destined to be professional musicians, failure enervated me and stymied my progress. Playing poorly produced a catalytic shame in better students, but plunged me into a debilitating sense of helplessness. After a poor performance, I would pout and look around for explanations beyond the obvious fact that I wasn't working as hard as I should.

"You were a nervous boy," said Joe, years later.

I'm nervous on the train, heading north from New York City to the town where I once lived. Joe is the last of my friends there, and for many years, he was the only reason I visited Schenectady. After a month of focused practice on the variations, I've decided—for reasons that are mysterious even to me—that I want to play them for him. I have a vague fantasy that I will take a lesson, just as I did thirty-five years earlier, and that this lesson will lead to a breakthrough. Perhaps he can impart some wisdom that will magically transform tenuous knowledge to something more certain, reliable, and fixed. The music is in a maddening "almost there" stage of learning, much of it mostly memorized, with my fingers sufficiently trained so that from time to time it actually sounds like music. But the slightest distraction, from a small change in tempo to any passing mood, makes my mind fly elsewhere, and my playing immediately becomes clumsy, approximate, and laden with mishaps. When I proposed coming up to play for him, he said he'd be happy to hear anything I wanted to play, but resisted taking payment for a lesson. So this is now established: he is happy to listen, but we aren't going backward to some preexisting stage of our relationship in which I am the student and he is the teacher. We have been friends too long for that.

On the train, a young woman notices that I'm studying the *Gold-berg* score and asks if I'm a musician. The question takes me by surprise and I don't honestly know how to answer it. I'm a writer and make my living as a writer. But I knew how to play music before I knew how to read, and music has been a constant companion throughout my life. I'm tempted to answer, "No, I'm just a music lover." But that isn't true in at least two ways. It suggests that I am primarily interested in listening to, rather than making music. In fact, I don't listen to music all that often. I go to occasional concerts but never walk around plugged into headphones or listen to it in the background. I'm also not sure I love music at all, at least not in the sense that people will say, "I love Paris" or "I love sushi." Music is not a pleasure in any simple sense of the word. It is an obligation, a duty, an obsession, an ineradicable part of my life. It occupies every empty mental moment, when I'm walking, standing, waiting, driving, exercising, and all too often even when I'm trying to be social and attend to other people. I wake up in the middle of the night with my muscles and tendons twitching an unconscious recollection of the previous evening's practice. On the train north, as the green banks of the Hudson pass by, I am focused on how much musical work is left to do, how many variations remain only half memorized, how much my performance the following morning will be dependent on the pure momentum of semiautomatic finger memory. There are dozens of moments in the canons where I haven't bothered to disentangle the two lines such that they live in true independence of each other. Remembering Joe's unflinching view of human nature, I wonder if I'm making this visit in order to fail, to demonstrate once again that I'm unequal to the challenge I've set for myself. As the train brings me closer to the derelict town where I grew up, I am sick of myself, angry that there were so many evenings when I set the music aside thinking, *This can be solved later.*

"Yes, I guess I am a musician," I say to the woman next to me, wondering for a moment if she is one of those omniscient and impertinent Sybils of public transportation, and if she'll look me in the eye knowingly and say: "No, you're not." But a question that has addled me to the core was merely a conversation opener for her. She looks at the music, which I've closed on my lap, and says, "Batch. Botch. How do you say it?" So I muster my best avuncular self: "Actually, it's Bach, he was a very famous composer once upon a time."

"Bach. I've heard of him."

———

WHEN BACH WAS in his mid-thirties, he traveled to Hamburg, where he performed for an audience of local dignitaries, including the composer Johann Adam Reincken, who was then about eighty years old, or perhaps even older if one believes a contemporary account. As a student, he had admired Reincken, and traveled several times from Lüneburg to Hamburg to hear the esteemed organist play. Reincken had served for decades as the organist of St. Catherine's Church, a prestigious post and home to a large, sophisticated, and widely admired organ. It was certainly among the most splendid instruments in Germany, and Reincken's performances on it had made a profound impact on the young Bach, when he was still a teenage boy. Bach's students remember their teacher's lavish praise of Reincken's playing and the organ of St. Catherine's, both of which remained for him standards of excellence throughout his life.

Reincken was a worldly figure, widely knowledgeable about music, intellectually cultivated, a fluent composer, influential and connected within the north German music world. A 1674 painting shows Reincken dressed in a sumptuous red kimono, tied with a belt, sitting at the harpsichord, surrounded by musicians of both sexes and an African servant. The atmosphere is one of leisure, sophistication, and refinement. If Bach met him during his youthful visits to Hamburg—and it's reasonable to assume that he did—he must have found Reincken as exotic as one of the Magi in an Old Master painting. No matter what he made of Reincken's personal style, or his theatrical personality, Bach would have deeply admired his depth of learning and range of reference.

So Reincken's response to Bach's performance in 1720 was obviously deeply gratifying. By then, Bach was the foremost organ virtuoso in Germany, and perhaps Europe. He had earned a well-deserved reputation as one of the leading organ consultants of the day, traveling widely within Germany to advise municipalities on the construction and renovation of church organs. Not only had he composed many of his most significant organ compositions, he was renowned for the complexity and sophistication of his improvisation, which was an essential skill for a church organist. With Reincken in the audience, Bach performed for more than two hours, including, by request, an improvisation, which lasted for almost half an hour, on a popular chorale tune. Bach knew this chorale well, and by all accounts he was astonishingly good at seeing the polyphonic potential in any theme or idea presented to him. So his improvisation on "An Wasserflüssen Babylon" wasn't entirely off the cuff. Indeed, this particular chorale may have had special meaning for him. Johann Christoph Bach, the musically brilliant cousin of Bach's father, had written an organ work based on the hymn, and Bach also knew Reincken's own enormously elaborate and extended variation on the melody. In 2005, a manuscript that may be in Bach's hand was discovered, suggesting that when Bach was about fifteen years old he owned a copy of Reincken's work. The hymn's theme of loss, exile, and the pain of being forced to make music during a time of grief may have particularly touched the adolescent Bach, who had lost both his parents, left his brother's home and the region where he grew up, and was surviving as a student contingent on his service as a musician in Lüneburg:

By the waters of Babylon
we sat down and wept,
when we remembered thee O
Zion. As for
our harps we
hanged them up upon the
trees that are therein.
For there they that led us
away captive required of us
then a song, and melody in
our heaviness: Sing us one of
the songs of Sion.
How shall we sing the Lord's
song in a strange land?

The anecdote about Bach's 1720 improvisation in Hamburg may be contrived. Was it just luck that whoever suggested he improvise on this hymn chose material known to be the subject of Reincken's earlier work? Were they setting Bach up for invidious comparison with the ancient master? Or, given how well Bach knew the music, lobbing him an easy pitch? In any case, Bach probably did produce something astonishing at that moment, an improvisation based on deep knowledge of the music, a lifetime of thought about its possibilities, familiarity with Reincken's own version, and the inspiration of his personal, emotional association with the music. And there was something else: Bach's first wife had died only a few months earlier, which was a terrible shock to him, leaving him with a house full of young children. So Bach, at the height of his powers and inspirited by grief, reached back to music from his youth and offered it up to an elderly man to whom he felt connected by bonds of admiration, memory, and discipleship. Reincken, who was more than capable of envy, was as astonished as anyone else, and his response to Bach's improvisa-

tion was rapturous: "I thought that this art was dead, but I see that in you it still lives."

This praise must have made a deep impression on Bach at a moment when he was particularly vulnerable to questions about his purpose and legacy. He was well situated as kapellmeister in the music-loving court of Anhalt-Cöthen, a position he thought he might keep until his death. Success, and some measure of security, may have made the ambitious composer wonder, *What's next?* And then he returned home one summer's day from the spa town of Carlsbad, where he was serving his prince and making music in one of the most cosmopolitan towns in Germany, to find his beloved wife dead and buried. Perhaps he asked himself, *What of her lives on in me?* Perhaps he followed that with the larger and more unsettling question, *What, if anything, in life persists?* And an eminent old man, whom Bach had admired since he was an adolescent, told him: Art, in you.

Bach remembered the story and must have recounted it in later years. Carl Philipp Emanuel and Johann Friedrich Agricola included it in the obituary they published after Bach's death. In their telling, Reincken became a man in his late nineties—"at that time [he] was nearly a hundred years old"—which may have been an honest mistake on their part, but a telling detail that dramatizes the historical passing of the torch between the aged master and his dynamic and ingenious successor. But if Bach the fast-rising kapellmeister took pride in Reincken's praise in 1720, over the next three decades these words—"it survives in you"—must have assumed a more subtle and sadder meaning. Throughout his career, Bach was an eminent teacher, working with students as the cantor of the choir and music director at St. Thomas's in Leipzig and as a composer who relied on university students to realize many of his works. He also worked as a private teacher who gave lessons to supplement his income and enlarge his circle of friends and allies, and some of his most important works were designed to serve both didactic and encyclopedic purposes. Bach was a devoted and methodical teacher, focused on the practical essentials of music making. But he was also an increasingly old-fashioned composer, who relied on his students not only to help keep him up to date, but to preserve his own musical ideas, which were increasingly out of step with prevailing taste.

He had dozens of students, many of whom went on to serious careers, as performing musicians, and as scholars and authors who specialized in the theoretical and scientific aspects of music. He taught his own children music and three of his sons, at least, went on to substantial careers as composers. But even if one includes his most prominent children, Carl Philipp Emanuel, Wilhelm Friedemann, and Johann Christian among his disciples, the legacy is ambiguous. Most of the composers who studied with him are minor figures, and Bach's imprint as a teacher is seen more in the loyalty and love of his disciples than in any direct impress on their musical style. Bach didn't leave behind a legion of imitators, but a wide network of well-trained musicians who revered him, without carrying on the musical tradition that their teacher embodied. Bach could never say of his students what Reincken had said of him: "I thought that this art was dead, but I see that in you it still lives."

EVERY TIME I visit the town where I grew up I feel the muscles in my body constricting, as if to shrink me back to the size I was when I left. I feel exposed and self-conscious, and I dread meeting by accident anyone whom I once knew, even though that hasn't happened in the thirty-five years since I fled. The landscape, which I remember perpetually locked in the afternoon gloom of gray winter days, refuses to assimilate to my memory, cycling through the seasons just as it does everywhere else on the planet. A few landmarks remain that I can still recall, a train crossing, a bridge over the river, the library where I played a recital years ago. The houses where I grew up are still there, though the neighborhoods have undergone a strange reversal: Homes that were new when I was a boy are now old and surrounded by mature trees, while the old houses that seemed more gracious and settled forty years ago now look barren and shabby. The street corner where my mother taught me the difference between left and right—left is down the hill to the railroad tracks, right is up the hill toward home—is now a traffic circle, and everyone must go right, even if they want to go left. The doctor's office where a cadaverous old man once proclaimed me "sickly" is no longer there, replaced by a half acre of asphalt and patchy grass. The house where I did yard work for an elderly widower survives, but the trash cans where he disposed of empty liquor bottles are gone. "He's a drunk, don't talk to him," my mother warned me, so I dutifully refused the lemonade this kind, forlorn man offered me every time I mowed his lawn.

I used to think I had left this place behind, but now I know I have dragged it with me for decades. And yet the city I have carried with me ceased to exist the moment I left it, and lives on only in me. I am the only one who knows that it was along this two-lane highway, just down the road from our old house, that my mother pulled the car off the road and slammed on the brakes and shouted at me, "What are you, queer?" She was angry that I had no date for a school dance, and she punished me in the most peculiar fashion: I would not be allowed to fulfill my duties as a Sunday organist at a local church, a job I held to make money for college. I was mortified to miss work and when I apologized to the choirmaster, who was more amused than angry, she asked me in a sly, conspiratorial voice, "What did you do?" I didn't know what to tell her. "Something bad."

This particular visit home, to see Joe, was in high summer, when the city was lush and green and the fields full of fireflies. When I was a boy my father would drive the family into the countryside on June evenings and park the car beside the road where we would watch the blinking of the lightning bugs, and these nocturnal shows delighted my mother. I hadn't thought of this in years, and the memory didn't fit the usual pattern of her unhappiness, so I left it beside the road as I drove from the train station on the evening of my arrival. The next morning, I was more nervous than I had been in years. I hadn't touched the piano in front of my old teacher for decades, and while we often speak about music, we rarely speak about the years when I studied with him. He arranged for me to play on a piano I knew well, in a large room at a local music school. We were both outside our usual haunts, on neutral ground, and the space was large enough that he could sit at a discreet distance. He was alert to my nerves.

The piano was sluggish under my hands. Two-thirds of the way through the aria I had to open the music and refresh my memory, and Joe interjected: "Don't fret so much." That helped, but even so, my playing was self-conscious, laborious, and indeed fretful. Some of the variations over which I had struggled for months went well enough; others fell apart. I played the aria and the first ten variations by memory, ending with the fughetta. "I should stop here," I said, because my concentration was shot and my playing increasingly sloppy.

"What do you want me to tell you?" he asked when I was finished. He then proceeded to make observations, incisive ones about the music and delicate ones about my playing, which he said was better than it had been when we studied together. Among them was a wrong note, a C sharp where it should be a C natural. His ear was always astounding, but this was also a generous way of saying that he could tell where I had dropped and missed notes in the heat of battle, which is a different thing than not having learned the music correctly. "I think I got about thirty percent of what I wanted," I said. "If you got thirty percent, that's good," he countered.

"Do you record yourself playing?" he asked. I said no. "I say this to all my students, no matter what age. You need to hear your own playing. It is invaluable." Then he moved on. "You aren't doing much with articulation." By this he meant shaping lines, breaking up long strings of notes into smaller ones, some of them smooth and connected, others played detached or with a sharp staccato snap to them. This isn't just surface detail, like choosing between matte finish or glossy paint on a wall. It is essential to the rhetorical power of the music, in some ways analogous to the difference between listening to a trained and untrained Shakespearean actor deliver a speech. Articulation, inflection, and pronunciation aren't just professional niceties applied to a recitation of iambic pentameter; they are essential to understanding the words at the most basic level.

I hadn't, in fact, put much effort into articulation, except in a few of the variations I knew well enough to play without fear of losing my way. It seems to put the cart before the horse to work out the details before the main substance of the music has been digested, and his advice ran counter to the misguided notion of musical learning into which I had lapsed long ago. It is easy to think that knowledge of a piece is built up in levels, beginning with getting the notes right, then speeding it up, then memorizing it, and finally adding in expression and highlights and other fine details. But the sooner one can integrate the mechanical aspects with the emotional and expressive features, the faster the music is mastered. "A better sense of articulation will help you with the memory," he said. And this is true, though not always intuitive. The difference between memorizing a random string of facts as opposed to a speech or poem that organizes information in a methodical or logical way is obvious. And it is much the same with music. An articulated, expressive line is more likely to stick in the memory than a string of undifferentiated notes.

We worked on articulation a bit, noting a few rare instances in the printed edition of the *Goldbergs* where Bach left definite instruction about how to shape phrases. Otherwise, Bach gives almost no guidance in these matters, trusting that performers will know the fundamental elements of style and make sensible decisions based on their own taste. We know from historical texts how contemporary harpsichordists fingered the music, which gives some guidance for where phrases naturally break. And Bach's son, Carl Philipp Emanuel, wrote a treatise on keyboard playing that is as close to a guidebook for the music of his father that we have. But subsequent generations of musicians have codified their own rules, not just about articulation but also about the critical question of how to play Bach's ornaments, whether they begin on or after the beat, how many notes they include, and whether they have little turns or twists or fillips at the end. Among the more sacred rules is the prescription that trills always begin on the note above the note indicated, a rule I would like to break in a couple of places.

"Do you think I can get away with this?" I ask, after introducing a few jaunty little on-the-note trills in the second variation, a detail that breaks with usual historical practice.

"Who's going to know?" asks Joe. It's a good question, and one that goes to the heart of why I'm learning the variations. To amuse myself? Provide pleasure to listeners? Impress connoisseurs? Or to prove something to myself? I say in response that anyone who knows the details of Baroque style will detect my sleight of hand.

"Fuck 'em." Joe's larger method has always been: know the rules, then break them if you wish. When I was studying with him as a boy, I never quite mastered the first part of this two-part dictum. Now, it seems, I have fetishized it to the point that I can't allow myself the freedom to indulge the second part. And yet the pianists whom I love regularly indulge the most eccentric variations on the rules of style and ornamentation.

"I was never good at getting the notes right, and now that's all I seem to care about," I say to him.

"You're not the same person you were." Perhaps only a teacher can make this observation. Parents are too close to their children, invested in snapshots that freeze static memories of a particular moment, an imago that preserves some idealized sense of their relationship. Good teachers are necessarily interested in something that parents all too often find terrifying, the freedom of the younger person. Only after a student has left the teacher and lived for a time in freedom can the teacher judge the success of the relationship. Perhaps the same thing is true for students: only after they have gained their freedom, can they judge the wisdom of those who taught them. I am struck during this lesson-that-was-not-a-lesson by how deft Joe was at managing the exchange, how well he said what needed saying without being dispiriting or cruel. A large part of teaching is about confirming what the student already knows in some inchoate way. It is about giving permission to advance to the next thing, to set aside doubts, to proceed unencumbered. Joe managed to say, in several different ways and without repeating himself, the same thing: You already know this.

Unspoken between us was the obvious fact: I had come to him for validation. Neither of us has any patience for pop psychology, and even less for self-delusion. But he deftly offered what I was seeking: a sense that this project wasn't futile or ridiculous. In little more than an hour, he communicated three basic things, which were always fundamental to his teaching: Listen to yourself; do what needs doing; feel free to move on and be your own person. Later we took a walk down to the river and sat on a bench as the sun went down, and I told him about the woman on the train who had "heard" of Bach. He laughed broadly and long. And then he said, "Most of my students don't want to study Bach." It was too much work, too much investment in music that channels emotion through complex rhetorical gestures that are terribly formal to many listeners today. A paper cup floating on the water was moving upstream, which seemed odd, and I remarked upon it, and Joe explained the peculiarity of the currents in this particular stretch of the river. While the main channel of the river flowed down to the Atlantic Ocean some 150 miles away, the water on its margins flowed backward. I was tempted to say, "It took me thirty years to really love Bach." But the air was hot and humid and the river was as lazy as I was, and I didn't bother saying it.

NINE

THE RESCUE SERVICE told us the puppy we were adopting was a Newfoundland, and would likely grow up to weigh around 140 pounds. The size was daunting, but the temperament sounded just about perfect: Newfoundlands are sweet, calm, loyal, and easy to train. In the pictures they sent us, he certainly looked like a budding Newfie, an amorphous fur-covered bundle with a prominent snout, but as the weeks passed he didn't put on sufficient weight. I downloaded a growth chart from the internet and every few days would scoop him up and place him on the scale, and every time I did, the results were more alarming. Our dog was voracious, and showed no signs of ill health, but if he was a Newfoundland, he was severely underweight.

Nathan turned out to be a border collie of some sort, with a temperament almost diametrically opposed to what we were expecting. He is a trickster, terribly smart, not very calm, and, as far as I can tell, entirely immune to training of any sort. And he has one salient character flaw that upended my life: He hates music. Not only does he hate music, he particularly hates classical music, despises music of the Baroque era, loathes anything played on the piano, and reserves especial animus for the music of Bach. Wagner makes him grumpy and elicits small groans of distress; Chopin on the piano will drive him from the room; Mozart makes him whimper and send us irritable looks of accusation. But when I play Bach, he howls unmercifully, as if on the rack.

I have taken to hiring a young woman from the neighborhood to take him on hour-long walks when I need to practice, and I encourage friends to borrow him for a few hours every now and then. But when it comes to the years-long battle between Nathan and the old Steinway grand piano in the living room, Nathan has effectively won. I don't use it unless he is out of the house, and I resort instead to a basic Yamaha electronic keyboard that lets me practice with earphones, causing no disturbance to the dog. Friends who have seen Nathan howl at my playing have suggested that it is perhaps simply jealousy: he resents my devotion to the beautiful black wooden box with its ornately carved legs and music stand, and he cries to attract my attention. But this isn't the case. When I practice on the electronic keyboard, he curls up at my feet and sleeps contentedly. Other observers, quite reasonably but with some malice, have suggested it is my faulty execution of the music that he dislikes. "He's a critic," they say, amused at a joke I've heard more than a few times. But Nathan will bark at the car radio if he hears Bach, no matter how great the pianist.

Others have suggested it is simply the noise he dislikes, and yet he tolerates loud noises with no fear or discomfort. Pop music rarely bothers him at all. It is classical music he hates, and he hates the work of music's Supreme Arbiter and Lawgiver more than anything else. Can a dog recognize Bach? In excerpts or paraphrases preserved from his lost "Treatise on the Influence of Melodies on the Soul of Animals," the great Arab mathematician and savant Ibn al-Haytham said that music can "affect a camel's pace, persuade horses to drink, charm reptiles and lure birds." Darwin observed that birds have a keen sense of what humans would call the aesthetic and credited them with "strong affections, acute perceptions, and a taste for the beautiful." Studies of individual species suggest that dolphins not only recognize individual melodies, but can distinguish them even when transposed to different keys. Cotton-top tamarins particularly hate uptempo music and generally prefer silence. The largest German-language dictionary in print during Bach's lifetime claimed that deer respond most keenly to brass instruments and that crabs are particularly susceptible to the flute. The French composer Camille Saint-Saëns, a committed misogynist and passionate animal lover, was a lifelong observer of animals and music, and once had a dog named Dalila, who hated the piano; another dog, he claimed, loved the piano but hated Chopin: "Before eight bars had been played, he had left the room, with dejected ears and his tail between his legs." And Nathan can absolutely recognize the music of Bach. Once, when I was watching *The Silence of the Lambs*, he pulled himself out of a deep slumber, traversed the room, and set himself before the television screen to bark imprecations at Hannibal Lecter, who was of course listening to Bach's *Goldberg Variations*.

Sometimes, as I watch Nathan lie on his back under the piano with his belly triumphantly exposed to the instrument that he has silenced, I wonder what he actually hears when I am playing. His brain can identify Bach as effectively as someone who hates cilantro can detect it in the mix of a soup or salsa. But does he in any sense understand or know music? Pain and aversion are a kind of knowledge, perhaps the first and most fundamental knowledge we gain when, for instance, we touch a hot stove as a child. But does he hear anything more than simply a noise he finds unpleasant? Or is he like a machine that barks mechanically when he hears certain kinds of music?

We might ask ourselves some of the same questions: What do *we* hear when we hear music? More fundamentally, what does it mean to "know" a piece of music? It seems a simple question. On television, people win money if they can recognize a tune in three notes. When music we "know" comes on the radio, we nod and say, "I know that." So to know a piece of music is simply to recognize it in some way. People who listen mainly to classical music, however, may use the verb "to know" slightly differently. They may have heard, and even recognize, an hour-long symphony by Mahler, but say that they don't really know it in the same sense as they know other works, meaning they haven't spent sufficient time with it to properly understand it. Before I had ever thought of learning the *Goldberg Variations*, I could have said without pretense that I knew the work well, having listened to it many times, more often than many other works I also know. I feel like I know Bach's Chaconne for violin, though I could never play it. In this sense, to know a piece of music means to know what comes next, to have a mental map of where it is going, to anticipate and enjoy the twists and turns of the music. One doesn't "know" Beethoven's Fifth Symphony, which is one of the best-known pieces of music in the world, until one knows that at the end of the scherzo there is a giant crescendo ending in an enormous C-major chord. Waiting for that moment, the knowledge that it is coming an essential pleasure of the music. And yet, even this knowledge, which is a form of expectation, is only part of what it means to know the symphony.

For a musician, the idea of knowing a piece of music is greatly more complicated. When I first studied with Myfanwy, she deemed my knowledge of a piece sufficient if I could play it to the end without stopping, even if I had to look back and forth from the music to my clumsy fingers as they picked their way haltingly through the notes. But other teachers had a higher standard for knowledge and would insist that I play a piece by memory before it was considered learned. Sometimes, to test my knowledge, they would take the music from the stand as I was playing and I would discover that I had indeed memorized it without quite realizing it. These moments were akin to a child's sudden discovery that his parent's hand is no longer steadying the bicycle, and that he has, for some time, been riding unassisted. Yet once I started to suffer nerves when I played for people, it was immediately clear that there were levels to memory, and that the muscle memory that came from repeatedly playing the same piece over and over again was very different from the mental memory that was essential to confident performance. And mental memory came with its own levels. There was an auditory component, the ability to hear in the mind what comes next, and an essential visual memory, the ability to see how the hands should be placed on the keys to do what they needed to do.

But even those deeper levels of memory might not be sufficient if someone placed me in a room and said, "Write out the Beethoven sonata you just memorized." Then I would struggle to remember which notes went where on the page, how the rhythms were structured, where the silences fell, and all the other details. I have tried this exercise from time to time, and found that the only way to do it is to "transcribe" the music from visual and auditory memory, as if one part of the brain is listening and watching some other part of the brain play the piece, and taking down notes. It is taxing and I've never produced a perfect copy.

And still we're not to the true depths of what it means to know music. Even if a musician can play a work perfectly, has memorized it thoroughly, and can transcribe that memory onto paper, there is still the question of why the composer wrote the piece in this particular way. Why these chords? Why these variations, juxtapositions, developments, and repetitions? This is the knowledge of musical architecture and syntax, and it, too, has its levels. One can analyze a piece of music by producing a detailed map of its progress, showing the harmonic progression, creating a taxonomy of its themes and their interrelations, and making connections between foreground detail and background structure. Some performers deem this analytical knowledge an essential guide to performance, because it helps them identify key moments in the drama of a piece, develop a sense of hierarchy about which events are more or less significant, and sometimes unearth hidden treasure, perhaps a small line buried in an accompaniment figure that, when highlighted, adds tension or nuance or underscores some emotional content. Other performers find this exercise academic and unrelated to the intuitive nature of making music. Both kinds of musicians can produce magnificent performances.

This level of knowledge also includes a sense of historical style, and an intimate familiarity with a composer's particular stylistic imprint. A good musician can look through a printed score of a Mozart sonata and quickly find mistakes in the copy, missing sharps or flats or misplaced notes, based on an infallible sense that Mozart wouldn't have written it that way. With the music of Bach, the historical, syntactical, and structural elements are particularly important because, like other composers of his day, he didn't leave a lot of explicit clues about performance. It is particularly difficult to play his music today without understanding its structure and historical context because so much of the music written since Bach died follows very different rules, raises and satisfies fundamentally different expectations. There is a temptation to "romanticize" his music, or connect it too explicitly to modernist ideas. And without some awareness of the basic formal ideas Bach used, his mastery of the fugue and canon, it is easy to squander hours making sense of complexities that are, in fact, quite manageable once one sees them in terms of counterpoint and polyphony rather than, say, melody and harmony.

Bach lived and composed near the end of a musical tradition that emphasized the weaving together of independent musical lines, worked out with varying degrees of elaboration, variety, and freedom. He was the consummate master of the fugue, a form in which multiple voices speak and answer each other, introducing new material, stacking new ideas on top of old, fracturing ideas and rearranging them, often in ways that reveal affinities between the subjects, countersubjects, and answers. The canon was even more strict, with the voices repeating the same material, though it could be at different pitches, or inverted such that every time one voice goes up, the other goes down, a form known as a canon in contrary motion. (The twelfth and fifteenth *Goldberg Variations* are both in contrary motion.) If one voice plays the same material backward while the other plays it forward, the piece was known as a retrograde canon. The permutations on this were endless. A mensuration canon involved using the same material set to different rhythmic divisions, so that one voice might play the melody twice as fast or twice as slow as the other. Different canon forms could be combined together. A table canon was simply a retrograde canon in contrary motion written on a single line. When that strip of music was placed on a table, two musicians could sit opposite each other and, as each read the same musical line as usual from left to right—thus both backward and upside down from each other—an appealing combination of two different voices was derived from the same material.

At some level, these were games, exercises in mental and musical acuity. But they were also deemed a science, a sophisticated kind of learning based on rigorous rules, posing problems and demanding solutions. In the Altes Rathaus in Leipzig is a portrait of Bach by Elias Gottlob Haussmann, in which the composer (who appears as "a fat-cheeked, broad-shouldered man with a wrinkled forehead," according to an entirely apt eighteenth century description) is holding a small piece of paper with three lines of music on it. This was an unrealized canon, which presents a kind of puzzle in which each line of music required the interpreter to suggest a matching line, such that a triple canon in six voices would result when they were performed together. Bach wrote this brief musical brain teaser as a gift to a group called the Society of Musical Science, created by one of his pupils—a group that was more than honored to have him and which Bach, who never fetishized the theoretical aspects of music, apparently joined somewhat reluctantly. The canon, clearly visible in the portrait, is derived from the first notes of the bass line that structures the *Goldberg Variations,* perhaps an indication of Bach's particular regard for this work's importance in his oeuvre.

While the "science" of writing fugues and solving puzzle canons could be esoteric, understanding the basic construction of these pieces is essential practical knowledge for musicians. In the *Gold-*

bergs, the tenth variation is labeled "Fughetta," or "short fugue," in this case a brief, buoyant fugue in four voices. It moves at a steady, even pace, with little rhythmic complexity, such that the voices are sometimes neatly stacked on top of one another rather like a four-part hymn. But if you attempt to learn it based on how the notes look on the page—as if this were a hymn with a homophonic texture—there's no hope of mastering it. Only when the ear can detect the horizontal lines moving independently does the piece make sense, and only when it makes sense is it possible to "know" it well enough to play it competently. Almost any time when Bach's music seems arbitrary or fussy, when an idea seems to be only half finished or a line heads somewhere and then abruptly breaks off, it is because you haven't been paying attention to counterpoint, the horizontal movement of voices; and once you do, not only do these apparent infelicities disappear, but you gain greater mental control over the matter at hand.

The little we know of Bach's teaching methods, derived from the Forkel biography and clues he left in compositions he designed as teaching tools, suggests that he moved quickly from the fundamentals of moving the fingers on the keyboard to teaching what was, in effect, compositional technique. On the title page of a collection of small pieces known as the Inventions and Sinfonias—instructional works, some written for his own children—Bach said that he created these works to teach keyboard players "a clear way not only (1) to learn to play clearly in two voices, but also, after further progress, (2) to deal with three obligato parts correctly and well; and along with this not only to obtain good *inventiones* [ideas] but to develop the same well." In Forkel's biography, Bach is said to have required his beginning students to do finger exercises "for months," after which he "immediately set his scholars to his own greater compositions." Bach seems to have pursued a particularly rigorous version of the standard eighteenth century practice, which was to teach theory and composition almost from the beginning of the student's study of an instrument.

This is a very different way of teaching music than prevails today. It's difficult to imagine children of the internet age would sit still for instruction in how to properly derive the harmonies from a figured bass line, or the fundamentals of harmonic progression or voice leading when what they really want is the means simply to make music. Theory and composition are something students do later, after they achieve substantial mastery of the instrument, or as a supplemental requirement to musical performance studies. When I was in college, they were effectively separate disciplines. There were performers who would begrudgingly take theory classes because they were obliged to do so, and budding musicologists who would learn the piano because it was a useful tool, but never intended to perform. I certainly balked at learning music theory when Joe tried to teach me, and I have had to play catch-up ever since.

This change in how music is taught suggests yet another question about what it means to know a piece of music. How has the idea of "knowing" music changed over time? We know a great deal about the history of music, but what about the history of listening? What musicians and listeners valued in music at different points in history is documented. But we have scant evidence to tell us anything about how they heard it, or the psychology of listening. Did knowledgeable auditors in Bach's day follow along, in their heads, every line of his fugues and canons? Could they detect each subject, countersubject, and answer in his fugues? Descriptions of Bach's music by contemporaries tend to emphasize his greatness, his astonishing dexterity at the keyboard, his mastery, artistry, and powers of invention. But these accounts are mainly a catalog of superlatives and unenlightening about the psychology of how music was perceived. There is, however, a rare episode from Bach's life, in the late 1730s, that gives us a few clues about how people actually processed the sound of his music.

In 1737, a former and apparently aggrieved student of Bach, Johann Adolph Scheibe, published an anonymous critique of his teacher's music, calling it "turgid" and overstuffed with an "excess of art." This led to a robust defense of Bach by his friends and students and further attacks by Scheibe, an exchange that lasted several years. In Scheibe's satirical attacks, and the lengthy, indignant responses from Bach's proxies, one gets a sense that music in Germany was at a crossroads: the complexity of Bach's style had overtaxed what many people were capable of comprehending.

Scheibe obviously felt that way. In a 1739 satire he adopted the first person to impersonate a composer of complicated music, and though he denied he meant Bach, it was almost certainly Bach he had in mind: "I compose so intricately and wonderfully that listening to my pieces makes people quite bewildered. Everything is intermingled. Everything is so completely worked out that one cannot tell one voice from another." Scheibe wasn't just a music critic, he was also a composer, and his own works are far simpler than those of Bach, sometimes charming in a naïve way, often clumsy, and rarely of much interest. But his criticism of Bach was in part a backhanded advocacy for the new, *galant* musical style. Bach's principal defender, Johann Abraham Birnbaum, addressed the same question of Bach's polyphonic complexity in an extended response to Scheibe's first attack:

> It is certain, by the way, that the voices in the works of this great master of music work wonderfully in and about one another, but without the slightest confusion. They move along together or in opposition, as necessary. They part company, and yet all meet again at the proper time. Each voice distinguishes itself clearly from the others by a particular variation, although they often imitate each other. They now flee, now fol-

low one another without one's noticing the slightest irregularity in their efforts to outdo one another.

Birnbaum denies what Scheibe asserts, that the music was bewildering. And his text is full of indications that he understood the complex art behind all this: the voices meet again "at the proper time" and follow one another "without one's noticing the slightest irregularity." He seems to be hearing the music in a fundamentally different way than Scheibe hears it, alert to its complexity but undaunted by any confusion. And yet his language is curiously similar to how a contemporary listener, unschooled in complex part writing, would probably describe the experience of listening to Bach. Some voices seem to answer each other, sometimes opposing, sometimes in sync, now they seem to flee, now to follow one another. This is a rather bland, spatial description of the experience and it makes one suspicious of Birnbaum's claim that the music unfolds without the "slightest confusion." In fact, Scheibe was more than a little right about Bach's having worked out his counterpoint to such a degree that one voice can't always be distinguished from the others: frequently, in the *Goldberg Variations*, one finds places where imitation between the voices, including the bass line, is so intricate that the effect and likely the intention is to make the voices blend into one another.

Scheibe's attack suggests that Bach had pushed polyphony to the point that even his contemporaries weren't entirely sure if they understood it. And Birnbaum's response gives us little sense of whether those who loved Bach's music were hearing it in a fundamentally more sophisticated way than we listen today. Many listeners were turning to a different musical paradigm, governed by different rules and expectations; others were struggling to find new metaphors and descriptive language for music that was overwhelming auditory comprehension. Within a century of this early debate about Bach's art, accounts of listening to it become so extravagantly spiritual and theological that it's hard to know what people were hearing. In 1827, Goethe remembered hearing an organist play Bach years earlier, and described it this way: "I said to myself, it is as if the eternal harmony were conversing within itself, as it may have done in the bosom of God just before the Creation of the world. So likewise did it move in my inmost soul, and it seemed as if I neither possessed nor needed ears, nor any other sense—least of all, the eyes."

This is inspiring language, but it isn't very helpful. Goethe was musically curious, and worked hard to be musically literate, but he wasn't particularly musically sophisticated. His memory of hearing Bach's music suggests more happy stupefaction than actual understanding. But by raising Bach's music to the level of "eternal harmony" and the "bosom of God," Goethe does what other listeners were doing in the nineteenth century, positing it as so great, and so beyond ordinary comprehension that it is essentially unknowable, except through a figure of speech, as resembling the mind of God. But as Bach's mind and the mind of God became functionally synonymous for many worshipful listeners, the fact of Bach's craft was discounted or ignored altogether. And Bach would have scoffed at the idea that he possessed superhuman or divine abilities. Forkel wrote that Bach "seemed not to lay any stress on his greater natural talents." Bach's own self-assessment wasn't necessarily an exercise in false modesty: "I was obliged to be industrious; whoever is equally industrious will succeed equally well."

I would be happy to know Bach's music in a far more basic way than Goethe experienced it. I would like to know it at the level of industriousness, rather than cosmic aspiration. I would like to know it well enough to play it. The curious thing, however, is that the more I have struggled with the music, the more I realize that there is no way to separate what it means to know it "in the fingers" as a performer, and know it "in the head" as an observer of its construction. To learn it, you must in effect "un-compose" it, breaking it down to its constituent parts even as you are struggling to master the notes. You must proceed rather as Bach is said to have taught his own students, progressing rapidly from the mechanics of how the fingers move to analysis of the structural and syntactical elements. Every variation begins with some muddling around that continues until you start sorting things out, noticing patterns, breaking down the larger structures into substructures, detecting the historical and stylistic formulas that govern many of the variations. The performer who sits down to study the twenty-sixth variation will see first an ominous thicket of notes in groupings of six, as if Bach were writing an étude for first the right hand, then the left. But above this, and then beneath it, he has also written a sarabande, which tracks so closely the sarabande of the opening aria that one might play the two together simultaneously with only a few notable misalignments or dissonance.

Other patterns are localized. In many of the arabesque variations, the patterns of one hand are replicated by the other later in the piece. In the twenty-sixth variation, this duplication is almost identical, so that in the first half of the variation, for example, the right hand plays a string of figuration that is repeated by the left hand eight bars later, only to deviate slightly so that it stays in alignment with the harmonies dictated by the *Goldberg* bass line. But in others, such as the fourteenth variation, the pattern is inverted, so that downward motions by the left hand in the first half of the variation becomes upward ones by the right hand in the second half. Some figuration evolves through several different formulas, say proceeding by thirds, then by reference to the harmony underneath, then stepwise. Noticing the joints between these different types of motion greatly speeds the mind's ability to commit the pattern to memory. Among several types of humor one detects in Bach's music is his occasional perversity with these patterns, where he uses one type of motion with regularity and then, just before a new musical event is about to happen, alters the figuration. These alterations arrive in unexpected ways, and it may seem as if he has thrown them in just to keep the performer alert.

In cognitive psychology, this part of the learning process is called "chunking," the mastery of a number of disparate things by grouping them in patterns. Memorizing the number 03311685 is a lot easier once you know that it's Bach's birthday, March 31, 1685. A pianist who can play a Mozart concerto isn't executing thousands of individual keystrokes according to a script, like a mechanical piano reads notes off a roll of punched paper. Rather, she is playing a series of scales, arpeggios, repeated accompaniment patterns, and recurring melodic lines, and these are stored in the memory not as discrete finger motions, but chunks of musical information logically grouped together. Much of what happens in the performance of a complex piece of music involves "ballistic" motions, rapid-fire gestures like a trill or scale figure that, once learned, are executed without conscious cognitive control, like a subroutine in computer coding. The more of these things that become second nature, the greater the artist's facility.

But for someone learning to play the piano, making them second nature is exhausting work, and there's no green light that flashes on to say that a pattern is now engrained and can henceforth be used infallibly. The process of making motions ballistic is essentially the same one that Bach used with his pupils: finger drills and repetition. Mindless repetition extends the process, sometimes indefinitely, while mindful repetition shortens it. The pattern is repeated slowly again and again, the eyes watch, the ears listen, and you find yourself hoping that this alien thing that is running the show—your brain— is being rewired in the process. Always, there is a tension between freedom and control. You play the recalcitrant musical phrase with strict control, note by note, until you can speed it up to the proper tempo. Then, perhaps, you play it—the trill, the arpeggio, the scale pattern—with greater freedom, as it was meant to be played, in its proper musical context, and sometimes it works, and sometimes it doesn't. These are the most onerous and dispiriting hours of practice, when the music seems fully known but not quite automatic, when it seems as if when you don't think about it, it works, but when you do, it doesn't. When will this come together?

Neuroscience is good at describing how we learn music in terms of where things happen in the brain, which cells are activated, and how different parts of the brain interact, and it has confirmed through scientific observation the efficacy of many things that have been standard practice since Bach's day and before. The "inhibitory function," for example, is essential to learning music. This is the same development process one sees in a baby learning to wave one arm at a time, rather than both in mirror motion, or use one finger to press a button rather than the whole chubby fist. In music, the inhibitory function allows the pianist to suppress the instinctive motion of four fingers so that one finger can perform a precise and independent action. "In the adult brain about 90% of the synaptic connections are inhibitory," according to one survey of the literature. The visual element in learning an instrument is also fundamental. Descriptions of Bach's pedagogy say that he often played for his pupils, as they watched, including in one case performing the entire twenty-four preludes and fugues of the first volume of *The Well-Tempered Clavier* three times, a demonstration that might have lasted more than five hours if he played them consecutively (which seems unlikely). And it turns out that watching is essential to learning an instrument, activating "motor co-representations." The mental practice that many musicians perform away from their instruments may look a bit like compulsive behavior, but it, too, is directly related to mastery: "When continuing mental practice over a period of several days, the involved brain regions showed plastic adaptations," according to a survey of music and neuroscience.

To a struggling musician, these observations feel a bit like lis-

tening to an engineer describe an engine he understands theoret-
ically but not practically, and not at all like a mechanic who can
lift the hood, size up the problem, and say, "You need a new fan
belt." Neuroscience can name a problem and find it on a map, but it
doesn't yet offer a satisfying account if you are a struggling musician
attempting to understand the process. Professional musicians who
have mastered their instruments don't often speak about the process
of that mastery, and for many of them it may have been unconscious,
forgotten, or consciously repressed. Hollywood depicts the miserable process of learning artistic technique with its usual license and
mythology, a montage of long and lonely hours spent practicing, followed by a blinding epiphany and brilliant success thereafter. These
dramas recycle the peculiar American ethos of hard work and prov-
idence: the artist invests labor in his or her discipline, and waits,
patiently, humbly, until divine reward is given.

But how one gets from practice to mastery is in fact a great deal
more complicated than these narratives, and far more complicated
than science has yet been able to explain. The philosopher Ludwig
Wittgenstein wrestled with a related dilemma—when can we say
we possess a skill?—in his *Philosophical Investigations* and came up
with an analogy based on reading. He imagines that human beings
("or creatures of some other kind") are being trained to be reading
machines, and he asks, at what point can we say they began to read?
At first a student might randomly hit upon the right sounds when he
sees a word, but would that be reading? Then the student begins to
get more and more words correct, but is he reading yet? Wittgenstein
asks, can we speak of a "first word" that he read correctly? If human
beings were reading machines, one might look inside the mechanism and detect the moment when real reading began. But we aren't
machines, so Wittgenstein suggests: "The change when the pupil
began to read was a change in his *behavior*; and it makes no sense
here to speak of 'a first word in his new state.'"

Picking up a skill, such as reading words or reading music, isn't the same as using that skill to master a particular task, such as learning a complex piece of music. But Wittgenstein's example and the question it raises gets something right about music: there is never a definitive moment when you can say, "I just mastered that." Even after hours of work on the tiniest detail of a piece, it is only in retrospect that you can say you've learned it. Things do become automatic, or ballistic, through practice, but the moment of mastery is elusive, and it is, in fact, a change in behavior that may alert you to having successfully fixed something. Over time, you notice that you are playing it *as if you know it*, and at that point you may begin to assume that, in fact, you do know it. Forgetting is in some ways a part of the process: As you master more and more details in a work, you forget how much trouble the earlier spots gave you, and this forgetting lessens the anxiety associated with them, and that, in turn, leads to even more positive changes in your behavior.

Much of the popular psychology literature about learning music is a sunny variation on Wittgenstein's insight. The essential message is: You can already do this. The music is already in you and awaits only changes to your behavior to come out. Play as if you know how to play, and the playing will take care of itself. But this model only gets half of the process right, that part which deals with the freedom side of the basic tension between freedom and control. Throughout the process of learning a piece of music, from the earliest repetitive efforts to make the notes automatic to the moment of public performance, there is a far more complex dialectic between learning and unlearning, familiarity and alienation, than the popular psychology model can comprehend.

Even after a particularly difficult passage has become ballistic, it never hurts to go back and interrupt the automatic nature of that process, introduce some new element or detail that defamiliarizes it, and then relearn it in its new, not-yet-automatic form. When Glenn

Gould was a student, he worked with a teacher who prescribed what seems at first a bizarre practice technique called "finger tapping." Gould was instructed to place one hand on the keyboard and then, with the other hand, tap the fingers of the playing hand finger by finger before striking the note. This is a bit like using the left hand to play on the right hand as if it were the keyboard of a typewriter, introducing a mechanical intermediary between the mental intention to strike a key and the physical act of striking it. I've tried this and it is extraordinarily effective at unmasking anything in the music that is imperfectly memorized.

The dialectic between mechanical mastery and the kind of freedom that one hopes to achieve in performance—to play freely, focused on things like expression and communication and the pleasure of the music—becomes far more than a question of how one practices or masters a particular piece. It becomes a matter of character, how one defines oneself as a musician. The "unlearning" process that destabilizes what is familiar, and forces the mind to higher levels of mastery and assurance, is a lifelong commitment, and it carries with it a great deal of potential for unhappiness. For every minute of freedom, there is a corresponding hour of self-criticism, analysis, and doubt.

The best musicians, or perhaps the happiest ones, are able to balance these aspects of life with poise. Bach was a perfectionist, and honored perfectionism in others. When one of his most diligent students, Johann Philipp Kirnberger, studied counterpoint "so strenuously that he fell ill with a fever and for eighteen weeks had to keep to his room," Bach offered to come by to overlook his student's lesson work, an honor that was doubtless flattering if not salubrious for the young man. When, at a large social gathering, another musician rose from the harpsichord and left a dissonance unresolved, Bach was so offended he "passed right by his host, who was coming to meet him, rushed to the harpsichord, resolved the dissonant chord, and made an appropriate cadence." He could also be severe in his oversight of other musicians, and in his conducting. A famous account published a century after his death describes his wrath in rehearsal: "The organist of St. Thomas's, who was in general a worthy artist, once so enraged [Bach] by a mistake on the organ, during a rehearsal of a cantata, that he tore the wig from his head and, with the thundering exclamation 'You ought to have been a cobbler,' threw it at the organist's head." But Bach was also accounted "peaceful, quiet, and even-tempered" except when "anyone slighted art, which was sacred to him."

But despite his perfectionism, there's no evidence that he suffered a self-lacerating excess of doubt or insecurity about his abilities. In a very rare account of Bach confronting his own musical failings, one gets the sense that he was ironic and bemused. Bach is said to have remarked to a friend that "he really believed he could play everything, without hesitating, at the first sight." The friend decided to challenge that, and so one day left as bait a difficult score on the harpsichord when Bach came to visit:

> Bach got to the piece which was destined for his conversion and began to play it. But he had not proceeded far when he came to a passage at which he stopped. He looked at it, began anew, and again stopped at the same passage. "No," he called out to his friend, who was laughing to himself in the next room, and at the same time went away from the instrument, "one cannot play everything at first sight; it is not possible."

This is small consolation for anyone who may resent the unequal apportionment of talent among humanity. Very likely, if the anecdote is true, the piece Bach encountered was badly written and unidiomatic for the keyboard.

Kirnberger said of his former master that he insisted "everything must be possible." When encouraging his students, he would point out that they had fingers, just like he had, so surely they must be able to master the music. In response to a compliment on his organ playing, he responded with a self-deprecation similar to the old joke about how Michelangelo sculpted his David: "It is easy, you just chip away the stone that doesn't look like David." Bach's riposte was: "There is nothing remarkable about it. All one has to do is hit the right keys at the right time, and the instrument plays itself." The joke is funny not just because it minimizes the enormous amount of skill it takes to "hit the right notes at the right time," but because it hints at the mechanical underpinnings of performance, the very thing that musicians must both strive for and resist.

Bach's enormous gifts didn't manifest themselves immediately. His early works can be plodding and dull. He was also a tireless editor of his own manuscripts, improving and correcting them, even adding important details to already published works such as the *Goldberg Variations*. If the fourteen canons that he wrote on his copy of the published *Goldberg* score were composed after the variations (he could well have had them "in his head" long before he wrote a note of the *Goldbergs*), then we have more evidence for thinking of this piece not just as a finished work of music, but as an ongoing set of musical problems with which Bach may never have been finished. For someone trying to learn the score, there is some small consolation in this: if Bach's understanding of this material continually evolved and accumulated even after the variations were published, then the performer's knowledge of it is likely to be a fluid thing, too, always subject to improvement, addition, and rethinking.

Late in the evening, hunched over the keyboard with the earphones hurting my ears from too many hours of practice, with Nathan lying silently at my feet, I'm struggling with one measure in the fughetta, with a trill on the second note of the last entrance of the tenor voice. All four voices are engaged at this moment, only four bars before the end of the variation, the bass adumbrating the basic line derived from the aria, the soprano descending from the apogee of its range, the alto finishing one thought before beginning another. Into this texture the tenor inserts one last statement of the subject, and Bach includes a trill exactly where he has included it in other iterations of the theme, but this time it falls in the most awkward place for the fingers, such that the only way to play it seems to be to divide the line between the hands, so that just as soon as the thumb and forefinger of the left hand finish the trill, the right thumb must jump in and finish the gesture. I have worked out a solution but I can't imagine the number of hours it will take to make it sound smooth.

I could say, at this moment, that I know the variation, not in the same sense as Bach knew it, or a great pianist knows it, but if I leave out this one ornament, it goes rather smoothly. And I love this moment in the cycle, the way Bach has compressed a tight little fugue into the familiar confines of his unchanging harmonic scheme, the way the fugue even obeys the two-part division of the variation form, starting over in the middle and yet without any undue disruption to the larger flow of the piece. If Bach disguises his canons so they don't always sound like canons, he puts forth this little fugue determined that it sound every bit the fugue, with clear and regular entry of the four voices, and a subject so clearly designed for fugal treatment that it might serve as the illustration in a textbook entry on fugue themes. So why not drop that one trill? If I did, I could add this variation to the collection of those I can play well enough to perform for other people.

The word "fugue" is from the Latin, to flee, which often describes the impression made by the voices as they seem to pursue each other, just as Birnbaum described the relation of voices in Bach's polyphony, "They now flee, now follow one another without one's noticing the slightest irregularity." But it would be an intolerable flight from self-imposed musical duty if I were to leave out that one ornament. I can't do it and so must hold this piece back, confined to the stable of variations that remain not thoroughly known in all their particulars.

And so, but for one small thing in a piece that is otherwise learned, I find that the pleasure I take in this variation is transformed into a nagging sense of frustration and inadequacy.

Nathan stirs at my feet, innocent of this self-flagellation. Music pains him, too, but in a way obviously different from how it pains human beings. Whether music reminds me of something sad, or returns me to a moment of pain in my life, or, as in the case of many of the *Goldberg Variations*, weighs me down with a sense of oppressive obligation and mediocrity, I keep coming back for punishment. Music isn't a pleasure, but essential to some part of my capacity for self-reflection. It isn't some kind of emotional massage or warm bath; it is a cognitive tool. It gives me perspective on my life, whether or not that perspective is one I enjoy or find flattering. But Nathan doesn't have that ability to step outside himself when he hears music. When he hears music that pains him, that pain is immediate and unmediated.

But why does it hurt him so grievously? It should have been obvious all along. When we adopted him, he was three months old, just old enough to be taken from his litter and placed in human care. He arrived during the first weeks that I was studying the *Goldberg Variations*, and he slept in a crate in the kitchen as I practiced in the living room. He was in a strange home, surrounded by new faces, and suddenly alone. Bach was the soundtrack to the most profound rupture in his life, the accompaniment to his confusion and his sorrow. When he hears this music, he misses his mother.

TEN

W HEN I WAS four or five years old, my grandfather took me to see the old locks along the Mohawk River, still active as a waterway a century and a half after the days of the Erie Canal. He was greatly interested in all things infrastructural—railroads, bridges, dams, and canals—and I adored him for his good humor and sense of adventure, and because he took joy in me, the only son of his eldest son. But when we got to the lock, he wanted to cross over its closed doors, a narrow passage with a flimsy guardrail. The giant gates of the lock towered over the turbid river, which ran in muddy brown torrents, and I was terrified of falling in. It was a foolhardy thing to do, but he was a fearless man, not in the sense of being particularly courageous, but rather he simply lacked the capacity for fear.

I would have none of it, and despite his cheerful coaxing and reassurance, I began crying and then screaming, and the noise must have been terrible, because the lockkeeper emerged to inquire what was the matter. I don't know if I embarrassed my grandfather, but my tantrum and the lockkeeper's concern managed to convince him not to attempt the crossing. My distress went deep, because I spoke of it to my mother later in the day, and there was drama in the house. At that point in my family's history, my parents argued behind closed doors, so the only clear memory I have is that something dramatic was happening far away, as if underwater, but no less intense for being muted and distant. I was too young to understand, but evidence pieced together later, along with reasonable extrapolation, suggests that my mother was furious with her father-in-law and demanded that my father intervene to prevent future danger to her child. After that argument my grandfather never invited me to do anything more risky than sneak under the old fence along the railroad tracks so we could place pennies on the rails.

Fear, along with illness, offered my mother a primal connection to her children that transcended any ambivalence she felt about motherhood. Happy and exuberant children were a nuisance, but a scared child always received comfort. She was intensely fearful herself. Her earliest memories, like mine, were memories of fear, of spiders lurking behind old armoires, of grave illnesses that threatened the family's survival, and of air-raid drills in Salt Lake City during the war, during which strange men chastised anyone who allowed light to peek through the window shades. She remembered the necrotic flesh on her sister's leg after a black-widow bite, the fear of polio contracted from the city pool, and the snake she encountered at eye-level when she went rock climbing with my father on their first date. She told us of the gold coins her Jewish grandfather had sewn into the hem of his jacket when he left for America, and she always said to never tell anyone this story. She said it in a way that left me unsure if it was the disclosure of a few gold coins among our treasures, or the fact of a Jewish ancestor that most worried her. She was also afraid of the weather, of the roads, of the telephone during lightning storms, of flash floods and tornadoes, two-lane highways, ice storms, sailing, homeless men, crowds of any sort, plague, killer bees, Arabs, dirty toilet seats, and any kind of colored stoneware, which almost certainly contained lead in its glaze and would leave a child gibbering and stupid.

Danger and death were her favorite subjects, and they were always close at hand. At the dinner table she spoke of car accidents, fires, floods, roof cave-ins, and the treacherous inner city, which we never visited but was the living instantiation of all the fears she had gleaned from television. She didn't believe in God, and would have scoffed at the idea that she believed in the devil, but her world was haunted by demonic figures who moved among mankind with malicious intent, distributing sickness, pain, and discord. No one became ill simply by chance or because of the onset of old age. Divorces didn't happen because people grew distant or matured into an awareness of irreconcilable difference. Children didn't fall through the ice and drown because of mere accidents. Something was causing this decay and destruction, something unknown, unspoken, and un-American. Heart attacks and strokes and cancer were a scandal, the malign work of shadowy agents who had set their sights on suburbia, on decent people, on good, honest families who had worked hard for their right to happiness. "She nicked her finger and it turned to gangrene. Now she's lost her whole arm, Christ almighty," she would say as we pushed half-boiled potatoes around the bottom of our soup bowls.

She was deeply impressed by stories of people outwitting great danger. Tales of motherly intuition triumphing over hidden threats were her favorite. There was a woman, a mother whom she knew, who came home one evening and took one look at her house in the gloaming and refused to let her family enter. Something was wrong, she didn't know what, but she just knew things weren't as they should be. She couldn't put her finger on it—there were no doors ajar or windows open—but still she crossed her arms and stood her ground and insisted, "We aren't going in there." She called the police, who chided her for succumbing to ungrounded fears, but they checked the house anyway . . . and found a serial killer inside. There was a mother who doubted the doctor's diagnosis of her child, and decided not to administer the medicine she was given. The doctor called only minutes later in a panic, telling her it was the wrong medicine and it would kill her child. "She just knew," my mother said, not with any satisfaction, not because the story confirmed the power of motherly love, but because it proved once again that the only defense in a world of irrational dangers was irrational intuition.

Her fears structured our lives. When the fondue pot bubbled

over and splattered the curtains, it could have caused a fire, and we never used it again. We always sat well back from the television when it was on, and withdrew from the microwave when it was cooking because of the radiation. She had heard that the snowplows that plied the streets of our town had once buried a child, so we were forbidden from playing in the front yard if there was more than a dusting of snow on the ground. We never ate food raw out of a can because of botulism, or pork that wasn't cooked to leather because of trichinosis. We lived only a few hours from New York City, but didn't go there, because of the crime. In the big city whole families had disappeared, their cars and luggage with them, and not a trace was ever found.

When I was a boy, she read to me poems of fear and danger, and they have stayed with me a lifetime. Our town began to decline when I was young, with old factories closing and industrial sites going to ruin. I can still recite the lines of Vachel Lindsay, from a well-worn book of greatest American poems:

Factory windows are always broken.
Somebody's always throwing bricks,
Somebody's always heaving cinders,
Playing ugly Yahoo tricks.

Factory windows are always broken.
Other windows are let alone.
No one throws through the chapel-window
The bitter, snarling, derisive stone.

Factory windows are always broken.
Something or other is going wrong.
Something is rotten—I think, in Denmark.
End of the factory-window song.

She patiently explained to me the meaning of "derisive," how a stone could snarl, and she tried to make sense of the reference to Hamlet. The truth of the poem was manifest every time we crossed the rusting bridge into the downtown of the nearby city, where old industrial buildings were pocked by hundreds of broken windows. But the irony was lost on both of us, I think, and we spent most of our time talking about Yahoo tricks. Who were these Yahoos? They lived in the city, no one taught them any better, they didn't have nice things like pianos in their houses, and they were very, very dangerous.

My mother passed on to her children not her particular fears, nor the curious mythological construct that animated them. But I received from her a template for fear, the habit of seeing the world in terms of fear, and from a relatively early age I have had to expend an enormous amount of energy battling the tendency to fear everything. In old paintings, the skull, a reminder of death, is seen on a desk or table, glowing in the candlelight before a person lost in thought. It is a spiritual warning to people who are inclined, by temperament, to take pleasure and revel in the world, a reminder that our existence is finite and there is always death around the corner, with its sobering theological implications. I've never had any need of this ostentatious memento mori, because I carry that fear with me every day, as if it's a small thing in my pocket, placed there by my mother at the same time that she taught me to remember my keys and lunch money.

In many ways, fear became my trusted guide. When I left home I was disgusted by my own fears, and could see a life as thoroughly delimited as the world my mother lived in if I couldn't overcome them. If I feared to do it, then it needed doing. I took up hiking and spent days in the backcountry, sometimes alone. I got a passport and traveled the world. I hitchhiked in New Zealand and took a bus across Australia, worked on a ranch, and labored on a sheep farm. I slept nights in ratty South American hotels with nothing but a bare mattress on the floor, traveled second and third class in trains across Asia, and once found myself being sick over the gunwales of a rickety dhow off the coast of Africa and thought: *If she could see me now.* I moved to the city and, despite a tremendous fear of talking to strangers, took up journalism, a profession in which one is obliged to talk to strangers on a daily basis. When my job took me to Afghanistan and Syria (before the civil war), I relished the chance to tell her I was going. I could never eradicate fear, but merely suppress it well enough to live a kind of life. But even well into middle age I took guilty pleasure in demonstrating to my mother that I wasn't afraid of anything—in part because it agitated her, but mostly because I wanted it to be true.

One of the few fears that I've never managed to beat back or hide is the fear of performing music in front of people. At one point in my battle against nerves, I decided to read about the phenomenon and found a curious book published in 1947: *Performer and Audience: An Investigation into the Psychological Causes of Anxiety and Nervousness in Playing, Singing or Speaking Before an Audience.* It was a small Freudian tract, written by a pianist and author who promised, in the dedication, something I craved: "To all those who have been led into the belief that their anxiety or nervousness is necessarily an inherited or constitutional factor and therefore incapable of modification or elimination, this book is dedicated in the author's belief that they are almost certainly wrong." One need only examine the roots of one's nerves, uncover the secret causes, and they would disappear. And what are the causes? Borrowing wholesale from Freud's *Civilization and Its Discontents,* the author blamed repression of primitive instincts, especially in "Anglo-Saxon countries" that have "succeeded in putting on the brake so efficiently that not only have those primitive, a-social or anti-social emotional drives been checked but also their socially acceptable and valuable modifications have been involved in the process, with the result that all freedom and spontaneity of every kind of emotional expression has been to some extent inhibited or even checked altogether."

In short, we are repressing far more than we need to repress to belong to civilized society, squelching more innocuous instincts in the process. This takes several different forms. Some musicians fear their own tendency toward exhibitionism, and so sabotage their performance as a form of self-punishment or compensation. Yet others are masochistic and revel in the pain of embarrassment after a bad recital. The association of words and ideas such as "play," "touch," and "hand" with childhood sexual expression leads the adult to anxieties about these concepts when trying to play the piano in public later in life. Fears can always be displaced from one cause to another, and so, like subterranean volcanic flows, what pops up into view may have its source miles away in the hidden depths of the traumatized, primitive self. As with many grand, airtight theories, the Freudian explication encompasses all possibilities and accounts for diametrically opposed causes that lead to the same effects.

As with many people of my generation, I spent a lot of time reading Freud when I was in college and in the years thereafter. When I finally had a little money set aside, I decided to undergo psychoanalysis, spending four days a week on the couch free-associating and waiting for transference to arrive, though it never did. When I told my mother that I was seeing an analyst, she was apoplectic. It was a waste of money, she said. "Didn't we knock any sense into you?" She had read enough in her college days to know all about the Oedipus complex: "Why would you believe all that sick, twisted stuff?" Years later, not long after her cancer diagnosis, I discovered that she had among her pills a bottle of antidepressants. She still had a few years to live, and despite everything she had already endured she was in relatively good spirits. Others in the family had noticed that, too. She seemed less nervous and angry, was thinking more clearly and with a newfound equanimity. I asked her about the medication, and she said the doctor had prescribed it for sleeping, so she took one tablet every evening and they seemed to work. I looked inside the bottle and saw that they were tiny little blue pills, smaller than the nail on my fifth finger, and I wondered what my life would have been like if she had begun taking them a half century earlier. When she learned that these were, in fact, a reliable and generally effective antidepressant, she discontinued their use.

———

O F BACH'S FEARS, and the darker side of his emotional life, we know very little. Since the popularization of Bach in the nineteenth century, and his assumption to the pantheon of genius, biographers have tended to gloss over his inner life, focusing on the tangible evidence of his faith and piety instead. From that, they have concluded that he was largely immune to the anxieties and perturbations that afflict modern man. He was devoted to God and devoted to his art, and whatever pain death brought to his family, he understood that within the larger cosmology of Christian submission and servitude. More recent biographers and historians have attempted to go deeper than that, to create a plausible though hypothetical sense of his emotional profile, extrapolating an inner life from the autobiographical accounts of his contemporaries and a broader understanding of the historical and social context in which he operated. Some of these writers have even dared to impute to him a radical normality: That he was merely human and must have experienced the same pains and pleasures visited on other human beings.

From Bach's own writing, we have a broad idea about his temperament, but only scant clues about specific emotional reactions. Most of his letters were professional recommendations for colleagues and students, testimonials about organ makers and their instruments, requests for preferment or professional posts, and often lengthy, lawyerly protests, especially to the town councillors of Leipzig, who were his employers for the last decades of his life. From these, one senses a man who was dutiful and even generous in his relationships with underlings and colleagues, especially those he felt worthy of assistance; prickly and slightly paranoid in his engagement with real and perceived rivals; fawning in his supplications to the powerful; and vigorously defensive of his prerogatives when dealing with his masters. There are a handful of letters that give a more specific sense of actual emotions, including spirited anger, as in a 1748 note to a local innkeeper (or the innkeeper's son), who had rented a harpsichord from Bach's collection and failed to return it. "My patience is now at its end," Bach begins, and concludes, "You must bring it in good order, and within five days, else we shall never be friends."

The grievance is more personal in a letter written to a town dignitary in Sangerhausen, where Bach had secured for his son Johann Gottfried Bernhard a post as organist. The young man, who was apparently more than adequately talented, may have been a wastrel, or at least not emotionally equipped to hold down a job, and shortly after his preferment he fled town, leaving behind a trail of debts. Bach carefully declines to pay any debts until he has confirmed his son in fact incurred them, but the father's pain and embarrassment are palpable: "What shall I say or do further? Since no admonition or even any loving care and *assistance* will suffice any more, I must bear my cross in patience and leave my unruly son to God's Mercy alone." Months after the letter was written, Johann Gottfried Bernhard began studying law at Jena University—perhaps an effort to escape the family trade, or the shadow of his father—and died at the age of twenty-four.

From letters written by Bach's contemporaries, court documents, official replies to his complaints, and other evidence, we get the sense of a man who had a temper, but was generally esteemed, whose early professional years were marked by a superfluity of talent and perhaps a lack of maturity, who grew in confidence and amour propre throughout his immensely productive career, who loved life, especially food, beer, and wine, and who suffered grievous loss, including the deaths of his parents, his first wife, and eleven of his twenty children. We know that when he was just twenty years old, and already serving as an organist in Arnstadt, he quarreled with a bassoonist named Geyersbach, and the two came to blows late one summer's night. Bach may have drawn a dagger. Some considered him puffed up and conceited; his defenders felt the world never sufficiently acknowledged his genius and contribution to German music.

More generally, we know that Bach's life spanned a period of rapid and unsettling change in Germany. He was born less than forty years after the end of the Thirty Years' War, which cost millions of casualties, bred famine and witch hunts, and devastated his part of Germany, with as much as 50 percent of the population of Thuringia lost to violence, malnutrition, and disease. It was, very likely, a traumatized landscape, and historical accounts suggest that even a half century later, especially in rural areas, there were towns and cities full of desperately impoverished widows and there was rampant hunger among the peasants. But Bach also spent half of his adult life in Leipzig, which was a flourishing center for commerce, home to diverse populations of foreign merchants and a major university, with a vital book trade and a rising middle class. In some ways, Bach was born in the Middle Ages and died in the Enlightenment. He was the product of a provincial backwater and was apprenticed into the family trade as young men had been for centuries before him; but he became an entrepreneurial burgher who published his own music, managed his own instrument rental business, and presided over a small empire of musicians and composers that included both his protégés and his children. The impact on his emotional life of these rapid changes in the world around him can only be guessed at. So along with all the things that he might have feared based on direct and indirect personal experience—war, famine, plague, disease, traveling by coach (Handel, his much-admired contemporary, suffered serious injury in a 1750 coach accident a few months after Bach's death), thugs and bassoonists in the street, prison (Bach was incarcerated for a month when he was in his early thirties), and unscrupulous innkeepers who refused to return harpsichords—he may also have felt deeper anxieties about a world that was rapidly changing, favoring a new class of men with different manners, expectations, and ideologies of art and music.

There is also the evidence of his music, his hundreds of church cantatas, many of which have an intensity of despair that may transcend religious sentiment, the great Mass in B minor, the emotionally lacerating Lenten music he wrote in his two surviving Passions, and the instrumental works that include minor-key episodes as anguished as anything in the larger vocal works. The *Goldberg Variations* include three variations in the minor key: the fifteenth, which uses a halting, dragging, two-note pattern to suggest a repetition of sighs and moans; the twenty-first, which introduces stepwise chromatic motion into the *Goldberg* bass line, a twist that Bach often uses to suggest anguish; and the twenty-fifth, an emotional black hole that opens up near the end of the variations, in which a soprano line becomes entangled in ever more radical chromatic thickets. Bach was more than capable of creating a middle ground of emotion, including melancholy, tempered sadness, and moments of sweet longing, but when his music goes to a dark place, it is as dark and unrelenting as anything created by any artist in any art form.

That intensity seems to beg for biographical explanation, though many scholars are reluctant to make connections between events in Bach's personal life and his musical output. Albert Einstein, who was a talented violinist, echoed the resistance to the psychologizing that prevailed in Bach studies for much of the twentieth century when he advised: "Listen, play, love, revere—and keep your trap shut." Others, however, argue that there's no reason to leave the music aside when attempting to construct a sense of Bach's inner life, and have attempted to bring its fraught evidence to bear on understanding his personality. One of the best equipped to do this is John Eliot Gardiner, a musician and historian who has conducted Bach for a lifetime, and who spent a year in 2000 (in honor of the 250th anniversary of Bach's death) performing all of Bach's church cantatas in a marathon tour of cities across Europe and the United States. More than a decade later, he published a biography of Bach based, in part, on an understanding of the composer that emerged from that immersion in his music, and though Gardiner acknowledged all the usual caveats about "the romantic view of music as autobiography," he argued for a more robust understanding of Bach's emotional life based on the music itself. He creates a sense of Bach more truculent and petty than others, and also more deeply wounded by the loss of loved ones. His Bach is subversive, encoding his music with his own theological understanding of the world, veiling his resentment of obtuse and philistine employers in musical eccentricities. He also finds evidence for a Bach deeply broken by the loss of his parents, broken and then, by force of will and great intellect, reassembled: "Some of his recollections were perhaps too painful to recall, yet they are all of a piece with the irascibility his music—joined with its text—sometimes exposes. Bach lived with indelible memories of his early childhood and surely brooded on the meaning of its events." This "persistent presence of death in his life—of parents, siblings, his first wife and then so many of his own children—may have led to an emotional reclusiveness or wariness based on his experience that loving intrinsically carries the risk of losing." Music was compensation, not because it consoled him in the trivial sense that we often think of, music as a balm, but rather because it enlarged his life, and gave him a handle on its unpredictability: "Perhaps music gave Bach what real life in many respects could not: order and adventure, pleasure and satisfaction, a greater reliability than could be found in his everyday life."

IF WE CAN only guess at whatever fears Bach may have faced, we can be more confident of the fears and larger cultural anxieties that Bach inspired. Revered as the founding father of the musical tradition that also gave us Mozart, Beethoven, and Wagner, Bach has settled into the collective memory as a patriarch, exerting on later generations a patriarch's intimidating sense of majesty. The greatness of his music has become conjoined with a sense of its fearsomeness and its difficulty. Not only was he accused of writing music that was overly complex by contemporary detractors, his posthumous reputation for intellectual rigor took on titanic proportions. His oeuvre became a figure for the classic sense of the sublime: exerting a power that dwarfs the merely human, that threatens to engulf us, and yet elevates us, as humans, to an almost divine sense of our autonomy in the universe.

Construction of this mythology dates back to his lifetime and the period shortly after his death, with the privileging of anecdotal material that stressed not only his superhuman abilities, but the fear they inspired. His astonishing talent was well known from an encounter with the king of Prussia, Frederick the Great, who asked Bach to play for him in May 1747. Bach obliged by improvising a complex fugue so well that "all those present were seized with astonishment." The setting, the king's palace in Potsdam, and the presence of the king himself along with his chamber musicians, including some of the most famous and distinguished performers and composers then alive, gives the drama of this encounter particular power. The episode allowed Bach to demonstrate his keyboard prowess in the most public way possible before the age of the large piano recital. The anecdote is a pendant to another one from thirty years earlier, when Bach served as concertmaster for the court in Weimar. In this case, Bach was encouraged to challenge one of the most famous organists of the day, Louis Marchand, to a duel of sorts, each improvising on some idea or in some fashion suggested by the other. Marchand, who was visiting Dresden, was noted for his arrogance, and the whole encounter may have been a setup—not by Bach, but by musicians in Dresden—to embarrass the French virtuoso. Bach sent his challenge, Marchand accepted, but in the end, Marchand never appeared. Bach's obituary elaborated: "Finally, the host sent to Marchand's quarters to remind him, in case he should have forgotten, that it was now time for him to show himself a man. But it was learned, to the great astonishment of everyone, that Monsieur Marchand had, very early in the morning of that same day, left Dresden by a special coach."

So Bach won by default. The anecdote was one of the most popular Bach stories circulating in the late eighteenth century and it prefigures a whole genre of stories about musical duels, including epic encounters between Mozart and Clementi, Beethoven and Daniel Steibelt, and Franz Liszt and Sigismond Thalberg. Some of these were deemed a draw, others a victory, and in the case of Beethoven, Steibelt supposedly fled the room. But only Bach's musical power is so great that the protagonist refuses even to show up. The story, much embellished in its retellings, served to demonstrate the superiority of German music over French, and the superiority of the diligent, brilliant, local hero over the world-traveling and glamorous *homme du monde*. But its larger effect has been to encourage an idea of music not as a discipline, or form of self-expression or artistic craft, but as means of self-assertion. Art is a contest, and only the strong survive.

It is a perverse, even tragic thing, to reduce music to struggle, but the idea has structured much of our relationship to the art form for centuries, from duels among great composers to the piano competitions of the Cold War era to the regular use of student competitions to motivate young people to practice. Even when music isn't perceived as competition against another person, it is understood as struggle against the recalcitrant, undisciplined self or a struggle with the music itself. One wrestles with Bach. Many are defeated. The idea that music is a tool with which one can assert oneself also took on new social importance during the later part of Bach's life, with musical literacy becoming just one more arena of contest in the cultural jungle.

When the *Goldberg Variations* were published, the title page said they were "composed for connoisseurs, for the refreshment of their spirits, by Johann Sebastian Bach." "For the refreshment of their spirits," which might also be rendered with more religious overtones— "for the soul's delight"—was a stock phrase at the time, but it wasn't meaningless. When Bach's predecessor as cantor at the Thomasschule in Leipzig published a set of keyboard pieces, his preface stated, "I have composed these new partitas, and published them myself, in the hope that those whose spirits have been tired out through other studies might refresh them at the keyboard." Another composer addressed his audience in similar terms, suggesting that through practice "they can refresh their spirits, when these have been exhausted through other studies and worthy activities." Music is seen as a healthy diversion from worthier but tiring pursuits, or at worst a minor vice that might draw one away from the indulgence of more serious ones.

But even as an expanding middle class was enjoying the luxury of a broader intellectual and cultural life, music was also being defined as something more suited to the female sphere, and for men a waste of time and energy. Men should know their music, and be competent judges of the finer things in life, including music. But learning an instrument was perceived as unnecessary. In 1705, young men were warned:

> To learn an instrument well enough to play in front of respectable people requires far too much energy and time. It is even worse to play poorly, and wound the ears of your listeners, because that can really lower your reputation . . . It is best to learn enough about music that you are able to distinguish the voice types, to know a good performance from a bad one, and to recognize skill and quality. That way, when you are in the company of your peers, and beautiful music is performed . . . you will be able to speak rationally and skillfully about it.

A host of anxieties and insecurities about music, still with us today, are present here: the fear of wasting time, the fear of humiliating one-self before an audience and losing standing, the fear of seeming igno-rant. Knowledge of music is a social grace, but making music is not a social asset. This view persists through the nineteenth century, and reappears in the self-loathing Thomas Mann heaped on one of his most pathetic characters, Hanno Buddenbrook, last of a great male line of German merchants, who is sickly, fearful, and weak, and finds meaning only in making music, a pastime that embarrasses his father. The same sensibility operates today, when young people, often in col-lege, give up instruments they have practiced for years, justifying the loss by saying something like: I was never going to be good enough.

Good enough for what? The old bourgeois ambivalence about music, nascent in the days of Bach, is lurking behind this curious phrase. If one can't perform brilliantly, then one shouldn't perform at all. When it comes to the music of Bach, there is a deeper fear lurking here as well. And that is the sense that because his music is sublime, it should surpass entertainment and leave the listener transfigured. It must be a matter of high seriousness, epochal and soul-shattering. This conceit is bound to leave many listeners disap-pointed, and has had a debilitating impact on the broader musical literacy of our culture. This isn't Bach's fault: he wrote the *Goldbergs* to refresh our spirits, not circumscribe them. Do any other compos-ers inspire such anxiety?

An episode from the 1820s, an essential moment in the can-onization of Bach's greatness, shows these anxieties in operation. By the end of the eighteenth century, the name "Bach" meant the next generation of the family, Johann Sebastian's sons Carl Philipp Emanuel, Wilhelm Friedemann, and Johann Christian. Bach him-self was known as "Old Bach," and while his music was studied and admired by connoisseurs, it was relatively little performed and gen-erally remembered as old-fashioned, arid, and difficult. That began to

---

change in March 1829, when Felix Mendelssohn led a performance of Bach's enormous *St. Matthew Passion* in Berlin, the first time it had been performed in a century. A later account of the event, written by one of the soloists who was a friend and admirer of Mendelssohn, presents the story as a heroic, against-the-odds narrative, and it has the dramatic arc of a Hollywood film. Mendelssohn's efforts to revive the work, which requires two orchestras, a skilled choir, and top-tier soloists, are resisted by an old curmudgeon, Carl Friedrich Zelter, the aging and irascible director of Berlin's Singacademie. As director of the Singacademie, a musical society that helped perpetuate Bach's work in the early nineteenth century, Zelter must be persuaded, but his devotion to Bach's memory is absolute: if it can't be done in a way worthy of Bach's majesty, it shouldn't be done at all. But Mendelssohn and his friend persist, they overcome objections, work heroically to master the music, and in the end they triumph. The audience listens "in deadly silence," a holy "solemnity" prevails, and the resuscitation of a "half forgotten genius was felt to be of epochal importance." In many ways it was. Hegel was in the audience when this new German spirit was birthed. Bach's large choral works haven't left the canon since.

Old Zelter's resistance operates in a small way every time I sit down to practice Bach. When you contemplate the complexity of what remains to be done and the near-certainty that you are unequal to the challenge, the project seems insurmountable, and with every increment of progress I'm aware of an even larger quantum of work that remains to be done. And even when things are going in the right direction, there is always the danger of backsliding and decay. For it is a curious phenomenon in music that as you learn and master new things, you often unsettle old things. You think, perhaps, that you can add subtlety and refinement like a painter adds highlights to a mostly finished canvas. But as the mind undertakes new challenges and discovers new aspects of the music, it also uncovers weaknesses and failings that bedevil its earlier efforts. It can be like one of those maddening mechanical puzzles in which one cannot move a single piece independently of all the others. It is easy, and sometimes infinitely tempting, to set it aside forever.

And what would be the harm in that? We give up on things all the time. We imagine that our lives are spent choosing to do things, deciding on action and undertaking new ventures. But we are defined just as much by what we choose not to do, by forgoing old pursuits, and by our half-finished endeavors and decayed ambitions. The larger hygiene of existence requires us to give up certain things before they become an encumbrance. A *galant* life demands we devote ourselves only to that which we can reasonably achieve in a reasonable amount of time. The older we get, the more subtly we must undertake the double exercise of shedding aspects of ourselves so that we have the capacity to develop new ones.

One of the things that most troubled me about my mother's life, the self-imposed smallness of it, became more poignant as she was dying. In her last days, she struggled to tell me stories, most of which I had already heard. There were no happy memories, just stories of fear and loss, among them an encounter with her father, a tyrannical and willful man whom she loved. The Navy had posted my father overseas, and she was about to move with her young daughter to a trailer in Corpus Christi, Texas, where she would have to care for that child on her own. Her father solemnly warned: "You have one duty in life, and that is to keep her safe." Her voice quaked as she recounted this injunction, delivered more than a half century earlier, and it clearly affected her deeply, because she repeated the story countless times over the years, especially as she came to the end of her life. It was, I think, meant to explain why she had been the mother she was, strict and quick to anger, to impress on her children the sacrifice she had made, which was real, and to remind us what was certainly true, that we had indeed been kept safe, and grew to adulthood in sheltered prosperity. But her father was speaking to a young woman with all her life before her, and he whittled it down to one thing alone, and grounded it in fear.

And now some remnant of that fear is mine, passed through the generations like an old set of spoons or a leather-bound Bible. It has taken root in me not as the pervasive fear of the world my mother felt, nor as the diverse fears I tried to master as a young man, but as a persistent fear that my life will end without having achieved any kind of significance. Many people feel this way. Given the way the world is made, it is almost inevitable that from time to time we will all feel this way, especially if we forgo the consolation of religion. I have tried to hide this fear away as much as I can, but perhaps the old Freudian author was right in some way: the repressed inevitably returns, and it seems to return, for me, when I grapple with music. Music is a strange place to cache one's anxieties, in something that should bring one pleasure. But perhaps because it is an art form that unfolds in time, one that makes us keenly aware of beginnings and endings, music leaves me deeply unsettled that my life will end before it is finished. If I could unlearn one thing in life, it would be this fear. When I started to learn the *Goldberg Variations*, years ago now, I saw it as a way of animating lively energies in the midst of grief. But over time, as I have moved on from grief, the music has become a reminder of how life often feels like a race against time, and there have been many evenings when I have thought that this project is crazy, and I should set it aside as one more graceful retreat in the face of the inevitable. And somehow it is fear, again, that comes to my aid, and requires me to make a last effort, the old, banal, ever-present fear of failure. It is time either to learn this music or set it aside.

ELEVEN

IT'S BEEN SEVEN years since my mother died, long enough for
Nathan to live half a dog's life, long enough for me to stop grieving. I will sometimes call my aunt to chat and it is uncanny how close
her voice sounds to my mother's voice, which I used to hear every
Sunday. There are a few odds and ends around the house that remind
me of her, a kitchen knife and colander that she gave me when I set up
a home for the first time, a lamp that used to sit on the piano in the
house I grew up in. Every so often, when I touch them, they will recall
her to mind, and more so when they break and I consider throwing
them away. When, through my own neglect, a fern my mother trans-
planted for me years ago came close to dying, I spent weeks anx-
iously nursing it back to life. Once, while going through old papers at
my desk, I found her handwriting on an insurance application filled
out thirty years ago. I could make no sense of the notes, which were
reminders to ask about details of the policy. But the familiar cursive
script startled me, so neat and old-fashioned, that I saved the paper
with my letters and photographs.

It isn't that these occasional reminders of her are in themselves
painful. Rather, it is the thinning out of these moments, the greater
infrequency with which they assert themselves, the certainty that
each time I stumble upon a memory of her it will be even longer
before the next time I am brought up short by something in the physical world that contains a trace of her existence. As the occasions for
thinking about her become rarer, there is the fear that at some point
in the future I will be the only bearer of her memory. A memory

contained in one mind alone is a fragile thing, so tenuous we may be hesitant even to recall it; and as we collect more and more of these artifacts, it becomes difficult to move around in our memory for fear that even the force of a footfall will leave nothing but dust. Of course, the fragility we fear is our own death.

When I started studying Bach after my mother's death, it felt like an effort to come back to life. But a curious thing happened: life came back of its own accord. The music now reminds me of some old friendships, which flourish again during visits to places where I once lived, and then fade into the background of life, relationships that will never die, and never grow. When I practice the piano, as when I exercise, it is no longer just about building up skill, strength, and control; it is also about taking stock of diminishing abilities. I felt a keen urgency to learn the *Goldberg Variations* in the months and years after my mother's death, an urgency prompted by incipient depression, and the fear that I might encounter my own death with the same weight of regret that she encountered hers. But as life returned, Bach returned to a more reasonable place in my life.

And then I spent my own season with the doctors, having blood drawn, images made, biopsies taken, waiting on test results, preparing for the worst. It was a scare, one of those chastening brushes with illness that are miserable in the moment, but may seem like a gift when they are over—if one can retain something of the hard-won wisdom that comes of fear. But when the "all clear" came, it was not the sweeping "all clear" as it has been with past scares, but only an "all clear for now." And that, too, was a blessing, because it helped me sustain the force of resolutions made while under the shadow. One of those was to finally grapple with the piano, resurrect my skills if possible, and learn the music as thoroughly as my brain and muscles are able. And it seemed to me that the only way to do that was to get away, shut out the distractions of life, and focus exclusively on this one thing, at least for a while.

So I packed up the electronic keyboard, loaded the dog into the car, and drove west to the Shenandoah Valley. For the better part of a month I had the run of an old house built by German settlers not long after Bach's death. It was one of the first sturdy houses set down in this part of Virginia, nestled into a green and stolid landscape of old magnolia and acacia trees, with rolling hills, remnants of thick forest, and placid streams that burst their banks during heavy summer downpours. I had the house entirely to myself and for weeks saw only anonymous faces in a few passing cars. I brought with me nothing but Bach, and though there was a television in the house, by the second day I couldn't watch it. I slept in a small, quiet room with narrow windows cut into the thick stone walls, and a fireplace close by the bed. Any number of generations have lived there, were born and died there, and some of those people must surely have died in that room, perhaps looking out the same window at the same hazy blue sky and thick foliage. For want of company, I tried to imagine them, quiet, sturdy, humorless people, always busy, always productive, but then these imaginary old Germans began to chastise me for what must have seemed to them the strange waste of my days, sitting alone at a keyboard, or lying on the sofa staring blankly at the ceiling, with nothing but snatches of music in my head.

On my first morning in this house, entirely alone but for Nathan sleeping at my feet, I lay in bed and daydreamed. Often since my mother died I have tried to imagine my own death, so as better to understand hers. I have tried to anticipate all the stages of dying, and think my way through the last hours of the process. And I always come back to a fundamental question: Does one feel a heightened intensity of the self as the self is extinguished? Or does the ego dissolve as one joins the rest of humanity in this universal, shared, perhaps even banal experience? Does our life "flash before our eyes," distilling our memories to their essence, or do we just "slip away," to borrow contradictory formulations for how people are supposed to experience death? And if our lives flash before our eyes, who is the author of this montage, and is it an accurate distillation of our existence, an arbitrary highlights reel, or a last, self-interested effort to give coherence to ourselves? These are questions I would like to ask someone wise, but if anyone has ever achieved this particular wisdom, it passed out of existence as soon as they did. My mother cannot enlighten me, not only because she is dead, but because morphine was her shepherd through that final hour.

I am about the same age my mother was when I dropped out of school and left home more than thirty years ago. When I find the chapter of life I inhabit bewildering, I often think about where she was and what she looked like at the same moment in her life, so I scrutinize old photographs of her to make sense of what it means to be thirty or forty or fifty or now fifty-two. With every passing year, there is a passive accumulation of understanding and sympathy for our parents that comes not from any mental effort or conscious empathy. Rather, the body explains things to us, how fatigue works, the operation of aches and pains, the reluctance to deviate from habits of food and sleep. As I lifted the electric piano out of the car, I made the same noise she used to make when picking things off the floor or moving heavy objects. My mother always wanted everyone in bed when she retired for the evening, which seemed an arbitrary rule. If I defied her and spent time studying or reading in the family room, I would have to sneak back to my room later in the evening, climbing to the second floor one stair at a time on my hands and knees, pausing at every creak and groan of the steps. No matter how quiet and meticulous my ascent, she would inevitably complain bitterly the next morning that I had woken her and she didn't sleep the rest of the night. Now, in this strange house, I find that I must have Nathan asleep in the room with me before I can settle down and sleep myself.

Only now do I have some vague understanding of a mystery that has always perplexed me: Why did she give up music? I can remember her playing the violin when I was a boy, and she played with pleasure; even into my early teens she would occasionally take the instrument off the shelf and play along to something I was learning. But as I got older and better at the piano, she played the violin less and less often. Her explanations shifted. At first, she didn't play because she was out of practice. Then, it hurt her left hand to press the strings to the neck of the instrument. Finally, her right hand was broken or damaged in some way that meant she couldn't hold a bow again with confidence. One of the last times we played together she stopped in the middle of a phrase, swore like a sailor, grabbed the violin by the neck, and began to swing it with the same force and intent with which she used to beat us, but she stopped just before she hit the edge of the piano, and then slowly and gently put the instrument back on the shelf.

During those weeks I had alone in the country, taking long walks, playing Bach, and lying under the stars at night, I may have made a more honest and consistent effort to understand my mother than I did when she was alive. Small things should have been obvious: that she was always happiest when she was away from her ordinary life; that she, too, struggled to find some kind of discipline or order in her life, and went to extraordinary lengths to institute regimes and policies for self-improvement; that when she couldn't bring order to one aspect of life, she asserted it ferociously over something else. Everyone around her was caught up in these things, unwittingly.

When my sisters and I were young, we would be summoned to the kitchen every month, where my mother would show us her meticulous account books. Therein she inscribed everything that had been spent on each of us, for our clothes, shoes, and textbooks, the school supplies and fees for the Girl Scouts, and the total for our lunch money. These evenings with the ledger, doubtless a relic of her having grown up in the Depression, left her children resenting each other, wondering why one of us had consumed more than the other, whether the dermatologist was a frill or a necessity, or if clarinet lessons were an educational expense or entertainment. As she read through the accounts she grew frantic. "We can't go on like this," she would say, and her lips would begin to quiver as she fought back panic. We would stand by, staring sullenly at the spiral-bound notebook in which she saw our family's ruin steadily accumulating, and sometimes she would weep, and then curse our indifference. Meanwhile, my father brought home his steady and ample paycheck, kept up on the mortgage, bought his cars with cash, put money aside for retirement, brought my mother small presents after many of his nearly weekly business trips, and saved enough for vacations and the occasional dinner out.

Her diets were legendary and sometimes bizarre. As we lived through months of austere meals, we would find hidden throughout the house candies and other delights, behind books, stuffed into the back of drawers that were rarely opened, tucked in the bottom of vases. Years after she gave up these diets we were still finding desiccated sweets, including some that were no longer manufactured, shriveled antiques wrought in corn syrup and food coloring. Her efforts to lose weight were for us merely episodes of privation, and we resented her weakness as though it were a more grievous form of hypocrisy; we never thought of her health or well-being. Throughout my childhood, she also took up new hobbies, and later she tentatively sought what had been unavailable to her when her children were young: a life outside the home. Sometimes her enthusiasms were driven by fear, as when she threw herself into gardening, carving up much of the backyard to put in strawberries, peas, beans, zucchini, and eggplant. The upheavals of the Nixon years, the gas crisis, wars in the Middle East, a partial nuclear meltdown at Three Mile Island, and then, worse than all of those combined, Jimmy Carter, whom she loathed, left her ever more pessimistic about the world. The garden was her hedge against starvation and chaos.

Other things, like exercise and volunteer work, she took up to enrich her life, and it shames me to remember that we were no more encouraging of these pursuits. She learned aerobics to maintain her figure, which also improved her mood, but when she showed us the exercises,

counting aloud in the family room as she bounced on the red shag car-
pet and thrust her arms perilously close to the low ceiling, we laughed.
Her exuberance was unexpected and unaccountable and we assumed,
when she quit classes not long after, that it was just a lack of determination and willpower, and had nothing to do with our mockery.

She also studied to be a children's advocate in the local court system, and told us solemnly that she was sworn to secrecy about her
cases, which she discussed nonetheless. This was in the early eighties when she, like the rest of the country, was growing more conservative. I was cynical about her court work and the stories she told,
because they seemed to reinforce prevailing ideas about the dys-
function of minority families and the laziness of the underclass. My
annoyance gathered to the breaking point one evening and I cut her
off in the middle of a story: "I thought you weren't allowed to talk
about your cases." She stopped sharing them with the family, and
eventually stopped volunteering as a children's advocate. One of my
sisters pointed out the oddity of my mother giving the court advice
on parenting, when she was not a natural parent herself. Looking
back, I realize now what we could not articulate then: because she
couldn't be a parent to us, we wouldn't let her be anything else.

═══

THE FIRST DAY I spent away from the city, I tried to take stock
of where I stood with the music. I got up early, made coffee, sent
Nathan out to explore the fields near the house, and then decided I
needed a plan. I wanted an honest, clear-eyed understanding of what I
had learned so far, and what remained to do, and also a list of specific
things to practice so that I would never sit down to work with a vacant
head or lack of purpose. I set up the keyboard at the edge of the stone
terrace, with my back to the house and nothing but green in front of
me. And then I played the variations through, the half dozen in the

beginning of the cycle that I knew fairly well, and then the next half dozen, which were mostly learned but not yet reliable. I took a short walk as the sun came up over the tops of the trees on the far hill, and braced myself for a more hopscotch survey of the second half of the cycle. I skipped the French Overture because I hadn't yet plotted out how to manage its clotted thickets of ornamentation, and some of the later arabesque variations that I hadn't even begun to explore. My efforts over the years had never been an orderly progression. Even the aria, which I love, wasn't memorized, perhaps because I always felt it so easy that I could memorize it quickly whenever I really needed to. By the end of the cycle, I estimated that after five years of sporadic work, I had learned about 30 percent of the music, and very little of it was thoroughly learned in a professional way.

My to-do list included things like: "Read, finger, learn, and memorize" for the half dozen variations that were entirely unknown to me; "Memorize" for at least a dozen others; and lots of items like "Clean up and bring to tempo" and "Fix potholes." In almost every variation, there were also passages I had learned incorrectly from the very beginning. At the end of the first half of the first variation—on a page now dog-eared from all the times I had turned it—I had taught my left hand to play the concluding D-major scale in the wrong direction, so that the hands played parallel lines rather than converged on the same note. I had stared at this measure countless times, heard it countless times, practiced it slowly and purposefully countless times, and all along it had been wrong. Undoing something like that, a musical gesture that has worn grooves in the memory through long usage, is ridiculously difficult and frustrating: learned right the first time, it is a simple matter; correcting it, however, requires major mental reengineering.

In some variations, I needed to get away from the keyboard and work on cleaning up and making sense of the chaos of notes I'd left in the musical score. Practice is all about good hygiene, never leaving a mess anywhere, never making changes without noting them down in the music. In many cases, I'd neglected to update old fingerings in the music, fingerings that now seemed so awkward I couldn't imagine how I ever thought they would work in the first place. They'd been superseded by new, more natural approaches, just as one often sees efficient networks of well-worn paths across a park that operate independently of the paved ones laid out by designers indifferent to human nature. Erasing the old markings isn't just fussiness. Not infrequently the eye will catch a glimpse of a page of music that has been thoroughly practiced and yet for some reason is lost to recall in the moment, and those old fingerings will flash like road signs and lead you astray.

And then there were the intractable problems, which persist like living sinkholes in the music, opening up again no matter how much effort one shovels at them. They require what I like least, the painstaking mental work of visualizing the hands in motion, playing the notes silently in the head, creating a full aural and sonic mental picture of the music. Sometimes, if you do this when your mind is clear, you may get the sense that you fixed the problem. It's not a strong fix, just a patch, but maybe if you're careful the patch will hold, and each time you traverse it successfully it will grow stronger and perhaps this little fissure in your knowledge of the piece won't open up again. You won't know, of course, until you drive over it at speed. There were dozens of these pitfalls throughout the variations, each one requiring hours of attention, and with each effort made, there was the need to sleep on it, and then try the thing again fresh in the morning to see if everything had set up nicely.

During my musical retreat from ordinary life, I tried to keep to a daily schedule. Mornings were for the hard mental practice of memorization and unlearning old mistakes, the afternoons for the more mechanical practice of strengthening passagework and material that was already familiar but not yet second nature, and the evenings for learning new variations and working out fingerings. But this proved more ambitious than I could manage. All told, I had about three hours of effective practice in me each day, and I know all too well how dangerous it is to practice when you are tired and inclined to carelessness. So I ended up in a curious state, with much of the day free, mentally but not physically exhausted, the brain too empty to do much of anything, but the body restless. So I went on long walks, with my mind full of music and almost nothing else.

After a few weeks of this there is progress. I can feel it, especially in the mornings when I play with the first and best of my energies, and I can almost measure it in one sense: The amount of time it takes to move each new bit of music through the levels of memory is decreasing. Most of the work is now done without looking at the score, except to check for errors. I can now move relatively rapidly from first working out the fingering to practicing passages without the music; and rather than play through each variation until I get to the potholes, I have most of those recurring trouble spots memorized, and can work on them in sequence, one after another, without being distracted by the score or the temptation to hear myself play what I already know. Some of them, I know, will probably always be intractable; others will return with atavistic menace from time to time; but many of them are slowly disappearing. When I first arrived, my lunchtime walk often felt like a juncture in the day, dividing the alert person who made progress in the morning from the wary, observant being who took stock of that progress in the afternoon. Now I sense things being stitched together, the music into a more manageable challenge, and my own sense of myself as a musician no longer divided by the meridian into an active agent pursuing a goal and a hapless creature who must put his hands to the keyboard to see if anything that was studied has, by chance, actually been learned.

It is a strange thing to sit in a landscape of green, with the wind blowing gently and the smell of cut grass in the air, and play over and over again a pattern of tones set down on paper almost three hundred years ago, music that no longer belongs to our time, that sounds to many ears as creaky and old-fashioned as the house behind me. After doing this at the same hour every day and in the same place, I have become part of the scenery, and the rabbits and birds are indifferent to the presence of this strange man silently flailing away at a plastic box on the edge of their domain. Nathan will take off after anything four-legged that comes too close to the keyboard, but he never catches them, and to call him back I simply unplug my headphones and the sound of Bach emerging from the speakers will break whatever spell the hares and voles and possums have cast, and he returns to bark his outrage at the music. As the days pass, the birds are ever more daring in their approach, venturing almost to my feet and sometimes clustering under a tree ten or fifteen feet away, like the avian audience gathered to hear the sermon of Saint Francis in the famous fresco at Assisi, generally attributed to Giotto. This is, perhaps, the perfect way to preach to them, without words or content of any sort, a silent communion that leaves them free to hear what they want to hear, and for me to say what I wish, with no harm done on either side.

The absurdity of these moments isn't lost on me, nor my good fortune to be in this place, to be able to escape my ordinary life and pursue something so selfish, so solipsistic, so quixotic. For the first time in years, at least since my mother died, I have been able to gather up a few beautiful things and add them to what I think of as my inner life. There is a passage from an Auden poem that describes a summer evening so perfect that for a moment all feelings of anxiety disappear: "The lion griefs loped from the shade / And on our knees their muzzles laid, / And Death put down his book." I don't know what other people mean by the word "happiness," but for me it is that, and several times in the last few weeks I've felt it. With just a bit of progress on this musical project, I've begun to feel a larger sense of control over my life, similar perhaps to that which John Eliot Gardiner ascribed to Bach through the medium of music: a sense of "greater reliability than could be found in his everyday life."

My sense of the inner life is simple, even primitive. It is the warehouse we stock with meaning as a hedge against pain and loss, death and the inherent isolation of being human. We may never be able to explain how or why something is meaningful to us, but we can at least be certain that whatever is meaningful must be cultivated and preserved until such time that we need it. Music and literature don't necessarily give me pleasure in the moment, but are things that I "put in there," things that can be held and conserved in a way that ordinary experience never can. Belief in this rudimentary interiority is the most important thing in my life, and yet I cannot say one meaningful thing about my mother's inner life. I have no idea of it and I never asked her about it, and even if I had, I feel quite sure she would have scoffed at the notion that she possessed one. When I tried to gain a sense of her memories, they were always fears, and little else. If she hoarded any pleasures or memories of meaningful moments that weren't rooted in fear, I knew little of them.

Often, when I have struggled to remember my mother, I find myself creating a plausible sense of a person who is unknown to me, a hypothetical mother whom I use to test various theories that would explain our history of anger and misunderstandings. To give a face to this conjectural mother, I look back to old photo albums; to understand the chronology of the life I posit for her, I interrogate my father, my aunt, and my older sisters; to make sense of her emotional life, I map her peregrinations against the broader currents of history, the Depression, the war, the fifties and sixties and seventies, and the cultural currents of those years; and to complete the picture, I muster all the documentary evidence I can, the marginalia in her books, the birthday-card messages and occasional letters from decades ago. And when I am done with this process, which is essentially the same one that biographers have used to make sense of remote figures like Bach, I have a fuller, richer, more human image of a woman I still don't know. It may even seem for a moment that this constructed figure is real, that my memories of a mother produced by the process of induction are like the memories that other people have of mothers they knew and loved with genuine intimacy.

Near the end of my time in this house, when I was already feeling the pangs of departure even though I had several more days before returning to the city, I worked on two of the variations that are among the most difficult in the cycle: the sixteenth variation, known as the French Overture, and the twenty-ninth, a virtuoso romp that drives with relentless high spirits toward the poignant final variation and repeat of the aria. Both of them hint at Bach's cosmopolitanism, the sixteenth variation through its use of the French style—a distinct dotted-note rhythmic profile, a pervasive sense of weightiness on the downbeats, a love of ornament, including extended trills—and the twenty-ninth variation through its use of virtuoso techniques associated with the Italian harpsichordist Domenico Scarlatti. Bach lived an isolated life, traveling as much as he could but never outside of Germany. Yet these variations show him looking to the wider world, expanding the range of his reference. One of the great unknowns of Bach's life is this hypothetical: Who would he have been if his career had, like those of Handel and Scarlatti and even Christian Petzold, the composer of the little minuets from Anna Magdalena's notebook, allowed him to travel? What would his music be like if he had spent time in London, or Paris, or Italy? Would the *Goldberg Variations* exist at all? Would they be even more variegated and brilliant in their compendium of keyboard possibilities? Is there a relation between Bach's genius and his isolation?

To the extent that I thought much of my mother's inner life, it always seemed to me small, which embarrassed me. When I was still in kindergarten, she went back to college to finish the degree that had been interrupted by her marriage at the age of nineteen. But she never remembered those two years of studying Russian and English literature at the State University in Albany with any fondness. It was windy and cold on the arid, modernist campus of the university, and she seems to have been an odd fit for university life in the 1970s. She would imitate her professors in a mocking voice, but the anecdote probably masked her embarrassment: "Mrs. Kennicott, do you remember anything significant on page 237 of *Moby-Dick*?" And then she would describe some overly subtle metaphor that was too arcane for a mature person to take seriously. She repeated this story, with its snarling professor, when I was studying literature and philosophy, and I often felt it was directed at me. But that was unfair. It was, instead, simply a painful memory: a woman in her forties had felt trapped in the spotlight of professorial inquisition, unable to answer a question, shamed and alone in a room full of people half her age. When I was a teenager, she pressed on me the books she had read in those years, Bertolt Brecht's *Life of Galileo*, Solzhenitsyn's *One Day in the Life of Ivan Denisovich*, and Ayn Rand's *Atlas Shrugged*. By the time I condescended to read these books decades later, she didn't remember them. Her nightstand had only two kinds of books on it, romance novels with embossed titles and books about birds.

Later in life, we learned not to talk about anything serious, including books, part of a larger rapprochement that took off the table most of the things that parents and children ordinarily speak of. We did our best to avoid politics, to skirt around the details of my private life, and never touch upon the complicated memories of our shared past. The uneasy truce was effected slowly, over time, and instead of months passing between phone calls, we eventually settled into a weekly ritual of Sunday afternoon banalities. I would ask her what she was doing, now that the house was empty, the children gone, now that she could pursue anything she wanted. I would ask if she was playing the violin, and the answer was invariably the same. "I'm working on the house." When the telephone rang on Sundays, I would put down my book, or get up from the piano, or disengage from the chatter of my friends, and try to imagine her life, far away, with its Sisyphean devotion to cleaning, proceeding methodically, room by room, day by day, until she arrived back at the starting place, only to begin again, week after week, year after year. It seemed to me terribly sad, and unnecessary, and perhaps even a form of revenge she was taking on her family: since we had not let her be who she wanted to be, she would remain forever who we made her. But when cancer had weakened her to the point where she could no longer leave her room, it became clear that she had kept her life small because that was the only way she could manage it. As she lay dying, she thought of the rest of the house, now beyond the ambit of her vacuum and sponge, going to ruin, and it only added to her anxieties. She had no faith in her survivors to keep the house up to the standard she had set because she knew that her passion for cleaning was never about having a clean house. What had seemed a reflexive impulse to clean was, in fact, life itself, an assertion of her presence and identity and control, and it was slipping from her.

She had risen up in the world so that I might have the freedom to roam in it more widely, but that roaming must have felt to her like a betrayal. When I was a boy, she loved music and read books and we went together to the ballet, evening concerts, and once to the opera, when a small traveling troupe came through town. As I grew older and took to these things with a passion that defied her sense of balance and decorum, it seems that I stole them from her. The more I worshipped what she merely loved, the less she loved those things, until our lives were defined by this strange, almost occult transfer of some part of her soul to mine. The gift of music offered by a mother to a child became, in the end, a chasm between us, leaving a vacuity on her side and what must have seemed to her an excrescence on mine.

None of this is entirely fair to my mother. This hypothetical understanding of her helps me answer painful questions, not just why she gave up music, but why it seemed that her life became more isolated and smaller as she got older. Her children grabbed from her all her dreams and to some extent made them real in their own lives. Her ambitions were thwarted even as they lived on in her offspring. But this reconstruction omits essentials, among them the birds. For as long as I can remember, she was passionate about birds, and throughout the decades of life she shared with her family, no one in her family shared that passion. We were uninterested in much of what she cared about, even to the point of hostility, and perhaps that drove her away from other interests and pursuits. But she never gave up on birds, and during her retirement she studied them, and went birdwatching, and served as a volunteer in a natural history museum, where her interest in all things avian was valued and put to good use. I don't think I ever asked her why she liked birds, and what they meant to her; one of the few times I discussed it with her, I told her that I liked birds well enough, as aesthetic objects, poetic devices, and objects of contemplation. But beyond that, aren't they all the same?

So I have no clue what kind of bird it was I found trapped in a piece of plastic netting alongside the road during one of my last lunchtime walks in the country. It was small and dark gray, with a slight dash of red on its wing. At first I couldn't see it through the tall grass, but I could hear the rhythm of its distress, a frantic, rapid flapping followed by silence, the sounds of exertion and exhaustion, the former yielding to the latter. I reached into the grass and exposed the animal, and worked for several minutes to disentangle it, while it pecked desperately at my hands. And then suddenly it was free and flew away, apparently unharmed but for its dignity. Normally I would not put this on the page, because it is a cliché and the sort of thing I hate in writing. But it is true, and it is the sort of thing my mother would have loved, and as I look back over a lifetime of writing, there isn't one thing I ever wrote for her. So I'll let it stand here in memory of a woman who loved birds because they were one of the few things that her family never took from her, that allowed her to enlarge her world and gave dimension to her inner life, whatever that may have been.

TWELVE

WHEN WE GRIEVE we want to be done with it, and when we care for those who are grieving, we hasten to reassure them that they will eventually come out the other side. We hope to minimize the presence and duration of grief in our lives, and a good life, it seems to us, is one in which there is hardly any grief at all. And yet nothing organizes our world quite like grief. It puts our priorities in order, and makes us impatient with trivial things. It may not free us from ordinary obligations, but it gives us permission to forgo caring about that which is insignificant or meaningless. It forms us into communities, and stirs all but the worst of us to be kinder. When we are older and more skilled at suppressing emotion, grief rekindles cathected memory and returns us to a state of vulnerability that reminds us what it felt like to be young. If we think back on grief long expired and periods of sorrow that are safely contained in the past, these may seem to us some of the most beautiful moments of our lives, especially our earliest experience of mourning, when we discover that our emotions cannot mar or alter the beauty of the world around us.

But grief is exhausting, and at some point we wake up impatient with it, and even think: *Grief is boring.* The blandishments of ordinary life reassert their appeal and we take interest in little things once again. What do we call this moment in the cycles of grief? I hate the word "healing." And even though it is almost impossible not to use the word "process" when we think of grief, that word is inadequate, too, as if there is some quantum of grief that must be run through the gin before we can move on. It isn't about forgetting, either. Forgetting is too passive. Grief begins to fade when we are finally exhausted by the intensity of meaning that it has brought us and choose the lesser life of daily distraction, small nuisances, and passing pleasures. Is it like hearing Haydn after too much Wagner?

Perhaps pseudoscience gives us better metaphors. Grief is like the ether of the heavens, or the phlogiston of combustible bodies, a mysterious, intangible substance that exists everywhere, ever the same, and becomes manifest to us only when we are forced to think of death in a concentrated way. Grief shatters or fractures into a kind of particulate matter that clings to everything, is ground into us, tracked into the recesses of our world like street dust, impervious to removal or cleaning, yet something that we learn to live with, a messy omnipresence. It is like the fluff of cottonwood trees, which we discover long after they have molted their seeds in spring, still swirling in some corner we haven't looked into in months. It never disappears, but remains mostly invisible during the happier moments of our lives, and only as we grow older and our losses accumulate do we realize that the world is forever glinting with it, on the bright days and the dark ones, too.

Like the aria on which they are based, Bach's *Goldberg Variations* grow more interesting as they go along. Just before his fifteenth birthday, Bach left his brother's house and began a life apart from his family and the world he knew in Thuringia. With the fifteenth variation, Bach introduces something new to the set, the first variation written in the minor key. This isn't the first time we've heard a minor tonality, because the harmonic line of the variations touches on the minor at several points, including a sequence in the second half of the aria that cadences in E minor. Following the aria's lead, the variations also make brief forays into the minor, and these are among the most beautiful moments in the entire work, inflecting even the most lively, cheerful, and boisterous music with darkness, sometimes strikingly so, sometimes like a small touch of salt that makes chocolate taste all the sweeter. If I could take only one small fragment of each variation with me to the proverbial desert island, it would be these moments when Bach works his way into and out of E minor.

But with the fifteenth variation, Bach moves resolutely into the minor key, the first of three variations that begin and end not in G major as the others do, but in G minor. The placement of these variations isn't accidental, but essential to the larger dramatic, emotional, and philosophical structure of the work. The minor-key variations highlight turning points in the cycle, or hearken back to the original aria in striking ways, or leave us with an uncanny sense that they are dark twins or shadows of what we have already heard. There is something excessive about them. Beyond their heightened emotionalism they have an abundance of curious, even bizarre details, gestures that become obsessive, statements that are left to trail off in midair. Only three out of thirty variations are in the minor key, but they have overwhelming power, and even if one doesn't believe there is a symbolic aspect to this power, they have extraordinary gravitas in purely musical terms.

Bach gives an uncommon amount of direction when it comes to how one should play the fifteenth variation, labeling it "andante," which suggests both a tempo that is moderately slow, or at a walking pace, and a manner of playing that is clear and deliberate. He also places small indications of articulation in the original printed score, to be sure the performer breaks up a common note pattern into repeated, two-note sighing motifs. This is the "dragging motif," which suggests a slow, belabored motion, a trudging of sorts, and it is found in other works of Bach where the composer wants to suggest a painful deliberation to the forward motion. The little slurs that connect these two-note fragments are also indicated in the bass line, which takes up material from the two canon voices above, and refuses to be merely a harmonic pedestal to the upper-level discourse.

In both the fifteenth and the twenty-first variations, the basic shape and even vestiges of the *Goldberg* bass line's major key origins are maintained, even as the music grows more anguished. If Bach had any symbolic intention in this, it might be to say that it will take more than a few shocks to undermine the strong, major-key foundation of the variations. Neither the weariness and struggle of the fifteenth variation, nor the mournful dialogue of the twenty-first variation (in which the two canon voices separated by a seventh are entangled in a gathering, mutually reinforcing sense of sorrow) will entirely shatter the ground upon which the music is based. But by the twenty-fifth variation, the third in the minor key and for many listeners the emotional climax of the whole work, the lower line has succumbed to the misery and is overwhelmed by chromatic motion—the use of half steps, which, for Bach, is a recurring expressive device in his most agonized and introspective music. In the second half, instead of heading toward the relative major of E flat, the soprano line passes through the remote and anguished key of E-flat minor, an extraordinary gesture of avoidance that suggests all light has been extinguished. The texture of the music, with a soprano line articulating a florid cantilena above two voices below, sounds like a lacerated and emotionally broken version of the far sweeter thirteenth variation. Performers are inclined to take enormous liberties with this piece, which the harpsichordist Wanda Landowska called "the black pearl" of the set, drawing it out to seven or eight minutes or more, sometimes to almost double the length of any other variation, which only emphasizes the apparent breach with the *Goldberg* bass line, and indeed with all the rest of the *Goldberg* set. The music gets lost in grief, becomes almost static in its self-absorption, with every motion and event localized, as if the subject who sings this dirge can no longer see outside the immediacy of pain.

The shift to the minor key allows Bach to reverse the music's polarities in striking ways. If the weather in the other twenty-seven variations is mostly sunny with a chance of clouds, in the minor keys this becomes mostly cloudy with a few bright moments in the fifteenth and twenty-first variations. But these bright moments are exquisite, aching moments, as in the second half of the fifteenth variation, where, when the music resolves to E-flat major, the old bones of the dragging motif become momentarily agile and spry. Perhaps inspired by the image of Christ carrying the cross, the music adumbrates a narrative idea, and a deeply spiritual one. No specifics are given, no names or context, but the ear detects the fragment of a story: a great weariness momentarily eased, a burden lifted. Something is shining through the gloom, something insistent.

The fifteenth variation is the last one of the first half of this great musical diptych, the closing aria of the first half of the show, and the transition from the fifteenth to the sixteenth variation is among the most memorable moments in a complete performance of the *Goldbergs*. The fifteenth variation is one of the canons—at the fifth—and it concludes with the lower of the two voices descending to the tonic and dying out, while the upper one continues on to finish its material, ascending upward to a high D until it is heard alone against the bass. These two notes are widely separated, forming a spaced-out "open fifth," an unsettling and ambiguous interval which can suggest something open and spacious (when Aaron Copland uses it), but more often sounds as it does here, thin, uncertain, tentative, and archaic. The upper note feels particularly exposed and frail, and the canon doesn't seem to fully resolve, but simply fades away. And then the sixteenth variation begins with one of the biggest sounds Bach's harpsichord could make, a fully fleshed-out four-note G-major chord in the left hand and a roaring upward G-major scale in the right hand, followed by great flourishes of ornament. If Bach had an orchestra play this, it would be full of timpani and trumpets. So at the halfway point of the cycle, the dragging gait yields to a stylized swagger, the two-note trudging motifs to an assertive, broad motion that bestirs the whole body, and the music, which seemed to ache only moments earlier, throbs with new excitement.

In the 1741 score of the variations, Bach makes it more than obvious that this is a new start. He indents the beginning of the music, writes in the word "ouverture," and when it is over, after a brilliant episode of pageantry followed by a crackling, fleet fugue, he writes the final chord in large notes and leaves a blank line at the bottom of the page. These visual cues are obviously not available to the listener, but they aren't necessary, either, to hear the overture as a rebirth after the first of the darker, more anguished variations. And while the second half of the variations is constructed the same as the first half, it is quickly obvious that something has changed, the virtuoso variations are even more challenging, the boisterous ones even more boisterous, the seemingly naïve ones even more direct in their insouciant appeal. Gould was skeptical about these later variations, sensing that in some cases Bach was playing to the crowd, indulging the capacities of his instrument, and demonstrating the limits of technique. The ideal of "pure" music has given way to something more demonstrative.

But one might also hear these earthy, eager, and exuberant variations as a natural development of the work's larger emotional logic. As pain gathers in our lives, joy is harder won. The idea that happiness, though occasionally shaken by sadness, is our natural condition, gives way to an understanding that happiness is something we work to achieve, something we build and shore up, a bulwark against sorrow that gathers relentlessly over time. If the fifteenth variation yields to the sixteenth as a constitutionally cheerful person shuts the door on dark thoughts, the twenty-fifth variation gives way to the twenty-sixth with a frightfully manic determination. The twenty-fifth variation, a subject of sometimes embarrassing hyperbole, uses all of the expressive devices available to Bach to present an aural image of suffering, rising up by ungainly intervals and then descending in protracted chromatic motion, leaps and stepwise progressions that iterate and reiterate the tritone, an interval so unstable that it was known as the "*diabolus in musica*," or the devil in music. At the end, the upper line descends through six nearly identical scale figures, the repeated downward musical motion an analogue for the idea of death as a sinking, or falling. It is a gripping and morbid gesture. The passage from the twenty-fifth to the twenty-sixth variation is more than just an ordinary succession of one idea by another, and the drama of this moment extends beyond the thrilling contrast in tone, mood, and texture between the two variations. The opening of the twenty-sixth variation also commences a rush to the end of the cycle, with the canon of the twenty-seventh variation stripped down to its aerodynamic essentials and the twenty-eighth and twenty-ninth variations outvying each other in their display of technical fireworks.

There is a sense of demonstrative hilarity in these last variations that prefigures the end of Mozart's greatest operas, including his *Così fan tutte*, in which characters who have just brutalized each other with psychological torture cry out together, "Happy is he who always sees something good in everything" and "Things which make others weep are for him a cause of laughter, and amidst the storms of life he will always find his peace." But Bach is never more serious than he is in the final pages of the *Goldberg Variations*, where the jarring juxtaposition of black-pearl depths with high-minded keyboard frivolity is elevated to spiritual dimensions. It would be anachronistic, a modernist distortion of eighteenth century aesthetics, to think that the energy and ebullience of the last variations are an absurdist riposte to the despair of the twenty-fifth variation. But Bach intends the contrast to be striking, so that he can better underscore the philosophical and psychological power of the final variation, a masterstroke of invention and emotional finesse, known as the quodlibet.

The quodlibet is a sophisticated medley of popular tunes, heard in fragmentary form and assembled into one of the richest and most integrated of all the variations, and at times it sounds like a hymn with its full, four-voiced texture. The motifs are simple and easily singable, and though their origins are in the world of what we would now call popular, or folk, music, they have a striking grandeur to them. Not all of the music fragments in the quodlibet have been identified, but scholars are relatively confident of some of them. Philipp Spitta, writing in middle of the nineteenth century, identified the melodies of two songs, the latter of which was used in full by Bach:

> *I long have been away from thee,*
> *I'm here, I'm here, I'm here,*
> *With such a dull and dowdy prude,*
> *Out there, out there, out there.*

And:

> *Kail and turnips,*
> *Don't suit my digestion;*
> *If my mother cooked some meat*
> *I'd stay here without question.*

"Cabbage and beets have driven me away" is a more common contemporary translation of the first lines of the second song, heard in the alto and then the soprano voice in the second and third bars. Bach could have used both songs simply for their robust musical appeal and because they fit his harmonic scheme. Did he intend anything at all by the words that were often sung to these melodic lines? He belonged to a musical tradition that frequently repurposed melodic ideas without concern for their original texts, something he did relatively often in his cantatas, where it is dangerous to read too much into the recycling of a melody that may have been associated with strikingly different words and sentiments in an earlier context. But both songs touch upon themes from Bach's life for which there is evidence even in the scant anecdotal material we have, including his having left home at a young age and the experience of early poverty and even hunger.

Bach could have used this material without labeling it a quodlibet, simply embedding the melodic fragments into the variation and leaving it to listeners to detect their origins. But given how rarely he attaches labels or any other interpretive clues to the variations, we can assume he had some other intent when he wrote "quodlibet" on the page. In using it to distinguish the last variation from the others, he recalls a historical tradition of musical thrift, conserving and reiterating sacred and popular musical themes in the creation of new works. Since the Renaissance, composers would not only appropriate melodies from one context to another, but combine multiple melodies together in elaborate, even ostentatious displays of counterpoint. In Germany, by Bach's time, this had become its own form of musical humor, with a rough-and-tumble quality, and new, often ribald texts set to the borrowed melodies. These mash-ups might be improvised if the musicians were particularly skilled or willing to take chances with their impromptu melodic cobbling, or they could be pulled together quickly for party entertainment. The more incongruous the music and the more ridiculous the words, the better the results. From Forkel's biography of Bach, we know that this entertainment was a favorite pastime for the larger Bach clan, and it must have produced delightful and bawdy excesses when they gathered for reunions.

Bach was referencing that tradition, and the genial frivolity that comes with it, when he finished his variation cycle with a quodlibet. But the quodlibet he wrote at the end of the *Goldbergs* doesn't necessarily sound crude or funny in performance. While it can be played quickly, with animation and perhaps with a slightly drunken stagger, it also sounds very well when played with a stately formality. The melodies chosen are merry enough in isolation, but in Bach's setting they want a little air, and with a slight breadth to the tempo they begin to soar. This need not sound like a nineteenth century

chorale or symphonic hymn singing, slow to the point of being lugu-
brious, but with just a touch of spaciousness and nobility this medley
has some of the same emotional grandeur as the end of Beethoven's
Ninth Symphony, or Brahms' First. The spacing of the voices also
seems to demand this, with Bach testing the player's ability to span
wide intervals in one hand, or divide up lines between the hands to
facilitate smooth rendition, which makes a deliberate tempo all the
more reasonable a choice.

We will never know the particulars of Bach's sense of humor,
though we have more than ample evidence to prove he had one, and
that it was well developed and fundamental to his understanding of
the world. He was extraordinarily hardworking and diligent, so was
it the messy humor of blowing off steam, a giddy or perhaps drunken
punctuation to sober life, like the humor of Bruegel the Elder or Jan
Steen? Or was it the existential laughter that nineteenth century phi-
losophers would anatomize, the laughter of wisdom, the humor of
the heights, not the herd? Whatever it was, the quodlibet exists to
connect laughter to ideas of transcendence or philosophical acceptance. Bach wants to tether one of his most ambitious musical cre-
ations to memories of a family gathering, not to keep it earthbound,
but to insist on an essential connection between lightness of spirit
and greatness of spirit.

＝

NEITHER KALE NOR turnips nor cabbage nor beets would drive
me away, but eggplant was a source of despair. It grew in abundance in my mother's garden, and she was partial to the vegetable.
By early August the crop was voluminous, but we often missed them
in the thick midsummer foliage of zucchini and pumpkin vines, and
there was always a sinking feeling when you chanced upon a forgotten aubergine, fat and purple in the shade, and full of tough seeds and

woody flesh. If we were harvesting without my mother's oversight, we would haul these lazy monsters to the far edge of the yard and dump them in the grass and bushes that lined the muddy flats of our small, polluted creek. But all too often we were obliged to add them to the dispiriting cornucopia of vegetable matter that regularly made its way to the kitchen, where it formed the better part of our daily sustenance for months at a time.

When my sisters and I gather for family celebrations, we still joke about my mother's cooking. She was more than capable of pulling together a fine meal on holidays, but the rest of the year she cooked with ferocity and resentment. After her nightly whiskey sour, she would proceed to the kitchen, cast a gimlet eye on the contents of the refrigerator, and pull out the hapless stuff of our evening meal as if culling a herd of sick animals. The preparations were limited, the noise deafening, and within half an hour or so we would be called to the table, where she would announce, "It's crap, but you're going to eat it anyway." My father inevitably responded, "Smells good, honey." Over time, her recipes all tended to the same place, vegetables and perhaps some rubbery meat cooked with a dash of soy sauce and ladled over egg noodles, and eventually even her fanciful references to actual dishes—ratatouille, goulash, fricassee, casserole—were forgotten and the meals were called simply "cook-up." For weeks after Thanksgiving we ate turkey cook-up, beef cook-up after Christmas, indeterminate meat cook-ups much of the rest of year, and vegetable cook-up during the garden season.

But there was one exception to the generic cook-ups: eggplant parmigiana. Made from thick slabs of the most venerable eggplants stewed with a can of tomato sauce and covered with a sprinkling of desiccated Italian cheese from a green columnar container, this dish bore a consistent but satirical relation to its namesake. Even if something about the taste of eggplant didn't tickle my gag reflex, these tree-sized rings of gray pith covered in thin tomato brine would have been inedible to me. I was young and by the end of the day I was always ravenous, and the news that it was eggplant parmigiana for supper was enough to make me weep. My mother seemed to save this dish for evenings when she was feeling particularly saturnine, brooding darkly, but full of the fighting spirit. We were never allowed to decline the main dish, nor any other dish, and if I graciously said I would sacrifice my portion to my dearest sister who looked more than usually peckish this evening, my mother saw through the ruse and laid down the law: "You're both going to eat every goddamned bite of it."

And then the grim vigil began, and we would stare down the meal until it was cold and the sun had set and well after my father had finished the dishes and my mother retired to watch television. We were inventive in our attempts to clear our plates, but eventually every stratagem was discovered. If we were eating outside on the patio, we would surreptitiously form a bolus of the matter in our hands and then drop it through the wooden rails of the deck. For a while, we managed to secret it into napkins, beg for a bathroom break, and then flush it down the toilet. Our dear dog Smokey, a toy poodle my mother kept mostly confined to the basement and who was often as hungry as we were, was an ally for a while, gobbling down handfuls of our unwanted dinner. But one evening he decided to enjoy it in the manner of the ancient Greeks, and carried off a large slab of eggplant to the family room, where he took a recumbent position on the sofa and commenced to savor it in leisurely fashion while my mother enjoyed her game shows.

When she saw what was happening, poor Smokey had to forfeit his portion, which was brought back to the dinner table and laid in front of us like the dead swan before Parsifal. Why was the dog eating our dinner? "Smokey can't resist your parmigiana," I said, but this only inflamed the interrogation, which escalated rapidly. Speaking a truth I thought was shared by all, I borrowed my mother's own description of the meal and said, "I can't eat this crap anymore." I was told in a solemn, shocked voice to repeat what I just dared to say, which I did with a desperate variation. "I can't eat this shit anymore." And so, for what would be the last time in my childhood, I had my mouth washed out, a ritual that involved forcing a wet bar of soap into the orifice, twisting it around violently, with some occasional banging of the head on the sink, until a rich lather emerged. Depending on the soap, the taste disappeared in a matter of hours or days. Irish Spring was the worst. I was then sent back to the table, and Smokey's half-finished meal was re-plated and placed before me and I was told that if I was going to feed my dinner to the dog, I could eat the dog's dirty leftovers. "But you've just cleaned my mouth," I protested. And I laughed, and couldn't stop laughing, and though she was furious with me, she never again repeated that particular punishment.

Eggplant parmigiana, however, remained a recurring trauma until I learned in biology class the basics of plant reproduction and pollination, and realized that with timely horticultural intervention the entire eggplant crop would simply disappear. This became an annual rite of spring when the plants blossomed. While pretending to weed them, I would pluck out the pistils and stamens and anything else that looked naughty inside the flower, and no one was the wiser. This neutering proved 100 percent effective, which led to long, serious, apocalyptic conversations about a supposed eggplant blight or contaminated soil or some other localized pestilence that had descended on our garden, and our garden alone. Not until I was in my forties did I confess what I had done. The whole family was gathered and we were reminiscing and my mother had some wine, which always put her in good spirits. After I told my story she took me by surprise and hit me on the head, with genuine anger but insufficient force to cause any pain. And though she glowered at us, we laughed and laughed to think of old times.

232 || *Philip Kennicott*

‛W E ARE A curious species. We spend much of our lives doing
one thing in order to do another, having children to fix
marriages, running marathons to heal psychic traumas, learning
music to lessen grief. No matter how skeptical we are, we never quite
lose faith in the magic that connects these disparate means and ends,
perhaps because it is the essential magic that makes life bearable,
connecting life in the biological sense to a host of unrelated ideas
about personal growth, meaning, and purpose. We muddle through
life in order to get somewhere, we suffer in order to be happy, we live
in order to have had a life.

Did learning the *Goldberg Variations* help me crawl out of the
hole I was in after my mother's death? Not at all, and the idea was
absurd. In emotional terms, I might be in the same exact place had
I studied ornithology or taken up a sport or played *Angry Birds*. The
best one can say of music is that it is a powerful substitution, direct-
ing mental energy away from thoughts of death and loss; but it also
makes us aware of our insignificance, our frailty, our susceptibility to
suffering. For every moment that working on this music has allowed
me to push aside existential anxieties, it has made me just as keenly
aware of the sad fact that the *Goldbergs*, like so many other things,
will be an unfinished project. How much time would it take to really
learn them? All the time I have, and even more.

I did, however, take my teacher's advice, and recorded myself
playing the music I have learned so far. It took me several days to have
the courage to listen to it, and when I did I heard two distinctly different things. One was a disheartening sense of my inadequacies, the
other a faint pleasure in accomplishment. After decades of neglect,
I have resuscitated some measure of my former skill at the instrument; my fingers are perhaps more independent than they were even

when I was playing regularly as a young man; and there is a stronger sense of visual and mental control over complex music. You can fake many things in life, but you can't fake playing Bach, and though I would never claim to have mastered this music, what I have learned is genuinely learned. A half dozen variations are, I think, permanently in my fingers, most of them are better sorted in my head, and all of them fit into a larger and richer picture of Bach's purpose and accomplishment.

But much of what I have recorded sounds mechanical. There are places where I have managed to master particularly difficult passages, but only if I approach them with deliberation, focused concentration, and a slight slowing of the tempo. Other places, where the fix is not quite so secure, inevitably make me rush forward, like a child hoping to spell a difficult word by blurting out its letters so quickly that he has no time to think about accuracy. My playing seems to me as primitive and distorted as an old film in which the timing is all off, herky-jerky and frenetic. The ornaments are a perpetual source of grief and in my hands they generally do exactly the opposite of what they are meant to do, making things sound cumbersome and labored rather than elegant and effortless. I also sense dozens of places where I have neglected to indulge what I love in this music, places where I could project more pleasure in a passing dissonance or the sweetness of a suspended line, places where I enjoyed the music more thoroughly when I was innocent of its technical challenges. This failure to collect what is beautiful is a larger character flaw. It is a shock to hear it so clearly present in my music making. Indeed, my musical failings offer a good snapshot of other failings: fear makes me skittish and I overcompensate; and I have a tendency to march grimly through the world even when I set out to enjoy a pleasant evening stroll. Recently I have tried to take this wisdom to heart, and my playing improves. Over time, I will neglect it again, and my playing will worsen. Is there any forward motion in all of this? Does it matter?

But I still love this music, and I don't regret a minute I've spent with it. The more intensively I work on Bach, the more I discover myself unconsciously at work on Bach, and it seems a far better thing that the brain should fritter its excess energies on this than on many other things that might occupy it. When I think of all the rest of Bach I've never touched, the partitas and *English Suites* and the *Italian Concerto*, I'm almost giddy. When I turn to these unsullied pages, there is the possibility that perhaps I will learn them more strategically, with greater self-consciousness about mistakes made in the past. Even in the *Goldbergs*, I am still finding new things, satisfying patterns and interconnections, sometimes in the variations I know best. There is a little three-note cell that runs throughout the fourth variation and just the other day I found two more instances of it hiding in plain sight. I took as much pleasure in this as I imagine Archimedes did in his bathtub. Having found these little phrases will make the piece better in the long run, once I integrate them into the whole, a process that requires a lot of work in the near term, as I reconfigure these passages to compensate for the new details. "You sneaky little bastards," I said to them, but it was said with love.

All this time spent with Bach has made me a superior bore. I am too delicate at parties to raise the subject, but woe to anyone who asks me about it. I am more than happy to defend the proposition that this is a great piece, one of the greatest ever written, and that it will add immeasurably to the richness of your life. I have strong feelings about some of the central questions raised by the work itself: Is it a coherent whole, or a collection of parts? Absolutely the former. Does the aria recur during the variations, or is it the absent parent that Gould claimed? I think Gould was wrong, and the DNA of the aria's melodic line is heard repeatedly throughout the variations. Is this a work of pure, abstract music, or does it have metaphorical, biographical, and symbolic content, too? With caveats and circumspection and less than total confidence in my judgment, I think this set of variations has a significance that surpasses musical matters. It is as full and rich and comprehensive an account of Bach as we will ever have, analogous, say, to discovering his personal journal, but written in a language that can never be translated.

I wish my playing of this music brought as much pleasure to human beings as my not playing it does to my poor suffering dog, Nathan. And sometimes it seems absurd to have spent so much time learning this one piece. The ability to play Bach at a mediocre level is a skill less valuable to society than the ability to change a tire. But this was a deeply selfish project all along, spurred as much by my own fear of death as it was by grief over the loss of my mother. I've known since I was in college that music is not how I am meant to serve other people. All along, this was about an atheist hoping to do an end run around the hard facts of life, and find some sense of higher spiritual value or purpose in my existence. And I've found none at all, which adds yet more absurdity to the project.

Sometimes, when I am feeling particularly morbid, I will look at my hands and imagine them after my death, as mere flesh to be disposed of, with no music in them. After my mother died, my father and I went to the funeral home to deal with the corpse. State law required that before cremation one of us identify the body, and my father asked if I would do it. When I went into the room, her body had been dressed, her hair brushed, and her face painted with cosmetics. The mortician, who had been trying to up-sell us on fancy urns while we kept insisting on a basic box for the ashes, lingered in the doorway, waiting I suppose for a nice word about his handiwork. I wanted desperately to say, "Sorry, I don't recognize her." So much effort had been wasted on an illusion, I thought, and perhaps it was my mother's voice speaking through me when I said to myself, *Christ almighty, you're just going to stuff it in the incinerator.*

I respect music too much to have any pretense about its power. That doesn't mean I've learned nothing in these past years, but the lessons aren't earth-shattering and perhaps I could have learned them in other ways. Bach is demystified for me, not in the sense that I can comprehend the magnificence of what he accomplished, but I don't expect from his music miraculous entrée to higher consciousness. I had hoped that the *Goldberg Variations* might be the key that unlocked all the rest of my musicianship, but they haven't been. I'm a better musician now than I was before, but there have been no great epiphanies or magic transformations. I am more comfortable now with the nonlinear nature of learning and mastery. There were times when I wanted to be done with this music, when I wanted to throw the score across the room and slam the keyboard with my fists. I am better now at detecting the difference between being lazy and the need to let something rest for a while, until the brain is better able to address the issue.

The most powerful of these lessons is simple to explain and incredibly difficult to put into practice. And that is: One must always move on. Motion is the only cure. After the morbid twenty-fifth variation comes the exultant twenty-sixth. And the twenty-sixth may be my favorite, something I hear in my head when I need to push forward with life, when I sit on the edge of the bed in the morning and struggle to remember what it is I must do for the day, when I read the newspaper and feel despair for my people, when sorrows crowd in and I feel I cannot pull myself off the sofa or make it out the door. I hope when I most need to hear it, whenever that time comes, it will be in my head, and I can use it to spur myself to a graceful and speedy exit.

I had hoped during these past years to clear my head, to find a bright, sunny, silent space in the brain that would make learning music easier. I had hoped to be done with my mother's voice, calling to me when I practice. But that hasn't happened. If anything, it is noisier upstairs than it has ever been, a side effect I think of feeling more compassion for the world, which is in turn a side effect of grief. Sometimes, when I practice, random people from all different times of my life will visit me and disrupt my fitful concentration, and I will sense not only their presence but see into them and detect a terrible sadness, people whose lives have not gone how they would wish, who crave companionship but have only solitude, who have devoted themselves to someone or something that returns nothing in kind, who are self-deluded in some way that has stunted their life or who walk on the razor's edge of an enlightenment that would annihilate them. The feeling is the same as when I look at Nathan the dog and contemplate the shortness of his life, the arbitrariness of his devotion to me, and the pathos of the particular way he stares into the distance and seems to remember a wildness that was domesticated out of his forbears ages ago. I think I saw into the life of my mother, and understood her sadness, long before I was able to acknowledge what I had seen, and it scared me.

Had she been merely cruel and capricious, I might have hated her. But all along I saw also the woundedness of her life. The resistance I needed to escape and become my own person, to salvage dignity from childhood, a resistance that was sometimes as ferocious and noisy as her cooking, only added to her suffering. When I sat by her deathbed, it wasn't just the fear of my own mortality that pierced me. It was the helplessness of watching an unhappy life come to an unhappy end.

But it is presumptuous, and rude, to dwell so long on death. After all of this, I have only one thing to offer, a small observation about fear and pain. Every grief is bearable but for the fear that there is a worse grief to come. When we are sometimes given a presentiment of pain that is unbounded and crushing, the fear of it can haunt our lives and drive away even the possibility of distraction and happiness. It may seem as if this dread thing that we know awaits us—the catastrophe of crushing sorrow—is everywhere, as if any fine breeze might pitch us into it. But when that great sadness finally arrives, a grief that casts us into a suffering deeper than the ameliorating power of any ordinary art or music, there is also a kind of awe. You can only stare into it, look upon its terrible majesty, and be stupefied by it. You can't back away, you can't minimize it. You must stand there, in its presence, undefended. And in that raw moment of openness there is, in fact, one tiny bit of consolation: a sense of our pitiful smallness. I have that same feeling when I listen to the aria of Bach's *Goldberg Variations* fade away at the end of one of the great emotional journeys in Western art. Bach brings us face-to-face with an emotional resignation that is beyond pleasure, or healing, or anything that can be captured in words. It exists outside of any ordinary sense of time. It existed for centuries before any of us were alive, and it will exist after we are gone, and it doesn't care about us one whit. It is wonderfully exhausting and perfectly beautiful, and if you haven't heard it, you should, before you die.

Acknowledgments

JOURNALISM IS RELENTLESS, and when my mother was dying in 2010, I was not only caught up in an emotional whirl, but behind on my deadlines. I used to write a monthly column for *Gramophone* magazine, and I had no choice but to write it, even as my mother was expiring and my mind was elsewhere. I could think of nothing to say except that I had fallen deeply in love with a piece of music by Bach, and could listen to nothing else. Somehow I managed to stretch that theme out to the usual eight hundred words. To my surprise, many of my regular readers said they enjoyed the column, and found it more meaningful than many of the others I had written. As a critic, I have always resisted the first person, but it was the first-person directness they seemed to enjoy. I thought perhaps of expanding on that column, written some ten years ago, and am deeply grateful to my agent Markus Hoffmann not only for encouraging the idea, but improving it, along with many drafts of a first chapter. I am also grateful to John Glusman, my editor at Norton, for taking a chance on it, and helping a first-time author give it focus.

My partner Marius is infinitely supportive, and perhaps he is right: this book would have been much improved by the inclusion of vampires. But it is haunted by other things, more ordinary, but perhaps more familiar to the reader. Each of my sisters has her own understanding of our family, but they have all supported this venture, which will lay before the public just one, mine. My mother is no longer alive, but I would thank her, too, if she was. She brought music and celebrated our successes.

My teacher Joe Fennimore is one of the finest pianists and composers living today, and I have been lucky to learn from him for some forty of the more than fifty years I have been alive. My colleagues at the *Washington Post* are a source of inspiration and enlightenment and I am particularly grateful to all of them. I want to thank Paige Warren, for allowing me to stay in her beautiful house while finishing the draft of this book, and for being an indefatigable and ebullient host to a group of friends whom I cherish dearly. The staff at the Library of Congress's Music Division have been consistently helpful and I am indebted to Vincent J. Novara, curator of Special Collections in Performing Arts, at the Michelle Smith Performing Arts Library of the University of Maryland, for help with a difficult question: Just how many people actually took piano lessons when I was a kid?

Finally, I want to thank my father. This is a book largely about my mother, but I hope the essentials of my father's character are evident from his occasional appearances here. He is kind, thoughtful, honest, and self-sacrificing, and he held his family together.

Notes

4   **The Chaconne was based on an early dance form:** For a summary of speculation about the origins of the dance and its name, see Richard Hudson, *Passacaglio and Ciaconna: From Guitar Music to Italian Keyboard Variations in the 17th Century* (Ann Arbor, MI: UMI Research Press, 1981), 4.

29 **"For this [work] . . . we have to thank":** J. S. Bach, *The "Goldberg" Variations,* ed. Ralph Kirkpatrick (New York: G. Schirmer, 1938), vii.

30 **"'Dear Goldberg, do play me'":** The original German is, "Lieber Goldberg, spiele mir doch eine von meinen Variationen," from J. N. Forkel, *Ueber Johann Sebastian Bach's Leben, Kunst und Kunstwerke* (Leipzig: C. F. Peters, 1855).

34 **"The age of the doubtlessly gifted":** Christoph Wolff, *Bach: Essays on His Life and Music* (Cambridge, MA: Harvard University Press, 1991), 213.

49 **"It must certainly have been orginally written":** Philipp Spitta, *Johann Sebastian Bach: His Work and Influence on the Music of Germany, 1685–1750,* vol. 3, trans. Clara Bell and J. A. Fuller Maitland (London: Novello, 1899), 171.

49 **"is quite certainly not by Bach":** Frederick Neumann, "Bach: Progressive or Conservative and the Authorship of the Goldberg Aria," *Musical Quarterly* 71, no. 3 (1985): 281.

51 **Piano lessons as a cultural phenomenon:** Piano lessons in America have been given both privately and, during periods in the twentieth century, for free in the public schools. Good numbers aren't available for how many students availed themselves of lessons, but estimates for the production of pianos give a sense of the appetite for home music-making, which peaked around 1910, fell off in the

1930s (during the Depression and with the advent of radio), and surged again after the Second World War. Production estimates are taken from Cyril Ehrlich, *The Piano: A History*, revised edition (Oxford: Clarendon Press, 1990), 222.

52   **"It is better, during the first lessons"**: François Couperin, *L'art de toucher le clavecin*, ed. and trans. Margery Halford (Van Nuys, CA: Alfred Publishing, 1995), 31.

53   **"For the fingers are little disobedient creatures"**: Carl Czerny, *Letters to a Young Lady on the Art of Playing the Pianoforte*, trans. J. A. Hamilton (Norfolk, UK: R. Cocks, 1848), 23.

54   **"If heaven has gifted you"**: Robert Schumann, *Music and Musicians: Essays and Criticisms*, trans. Fanny Raymond Ritter (London: Ballantyne, 1891), 417.

55   **"My hand gets so tired"**: Amy Fay, *Music Study in Germany: From the Home Correspondence of Amy Fay*, ed. Mrs. Fay Pierce (New York: Macmillan, 1922), 21–22.

87   **"Nothing prevents our keeping rooms"**: Walter Benjamin, *Reflections,* trans. Edmund Jephcott (New York: Schocken Books), 56–57.

96   **"I have tumbled from the superb peaks"**: Clive Bell, *Art* (Oxford: Oxford University Press, 1987), 32.

98   **"modifying the piece"**: Heidi Gotlieb and Vladimir J. Konečni, "The Effects of Instrumentation, Playing Style, and Structure in the *Goldberg Variations* by Johann Sebastian Bach," *Music Perception: An Interdisciplinary Journal* 3, no. 1 (1985): 99.

100   **"For if thought is like the keyboard of a piano"**: Virginia Woolf, *To the Lighthouse* (New York: Harcourt, Brace and World, 1927), 53–55.

105   **"the eye shares in the pleasure"**: Cuthbert Girdlestone, *Jean-Philippe Rameau: His Life and Work* (New York: Dover, 1969), 24.

118   **"Isn't it reasonable to think"**: Barry Green with W. Timothy Gallwey, *The Inner Game of Music* (New York: Doubleday, 1986), 14, 34.

122   **"Some accomplishments are essentially good"**: Immanuel Kant, *Education*, trans. Annette Churton (Ann Arbor, MI: Ann Arbor Paperbacks, 1960), 19.

133   **"permits you to cultivate a degree of textural clarity"**: The quo-

tation is from Geoffrey Payzant, *Glenn Gould: Music and Mind* (Toronto: Key Porter, 1984), 37.

133 **"It was playing of such uprightness"**: Cited from Paul Elie, *Reinventing Bach* (New York: Farrar, Straus and Giroux, 2012), 176.

134 **"A war," he said, "engaged"**: Quoted in Geoffrey Payzant, *Glenn Gould: Music and Mind* (Toronto: Key Porter, 1984), 120.

134 **He cut fourteen bars**: Kevin Bazzana, *Glenn Gould: The Performer in the Work* (New York: Oxford University Press, 1997), 26–28.

134 **"a grab-bag of subgrade Bach"**: The interviewer, Joe Roddy, is quoting or paraphrasing Gould in this passage, cited from Otto Friedrich, *Glenn Gould: A Life and Variations* (New York: Random House, 1989), 312.

138 **"erase all superfluous expression"**: Ibid., 54.

162 **"affect a camel's pace"**: Citations from Ibn al-Haytham and Darwin, and observations on Cotton-top tamirs, are from chapter 32, *Routledge Companion to Music Cognition* (Abingdon-on-Thames, UK: Routledge, 2017), 392.

163 **"Before eight bars had been played"**: Camille Saint-Saëns, *Outspoken Essays on Music*, trans. Fred Rothwell (London: Kegan Paul, Trubner, Trench, 1922), 133–35.

175 **"In the adult brain"**: *Neurosciences in Music Pedagogy*, eds. Francis Rauscher and Wilfried Gruhn (Waltham, MA: Nova Biomedical, 2007), 128.

175 **"When continuing mental practice"**: Ibid., 134.

176 **"The change when the pupil began"**: Ludwig Wittgenstein, *Philosophical Investigations*, trans. G. E. M. Anscombe (New York: Macmillan, 1953), 62–63.

188 **"To all those who have been led"**: James Ching, *Performer and Audience: An Investigation into the Psychological Causes of Anxiety and Nervousness in Playing, Singing or Speaking Before an Audience* (Oxford: Hall, 1947), 23.

192 **violence, malnutrition, and disease**: Cited in John Eliot Gardiner, *Bach: Music in the Castle of Heaven* (New York: Knopf, 2013), 22.

193 **"Listen, play, love, revere"**: Ibid., xxv.

194   "Some of his recollections": Ibid., 544–45.

197   "I have composed these new partitas": Both citations about music refreshing the spirit are from Andrew Talle, *Beyond Bach: Music and Everyday Life in the Eighteenth Century* (Urbana-Champaign: University of Illinois Press, 2017), 148.

197   "To learn an instrument well enough": Ibid., 147.

226   "Cabbage and beets": The translation of the quodlibet song is from Peter Williams, *Bach: The Goldberg Variations* (Cambridge, UK: Cambridge University Press, 2001), 90.